TIDES OF DARKNESS

WORLD OF WARCRAFT®

TIDES OF DARKNESS

AARON ROSENBERG

POCKET STAR BOOKS

New York London Toronto Sydney

Pocket Star Books
A Division of Simon & Schuster, Inc.
1230 Avenue of the Americas
New York, NY 10020

This book is a work of fiction. Names, characters, places, and incidents either are products of the author's imagination or are used fictitiously. Any resemblance to actual events or locales or persons, living or dead, is entirely coincidental.

First Pocket Star Books paperback edition September 2007
POCKET STAR BOOKS and colophon are registered trademarks of Simon & Schuster, Inc.

For information about special discounts for bulk purchases, please contact Simon & Schuster Special Sales at 1-800-456-6798 or business@simonandschuster.com

Cover art by Glenn Rane

Manufactured in the United States of America

10 9 8 7 6 5 4 3 2 1

ISBN-13: 978-1-4165-3990-2

ISBN-10:   1-4165-3990-5

To my family and friends and especially my lovely wife,
who help me hold back the tide.

For David Honigsberg (1958–2007)
Musician, writer, gamer, rabbi, and friend extraordinaire.
Teach Heaven to rock, amigo.

FIRST PROLOGUE

Dawn, and fog still shrouded the world. In the sleepy village of Southshore, people stirred, unable to see the dawn light but knowing night had ended nonetheless. The fog covered the world, draping itself over their simple wooden homes and concealing the sea they knew lay just beyond the town's edge. Though they could not see it, they could hear the water lapping at the shore, rippling up around the single dock.

Then they began to hear something else.

Slow and steady it came, floating through the fog, the sound reverberating until they could identify neither source nor direction. Did it come from the land behind them or the sea before them? Was it merely the waves striking harder than usual, or rain beating down upon the fog itself, or some trader's wagon rolling along the hard dirt path? Listening intently, the villagers finally realized the strange new sound came from the water. Rushing to the shore, they peered out into the fog, trying to pierce its gloom. What was this noise, and what did it bring with it?

Slowly the fog began to shift, as if pushed forward by the noise itself. The fog swelled and darkened, and then the darkness took on form, a wave rushing toward them. The villagers backed away, several of them crying out. They were masters of the water, these men, fishermen born and bred, but this wave was not water. It moved wrong for that. It was something else.

The darkness continued its approach, carrying the fog with it, the sound intensifying. Then finally it breached the fog, piercing its veil, and the shape divided into many and took on form. Boats. Many, many boats. The villagers relaxed slightly, for boats they understood, yet still they were wary. Southshore was a quiet fishing village. They had a dozen small boats themselves, no more, and had seen perhaps a dozen others through the years. Suddenly there were hundreds approaching them all at once. What did this mean? The men grasped short wooden clubs, knives, hooked poles, even weighted nets, whatever came to hand. And they waited tensely, watching as the boats drew closer. More boats were emerging from the mists, an unending procession, and with each new row of ships the villagers' shock grew. There were not hundreds but thousands approaching them, a veritable nation, more boats than they had ever seen before! Where had so many vessels come from? What could make them put to the water at once like this? And what could send them to Lordaeron? The villagers gripped their weapons more tightly, children and women hiding within their homes, and still the boats multiplied. The sounds were finally clear as the stroke of many oars striking the water out of rhythm.

The first boat beached itself, and only now could the villagers see the figures within it. They relaxed further, though their confusion and concern grew. There were men there, and women and even children judging by the size, with skin both pale and tanned and hair all the normal shades. These were not monsters, nor the other races the villagers had heard of but never seen. Nor did they seem armed for battle, for clearly most of these newcomers were not warriors. This was no invasion, at least. It seemed more a flight from some horrible disaster, and the villagers felt their fear turning to sympathy. What could have sent what seemed an entire nation into the sea?

More boats reached the shore, and people began to stagger out of them. Some collapsed on the rocky beach, crying. Others stood tall and took deep breaths, as if glad to be rid of the water. The fog was rolling back now, the morning sun beating it to thin wisps that faded before the strong rays, and the villagers could see more clearly. These people were no army. Many of them were women and children indeed, and many were poorly dressed. Most looked thin and weak. They were just people. People clearly stricken by some calamity, many of them so overwrought they could barely stand or stumble up the shore.

A few wore armor, however. One from the lead boat walked toward the assembled villagers. He was a large, stout man, almost bald, with a thick mustache and beard and a strong, stern face. His armor had clearly seen many battles, and above one shoulder rose the hilt of a massive sword. But in his arms he carried not weapons but two small children, and several more hurried alongside him, clinging to the warrior's armor, belt, and scabbard. Beside him walked a strange man, tall and broad-shouldered but slender, white-haired but with a strong stride. This one was dressed all in tattered violet robes and a worn rucksack, and carried a child across one shoulder while leading another by the hand. A third figure moved with them, a youth, brown-haired and brown-eyed and barely aware of his surroundings, one hand holding the large man's cloak like a small child clinging desperately to a parent's hand. His clothes were richly made but stiff with sea salt and worn from hard use.

"Hail and well met!" the warrior called out, approaching the villagers, his broad face grim. "We are refugees, fleeing a terrible, terrible battle. I beg you, any food and drink you might spare, and shelter if you can, for the children's sake."

The villagers glanced at one another, then nodded, weapons lowering. They were not a wealthy village but they were not poor either, and they would have to be far worse off to let children go unaided. Men came and took the children from the warrior and the violet-robed one and led them to the church, their largest, sturdiest structure. Already the village women were stirring up pots of porridge and stew. Soon the refuges were camped in the church and around it, eating and drinking, sharing donated blankets and coats. The mood would have been festive if not for the sorrow evident in every newcomer's face.

"Thank you," the warrior told the village headman, who had introduced himself as Marcus Redpath. "I know you cannot spare much, and I am grateful for what you have given us."

"We will not let women and children suffer," Marcus replied. He frowned, studying the other man's armor and sword. "Now tell me, who are you and why are you here?"

"My name is Anduin Lothar," the warrior answered, running a hand over his forehead. "I am—I was—the Knight Champion of Stormwind."

"Stormwind?" Marcus had heard of the nation. "But that is across the sea!"

"Yes." Lothar nodded sadly. "We sailed for days to reach this land. We are in Lordaeron, are we not?"

"We are," the violet-robed one commented, speaking for the first time. "I recognize the land, though not this village." His voice was surprisingly strong for one so old, though up close only his hair and the lines on his face suggested advanced age. Otherwise he seemed barely more than a youth.

"This is Southshore," Marcus told them, eyeing the

white-bearded young man warily. "You are from Dalaran?" he asked at last, trying to keep his tone neutral.

"Aye," the stranger acknowledged. "And do not fear— I will be returning there as soon as my companions can travel."

Marcus tried not to let his relief show. The wizards of Dalaran were powerful and he had heard the king treated them as allies and advisers, but for himself Marcus wanted no truck with magic or its wielders.

"We must not delay," Lothar was agreeing. "I must speak with the king at once. We dare not give the Horde time to move again."

Marcus did not understand this comment but he recognized the urgency in the stocky warrior's tone. "The women and children may stay here a time," he assured them. "We will care for them."

"Thank you," Lothar said with obvious sincerity. "We will send food and other supplies back once we reach the king."

"It will take you time to reach Capital City," Marcus pointed out. "I will send someone ahead on a fast horse to warn them of your approach. What would you have them say?"

Lothar frowned. "Tell the king that Stormwind has fallen," he said softly after a moment's pause. "The prince is here, as are as many of its people as I could save. We will need supplies and quickly. And we bring him grave and urgent news."

Marcus's eyes had widened at the list of troubles, and his gaze had gone quickly to the youth standing beside the big warrior, then moved away before his stare could become rude. "It will be done," he assured them, and turned away to speak to one of the villagers, who nodded and leaped onto a nearby horse, galloping away before the headman had taken two steps back to the church.

"Willem is our finest rider, and his horse the fastest in the village," Marcus assured the two men. "He will reach Capital City well ahead of you and deliver your message. We will gather horses and what food we can for you and your companions to take on your own journey."

Lothar nodded. "Thank you." He turned to the violet-robed man. "Gather those who would come with us, Khadgar, and make ready. We leave as soon as possible." The wizard nodded and turned away, heading for the nearest cluster of refugees.

A few short hours later, Lothar and Khadgar left Southshore, the prince Varian Wrynn beside them, leading threescore men. Most had chosen to remain behind, either from illness or fatigue or simply out of fear and shock and a desire to cling to those few survivors from their own land. Lothar did not begrudge them. A part of him wished he could remain in the small fishing village as well. But he had a duty to perform. As always.

"How far to Capital City?" he asked Khadgar, riding

beside him. The villagers had offered them the use of what few mounts and carts they had, which had proven just enough to manage. Lothar had hesitated about taking any more from the generous villagers but had finally accepted, knowing it would speed their process immeasurably. And time was of the essence.

"A few days, perhaps a week," the wizard replied. "I don't know this part of the country that well but I remember it on the maps. We should see the city's spires in five days at the most. Then we will have to pass through Silverpine Forest, one of the great wonders of Lordaeron, to skirt Lordamere Lake. The city stands along its north shore."

Khadgar fell silent again and Lothar studied his companion. He worried about the young man. When first they'd met he'd been impressed by the wizard's composure and easy self-confidence, and astonished at his youth. He had been only seventeen, little more than a boy, and already a wizard in his own right—and the first Medivh had ever deigned to accept as an apprentice! Subsequent encounters had shown him that Khadgar was bright, stubborn, focused, and friendly. He'd found himself liking the boy, the first time that he'd felt such friendship toward a wizard since—well, since Medivh himself. But after the events at Karazhan. . . .

Lothar shuddered, remembering the ugly, nightmarish conflict. He had found himself, with Khadgar, the half-orc Garona, and a handful of men, against Medivh himself. Khadgar had administered a lethal blow to his master out of necessity but it had been Lothar who had removed his old friend's head, a head he had protected many times in their youth. Back when he and Medivh and Llane had been friends and companions.

Lothar shook his head to drive away the tears. He had grieved many times on their long sea voyage, but still it felt as if the pain and rage and sorrow would overwhelm him. Llane! His best friend, his companion, his king. Llane, with the bright smile and the laughing eyes and the quick wit. Llane, who had carried Stormwind into a golden age—only to see it torn apart by the orcs, their Horde sweeping across the land and destroying everything in their path. And then to discover that Medivh had been responsible for it all! That his magic had aided the orcs in reaching this world, had given them access to Stormwind! And thus had led to not only the kingdom's destruction but Llane's death! Lothar bit back a cry at the thought of all he had lost, all his people had lost. Then he hardened himself to it, as he had so many times during their journey. He could not let himself succumb to such emotion. His people needed him. And so did the people of this land, though they did not know it yet.

And so did Khadgar. Lothar still did not understand everything that had happened in Karazhan that night. Perhaps he never would. But somehow, during the battle with Medivh, Khadgar had changed. His youth had been stripped away, his body aged unnaturally. Now he appeared an old man, far older than Lothar himself though Khadgar was the younger of them by almost four decades. And he worried what else it had done to the young wizard.

Khadgar, for his part, was too lost in his own thoughts to notice his companion's concerned gaze. The young-old wizard's thoughts were turned inward, though they ran along the same lines as his companion's. He was reliving the battle in Karazhan, and experiencing again that horrible wrenching sensation as Medivh drew from him his magic and his youth. The magic had returned—indeed, in many ways it was far stronger now than before—but his youth was gone, torn from him long before its time. He was an old man now, at least in appearance. He still felt hale and hearty, and had as much endurance and strength and agility as ever, but his face was lined, his eyes deep-set, and his hair and fledgling beard a stark white. Though only nineteen, Khadgar knew he looked three times that and more. He looked like the man in his vision, the older version of himself he had seen in battle through the magic of Medivh's tower. The older man who would someday die beneath a strange red sun, far from home.

Khadgar also studied the emotions within him, the ones that came from Medivh's death. The man had been evil incarnate, singlehandedly responsible for loosing the orc Horde upon the world. Yet it had not been the man, not truly. For Medivh had been subsumed by the titan Sargeras, who his mother had defeated millennia before. Sargeras had not died, only his body, and he had hidden away within Aegwynn's womb, infesting her unborn son. Medivh had not been responsible for his own actions, and his dying words to Khadgar had revealed that the Magus had been fighting the evil within himself for years, perhaps all his life. Khadgar had even encountered a strange phantom version of his dead master, shortly after burying the body, and that Medivh had claimed to be from the future and to be free of Sargeras's taint at last. Thanks to Khadgar himself.

So what should he feel, Khadgar wondered? Should he be sad that his master had died? At times he had liked Medivh a great deal, and certainly the world had lost much when the Magus died. Should he be proud of the role he had played in freeing the man and driving Sargeras from this world again, perhaps for good? Should he be enraged at what Medivh had done, both to him and to others? Or awed that one man could resist the influence of a titan for so long?

He could not tell. Khadgar's mind was awhirl, as was his heart. And added to all the thoughts of Medivh were more. For he was home. At least, he was back in his homeland, back in Lordaeron. And not in the way he had expected. When he had left to become Medivh's apprentice, at the behest of his previous masters in Dalaran, Khadgar had not expected to return until he was a master mage himself. He had thought to fly back on a gryphon, as Medivh had taught him, and land atop the Violet Citadel so that all his former teachers and fellows could marvel at his prowess. Instead he was riding a plow horse beside Stormwind's former Champion, leading a ragtag band of men to speak to the king about saving the world. Khadgar bit back a chuckle. Well, at least they would make a dramatic entrance, he thought. That was something his old teachers and friends would appreciate.

"What will we do once we reach the city?" he asked Lothar, startling the aging warrior from some reverie. His companion recovered quickly, however, turning to study him with those disarming storm-blue eyes that showed the warrior's emotions plainly but hid the sharp mind within.

"We will speak with the king," Lothar replied simply. He glanced at the youth riding silently beside them, and reached back to stroke the handle of his greatsword, its gems and gold gleaming in the afternoon sunlight. "Though Stormwind is lost Varian is still her prince and I am still her Champion. I have only met King Terenas briefly, and many years ago, but perhaps he will recognize me. Certainly he will know Varian, and the messenger will make sure he is aware of our arrival. He will grant us an audience. And then we shall tell him what has happened, and what must be done."

"And what must we do?" Khadgar asked, though he thought he already knew.

"We must gather the rulers of this land," Lothar answered, as Khadgar had thought he might. "We must force them to see the danger. No nation can stand alone, not against the Horde. My own land tried and is gone because of it. We must not let that happen here. The people must unite and fight!" His hands clenched on the horse's reins, and Khadgar could again see the powerful warrior who had led Stormwind's armies and kept its borders safe for so many years.

"Let us hope they listen," Khadgar said softly. "For all our sakes."

"They will," Lothar assured him. "They must!" Neither of them said what both were thinking. They had seen the power of the Horde firsthand. If the nations did not unite, if their rulers refused to see the danger, they would fall. And the Horde would sweep across this land as it had across Stormwind, leaving nothing behind.

SECOND PROLOGUE

A dark figure stood upon a tall tower, gazing out at the world below him. From his vantage point he could see the city beneath and the countryside around it. Both were covered in swirling, shifting darkness, a tide that swept across the land and covered the buildings, leaving them in ruins.

The figure watched. Tall and powerfully built, massively muscled, he stood motionless upon the stone peak, his sharp eyes studying the scene below him. Long dark hair swung in braids about his chiseled face, the tasseled ends occasionally striking the long tusks that jutted up from his lower lip. The sun beat down upon him, making his skin glow emerald in the light, and creating a glare from the many trophies and medallions he wore about his neck and across his broad chest. Heavy plates covered his chest, shoulders, and legs, their scarred surfaces gleaming black except where heavy bronze knobs studded them. Gold gleamed along the edges, proclaiming his importance.

At last the figure had seen enough. He raised the enormous black warhammer he had been leaning upon, its stone head absorbing rather than reflecting the sunlight, and bellowed. It was a warcry, a summons and an exclamation, and the sound swept forth, slamming into the buildings and hills around him and echoing back.

Below him, the dark tide ceased its movement. Then it rippled, as faces turned upward. Every orc in the Horde stopped and looked, staring up at the solitary figure high above.

Again he shouted, his hammer held high. And this time the tide erupted in cheers and shouts and answering cries. The Horde acknowledged its leader.

Satisfied, Orgrim Doomhammer let his signature weapon drop back down to his side, and the dark tide below resumed its destructive motion.

Down below, beyond the city's gates, an orc lay upon a cot. His short, scrawny frame was covered in thick furs, a sign of high status, and rich clothing lay in a pile nearby. But the clothing had not been touched, not in weeks. For the orc lay without stirring, as if dead, his ugly face scrunched in pain or concentration, his bushy beard bristling about his snarling mouth.

Then, suddenly, all changed. With a gasp the orc sat bolt upright, the furs falling away from his sweat-drenched body. His eyes opened, glassy and unseeing at first, then blinking away the long sleep and glancing around him.

"Where—?" the orc demanded. A larger figure was already moving to his side, both heads registering pleased surprise, and as the orc's gaze caught him the eyes sharpened, as did the features. Whatever confusion had lingered was gone, replaced by cunning and rage. "Where am I?" he demanded. "What has happened?"

"You were asleep, Gul'dan," the other creature replied, kneeling by the cot and offering a goblet. The orc grabbed it sniffed it, and tossed back the contents with a grunt, wiping a hand across his mouth afterward. "A sleep like death. For weeks now you have not moved, have barely breathed. We thought your spirit gone."

"Did you, now?" Gul'dan grinned. "Were you afraid I would leave you, Cho'gall? Abandon you to Blackhand's tender mercies?"

The two-headed ogre mage glared at him. "Blackhand is dead, Gul'dan!" one head snapped. The other frantically nodded agreement.

"Dead?" At first Gul'dan thought he had misheard, but Cho'gall's grim expressions convinced him even before both of the ogre's heads nodded. "What? How?" He pulled himself up to a sitting position, though the motion made him reel and break out in a cold sweat. "What has happened while I slept?"

Cho'gall began to answer but his words died as someone thrust aside the tent flap and burst into the small, dim space. Two burly orc warriors shoved Cho'gall out of the way and roughly grabbed Gul'dan's arms, hauling him to his feet. The ogre began to protest, rage darkening his twinned features, but two more orcs squeezed into the tight space and barred his path, heavy battleaxes at the ready. They stood guard as the first two dragged Gul'dan from the tent.

"Where are you taking me?" he demanded, trying to wrest his arms free. It was no use, however. Even at full health he would not have been a match for either warrior, and now he could barely hold himself upright. They were dragging him as much as leading him and he saw that he was being taken toward a large, well-crafted tent. Blackhand's tent.

"He took control, Gul'dan," Cho'gall said quietly, pacing beside him but staying beyond the warriors' reach. "While you were unconscious! He attacked the Shadow Council and killed most of them! Only you and I and a few of the lesser warlocks remain!"

Gul'dan shook his head, trying to clear it. He still felt fuzzy, unfocused, and from what Cho'gall said this was not a good time to lack clarity. But what the ogre had said made him more confused rather than less. Killed Blackhand? Destroyed the Shadow Council? It was insane!

"Who?" he demanded again, twisting to face Cho'gall over the warriors' broad shoulders. "Who did this?"

But Cho'gall had slowed his steps, falling back, a look of surprising fear crossing both his faces. Gul'dan turned back around just as a powerful figure strode forward. And at once, seeing the massive warrior in his black plate armor, the colossal black warhammer held so easily in his hands, Gul'dan understood.

Doomhammer.

"So you are awake." Doomhammer all but spat the words as the warriors stopped before him. They released Gul'dan's arms suddenly and the orc warlock was unable to stop himself from crumpling to the ground. He looked up, on his knees, and gulped at the naked fury and hatred he saw in his captor's face.

"I—" Gul'dan began, but Doomhammer cut him, backhanding him hard enough to lift him off the ground and drop him in a heap several feet away.

"Silence!" the new Horde leader snarled. "I did not say you could speak!" He strode closer, raising Gul'dan's chin with the head of his fearsome weapon. "I know what you have done, Gul'dan. I know how you controlled Blackhand, you and your Shadow Council." He laughed, a harsh sound filled with bitterness and disgust. "Oh, yes, I know about them. But your warlocks will not help you now. They are dead, many of them, and the few who remain are chained and watched." He leaned closer. "I rule the Horde now, Gul'dan. Not you, not your warlocks. Doomhammer alone. And there will be no more dishonor! No more treachery! No more deceit and lies!" Doomhammer rose to his full impressive height, towering over Gul'dan. "Durotan died from your scheming, but he will be the last. And he will be avenged! No more will you rule our people from the shadows! No more will you control our fate and direct us for your own sordid purpose! Our people will be free of you!"

Gul'dan cowered, thinking fast. He had known Doomhammer could become a problem. The powerful orc warrior was too intelligent, too honorable, too noble to be easily swayed or controlled. He had been second to Blackhand, the powerful Blackrock leader Gul'dan had chosen as his puppet for the Horde leadership. Blackhand had been an extremely powerful fighter but had thought himself clever and thus had been easily controlled. Gul'dan and his Shadow Council had been the real powers, and Gul'dan had ruled the council as easily as he did their warchief.

But not Doomhammer. He had refused to follow, carving his own path with reckless abandon equaled only by his loyalty to their people. Clearly he had seen what occurred behind the scenes, witnessed what he considered corruption. And when he had finally seen enough, when he could endure no more, he had acted.

Clearly Doomhammer had chosen his moment carefully. With Gul'dan out of the way, Blackhand had been vulnerable. How he had discovered the Shadow Council's location was unclear, but obviously he had done so and then had eliminated most of them. Leaving Gul'dan, Cho'gall, and who knew what others.

And now he stood over Gul'dan, hammer raised, ready to destroy him as well.

"Wait!" Gul'dan cried out, both hands raising automatically to shield his face and head from harm. "Please, I beg you!"

That made Doomhammer pause. "You, the mighty Gul'dan, beg? Very well, dog, beg! Beg for your life!" The hammer had not lowered, but at least it had not fallen. Yet.

"I—" Gul'dan hated him then, hated him with a passion he had never known for anything but power itself. Yet he knew what he had to do. Doomhammer hated him as well, for orchestrating his old friend Durotan's death and for transforming their people from peaceful hunters to raving warmongers. Given even the slightest excuse, that hammer would smash his skull in, coating itself with his blood and hair and brain. He could not allow that to happen.

"I bow to your might, Orgrim Doomhammer," he managed at last, pronouncing each word clearly and loud enough that all those nearby could hear him. "I acknowledge you as warchief of the Horde, and I pledge myself to you. I will obey you in all things."

Doomhammer grunted. "You have never demonstrated obedience before," he pointed out sharply. "Why should I believe you capable of it now?"

"Because you need me," Gul'dan replied, raising his head to meet the warchief's glare. "You have slain my Shadow Council, yes, and consolidated your power over the Horde. That is as it should be. Blackhand was not strong enough to lead us on his own. You are, and so you have no need of a council." He licked his lips. "But you do need warlocks. You need our magic, for the humans have magic of their own and without us you will fall to their power." He shook his head. "And you have very few warlocks left. Myself, Cho'gall, and a handful of neophytes. I am too useful to kill simply for revenge."

Doomhammer's lips pulled back in a snarl, but he lowered the hammer. For a moment he said nothing, simply glaring at Gul'dan, his gray eyes filled with hate. But finally he nodded.

"What you say is true," he admitted, though the words clearly took enormous self-control to utter. "And I will place the needs of the Horde over my own." He bared his tusks. "I will allow you to live, Gul'dan, you and those of your warlocks who remain. But only as long as you prove useful."

"Oh, we will be useful," Gul'dan assured him, bowing low. His mind was already working. "I will create for you a host of creatures such as you have never seen before, mighty Doomhammer—warriors who will serve you alone. With their might and our magic we will crush this world's magi even as the Horde tramples its warriors into the dust."

Doomhammer nodded, his snarl fading to a thoughtful frown. "Very well," he said at last. "You have promised me warriors who can combat the humans' magic. I will hold you to that." Then he turned and walked away, clearly dismissing him. The orc warriors departed as well, leaving Gul'dan still on his knees with Cho'gall not far away. The orc warlock thought he heard them laughing as they left.

Damn him! Gul'dan thought, watching the warchief disappear back into his tent. And damn that human wizard as well! Gul'dan shook his head. Perhaps he should be cursing his own impatience instead. It had been that which had driven him to enter Medivh's mind, seeking the information the Magus had promised but thus far withheld from him. And it had merely been bad luck that Gul'dan had been inside Medivh's mind when the human had died, his own spirit weakened by the sudden violence. He had been trapped, unable to return to his body all this time, unaware of the world around him. And that had given Doomhammer the opportunity to seize control.

But now, at last, he was awake again. And once more he could pursue his plans. Because at least that desperate, dangerous act had not been wasted. Gul'dan had the information he needed. And soon he would not need Doomhammer or the Horde any longer. Soon he would be all-powerful without them.

"Gather the others," he told Cho'gall, pushing himself up off the ground and testing his limbs. He was weak, but he would manage. He had no time to do otherwise. "I will forge them into a clan in truth, one that will serve my own ends and protect me from

Doomhammer's wrath. They shall be Stormreavers, and they will show all the Horde what we warlocks can accomplish, until even Doomhammer cannot deny their worth. Gather your clan as well." Cho'gall led the Twilight's Hammer clan—they were obsessed with the end of the world but were fearsome fighters. "There is much to do."

CHAPTER ONE

Despite himself, Lothar was impressed.

Stormwind had been a towering, imposing city, filled with spires and terraces, carved from strong stone to resist the wind but polished to a mirror sheen. But in its own way Capital City was equally lovely.

Not that Capital City was the same as Stormwind. It was not as tall, for one. But what it lacked in height it made up for in elegance. It sat on a rise above the north shore of Lordamere Lake, gleaming all in white and silver. It did not glitter as Stormwind had, but it glowed somehow, as if the sun were rising from its graceful buildings instead of beating down upon them. It seemed serene, peaceful, almost holy.

"It is a mighty place," Khadgar agreed beside him, "though I prefer a little more warmth." He glanced behind them, toward the lake's southern shore, where a second city rose. Its outlines were similar to those of

Capital City, but this mirror image seemed more exotic, its walls and spires suffused in violet and other warm hues. "That is Dalaran," he explained. "Home of the Kirin Tor and its wizards. My home, before I was sent to Medivh."

"Perhaps there will be time for you to return, at least briefly," Lothar suggested. "But for now we must concentrate on Capital City." He studied the gleaming city again. "Let us hope they are as noble in their thoughts as they are in their dwellings." He kicked his horse into a canter, and rode down out of the majestic Silverpine Forest, Varian and the mage right behind him and the other men trailing them in their carts.

Two hours later they reached the main gates. Guards stood by the entrance, though the double gates were wide open and large enough for two or even three wagons to pass abreast. The guards had clearly seen them long before they reached the gates, and the one who stepped forward wore a crimson cloak over his polished breastplate and had gold traceries in his armor and helmet. His manner was polite, even respectful, but Lothar could not help noticing how the man stopped only a few feet away, well within sword range. He forced himself to relax and ignore the laxity. This was not Stormwind. These people were not seasoned warriors, hardened by constant battle. They had never had to fight for their lives. Yet.

"Enter freely and be welcome," the guard captain stated, bowing. "Marcus Redpath warned us of your arrival, and your plight. You will find the king in his throneroom."

"Our thanks," Khadgar replied with a nod. "Come, Lothar," he added, nudging his horse with his heels. "I know the way."

They rode on through the city, navigating its broad streets easily. Khadgar did indeed seem to know the way, and never slowed to ask directions or puzzle over a turn until they had reached the palace itself. There they surrendered their horses to some of their companions, leaving them to mind the steeds. Lothar and Prince Varian were already striding up the palace's wide steps and Khadgar quickly joined them.

They stepped through the palace's outer doors and into a wide courtyard, almost an outdoor hall. Viewing boxes lined the sides, and though empty now Lothar was sure they filled with people during celebrations. At the far end another short flight of steps led up to a second set of doors, and these opened onto the throneroom itself.

It was an imposing chamber, its arched ceiling so high overhead its edges were lost in shadow. The room was round, with arches and columns everywhere. Golden sunlight streamed down from a stained-glass panel set in the ceiling's center, illuminating the intricate pattern in the floor: a series of nested circles, each one different, with a triangle at their middle overlapping the innermost ring, and the golden seal of Lordaeron within that. It had several high balconies and

Lothar guessed these were for nobles but also appreciated their strategic value. A few guards with bows could easily strike anywhere in the room from those vantage points.

Just beyond the pattern stood a wide circular dais, its concentric steps rising up toward a massive throne. The throne itself looked carved from glittering stone, all sharp edges and planes and angles. A man sat there, tall and broad, his blond hair only lightly touched with gray, his armor gleaming, the crown upon his head shaped more like a spiked helmet than a coronet. This was a proper king, Lothar knew at once, a king like his Llane who did not hesitate to fight for his people. His hopes rose at the thought.

There were people here, townsfolk and laborers and even peasants, gathered facing the dais from a respectful distance. Many carried items, scraps of parchment, even food, but they parted before Lothar and Khadgar, falling away from the pair without a sound.

"Yes?" the man on the throne called out as they approached. "Who are you and what do you wish of me? Ah." Even from here Lothar could see the king's strangely colored eyes, blue and green swirled together—they were sharp and clear, and his hopes rose still further. Here was a man who saw well and clearly.

"Your Majesty," Lothar replied, his deep voice carrying easily across the large room. He stopped several paces from the dais and bowed. "I am Anduin Lothar, a

Knight of Stormwind. This is my companion, Khadgar of Dalaran." He heard several murmurs from the crowd now behind them. "And this"—he turned so that the king could see Varian, who had been standing behind him, unnerved by the crowd and the strange trappings—"is Prince Varian Wrynn, heir to the throne of Stormwind." The murmurs turned to gasps as people realized the youth was visiting royalty, but Lothar ignored them, concentrating only on the king. "We must speak with you, your Majesty. It is a matter of great urgency and major import."

"Of course." Terenas was already rising from his throne and approaching them. "Leave us, please," he asked the rest of the crowd, though it was an order despite its polite wording. The people obeyed quickly, and soon only a handful of nobles and guards remained. The men who had accompanied Lothar faded back to the sides as well, leaving only Lothar, Khadgar, and Varian when Terenas closed the distance between them.

"Your Majesty," Terenas greeted Varian, bowing to him as to an equal.

"Your Majesty," Varian replied, his training overcoming his shock.

"We were grieved to hear of your father's death," Terenas continued gently. "King Llane was a good man and we counted him as a friend and an ally. Know that we shall do all in our power to restore you to your throne."

"I thank you," Varian said, though his lower lip trembled slightly.

"Now come and sit, and tell me what has happened," Terenas instructed, gesturing to the dais steps. He sat on the top one himself and motioned for Varian to sit beside him. "I have seen Stormwind myself, and admired its strength and beauty. What could destroy such a city?"

"The Horde," Khadgar said, speaking for the first time since they had entered the throneroom. Terenas turned toward him, and Lothar was close enough to see the king's eyes narrow slightly. "The Horde did this."

"And what is this Horde?" Terenas demanded, turning first to Varian and then to Lothar.

"It is an army, more than an army," Lothar replied. "It is a multitude, more than can be counted, enough to cover the land from shore to shore."

"And who commands this legion of men?" Terenas asked.

"Not men," Lothar corrected. "Orcs." At the king's puzzlement Lothar explained. "A new race, one not native to this world. They are as tall as we are, and more powerfully built, with green skin and glowing red eyes. And great tusks from their lower lips." A noble snorted somewhere, and Lothar turned, glaring. "You doubt me?" he shouted, turning toward each of the balconies in turn, looking for the one who had laughed. "You think I lie?" He struck his armor with his fist, near one of the more prominent dents. "This was made by an orc warhammer!" He struck another spot. "And this by an orc war axe!" He pointed to a gash along one forearm. "And this came from a tusk, when one jumped me and was too close for our blades to strike one another! These foul creatures have destroyed my land, my home, my people! If you doubt me come down here and say so to my face! I will show you what sort of man I am, and what happens to those who accuse me of falsehood!"

"Enough!" Terenas's shout silenced any possible reply, anger plain in his own voice, but when he turned to Lothar the warrior could see that this king's anger was not directed at him. "Enough," the king said again, more softly. "None here doubt your word, Champion," he assured Lothar, a stern look around daring any of his nobles to disagree. "I know of your honor and your loyalty. I will take you at your word, though such creatures sound strange to us." He turned and nodded at Khadgar. "And with one of the wizards of Dalaran beside you as a witness, we cannot discount what you say, nor the notion of races never seen here before."

"I thank you, King Terenas," Lothar replied formally, reining his anger back in. He was not sure what to do next. Fortunately, Terenas was.

"I will summon my neighboring kings," he announced. "These events concern us all." He turned back toward Varian. "Your Majesty, I offer you my home and my protection for as long as you shall need it," he stated, loud enough for all to hear. "When you are ready, know that Lordaeron will assist you in reclaiming your kingdom."

Lothar nodded. "Your Majesty, you are most generous," he said on Varian's behalf, "and I can think of no safer and finer place for my prince to reach his maturity than here in Capital City. Know, however, that we did not come here merely for sanctuary. We came to warn you." He stood tall, his voice rumbling across the room, his eyes not leaving Lordaeron's king. "For know this—the Horde will not stop at Stormwind. They mean to claim the entire world, and they have the might and the numbers to make their dream a reality. Nor do they lack magical might. Once they have finished with my homeland—" His voice grew deeper and rougher and he forced himself to continue. "They will find a way across the ocean. And they will come here."

"You are telling us to prepare for war," Terenas said quietly. It was not a question, but Lothar answered nonetheless.

"Yes." He looked around at the assembled men. "A war for the very survival of our race."

CHAPTER TWO

Orgrim Doomhammer, chieftain of the Black-rock clan and warchief of the Horde, surveyed the scene. He stood near the center of Stormwind as his warriors destroyed the once-great city around him. Everywhere he turned there was destruction and devastation. Buildings burned despite being made of stone. Bodies and rubble littered the street. Blood flowed across the flagstones, pooling here and there. Screams indicated that survivors had been found and were being tortured.

Doomhammer nodded. It was good.

Stormwind had been an imposing city and a powerful obstacle. For a time he had not been sure they could topple its great walls or overwhelm its stalwart defenders. Despite the Horde's superior numbers, the humans had fought back with skill and determination. Doomhammer respected them for that. They had been worthy opponents.

Yet they had fallen, as all must, before his people's might. The city had been breached, its defenders killed or run off, and now this land was theirs. This rich, fertile land, so like their own homeworld had been before the cataclysm. Before Gul'dan and his folly had destroyed it.

Doomhammer's thoughts turned grim and his grip tightened on his fabled hammer. Gul'dan! The treacherous shaman-turned-warlock had caused more trouble than he was worth. Only his opening the rift to this new world had saved him from being torn apart by enraged clansmen. Yet somehow the schemer had turned even that to his advantage. He had taken control of Blackhand—or perhaps he had always had it. Doomhammer had watched his former chieftain for years and knew the massive orc warrior had been smarter than he let on. But not smart enough. And by playing to Blackhand's ego Gul'dan had swayed him and taken control. He had been behind the plan to unite the clans into the Horde, Doomhammer was sure of that. And Gul'dan's Shadow Council had ruled from behind the scenes, advising Blackhand in such a way that he never realized they were in fact issuing orders.

Doomhammer grinned. That, at least, was ended now. He had not been pleased at being forced to kill Blackhand. He had been the warchief's Second and sworn to fight beside him, not against him. But tradition allowed a warrior to challenge his chieftain for supremacy and Doomhammer had finally been forced to take that route. He had won, as he knew he must, and with the blow that crushed Blackhand's skull he had taken control of their clan—and of the Horde.

That had left the Shadow Council to deal with. And that had been a pleasure.

He chuckled at the memory. Few orcs had even known of the council's existence, much less its membership and sanctuary. But Doomhammer had guessed whom to ask. The half-orc Garona had been tortured into revealing the council's location—no doubt her non-orc blood made her too weak to withstand much. The look on the warlocks' faces as he had burst into their meeting had been priceless. And even moreso their expressions as he had advanced through the room, slaughtering them left and right. Doomhammer had shattered the power of the Shadow Council that day. He would not be controlled as Blackhand had. He would choose his own battles and make his own plans, not to increase anyone's power but to ensure his people's survival.

As if thinking of him had been a summons, Doomhammer spotted two figures approaching him down the broad, bloodied street. One was shorter than an average orc, the other far taller and with a strange shape. Doomhammer knew them at once and his lips curled away from his tusks in a sneer.

"Have you completed your task, then?" he called out as Gul'dan and his lackey Cho'gall approached. He kept his gaze on the warlock, barely sparing a sharp glance at his hulking subordinate. Doomhammer had fought ogres all his life, as had most orcs. He had been disgusted when Blackhand had forged an alliance with the monstrous creatures, though he admitted they had their use in combat. But he still did not like or trust them. And Cho'gall was worse than most. He was one of that rare breed, the two-headed ogre, and had far more intelligence than his brutish brethren. Cho'gall was a mage in his own right, and the idea of an ogre with such power filled Doomhammer with dread. Plus Cho'gall had gained control of the Twilight's Hammer clan, and showed the same fanaticism as the orcs who followed him. That made the two-headed ogre very dangerous. Not that Doomhammer would ever let such concerns show, but he kept his grip on his hammer tight whenever the ogre mage was near.

"I have not, noble Doomhammer," Gul'dan replied, stopping beside him. The warlock looked thin but otherwise no worse for his months-long slumber. "But I have at last shaken off the last effects of my prolonged slumber. And I bring powerful news drawn from that same long repose!"

"Oh? Your sleep has brought you wisdom?"

"It has shown me the path to great power," Gul'dan admitted, lust clear in his eyes. But Doomhammer knew it was not an ordinary lust, not for females or fine food or wealth. Gul'dan thought only of power, and would do anything to obtain it. His actions on their own world had proven that.

"Power for you or for the Horde?" Doomhammer demanded.

"For both," the warlock replied. His voice dropped to a sly whisper. "I have seen a place, ancient beyond imagining, older even than the sacred mountain of our homeworld. It lies deep beneath the waves, and within it rests a power that could reshape this world. We could claim it as our own, and none can stand against us!"

"None can stand against us now," Doomhammer growled back. "And I prefer the honest might of hammer and axe to whatever foul sorceries you have uncovered. Look what your scheming did to our world, and to our people, the last time! I will not have you destroy them further or wreck this new world just as we have begun to conquer it!"

"This is far greater than your desires," the warlock snapped, his temper brushing aside any pretense of servility. "My destiny lies beneath the water, and there is little you can do to stop that! This Horde is but the first step in our people's path, and it shall be I who lead them beyond here, not you!"

"Have a care, warlock," Doomhammer replied, his hammer coming up to tap Gul'dan lightly on the cheek. "Remember what happened to your precious Shadow Council. I can crush your skull in an instant, and then where will your destiny lie?" He glowered up at the towering Cho'gall. "And do not think this abomination will save you," he snarled, raising the hammer higher and laughing as the ogre mage stepped back, fear washing across both his faces. "I have felled ogres before, even the gronn. I can and will do so again." He leaned in close. "Your goals are no longer important. Only the Horde matters."

For an instant he saw anger flicker in Gul'dan's eyes and thought the warlock might not back down. And a part of him rejoiced. Doomhammer had always admired and revered his people's shaman, as had all orcs, but these warlocks were something far different. Their power did not come from the elements or the ancestor-spirits but from some other, horrible source. It had been their magic that had turned his people from wholesome brown to gruesome green, and was killing their own world, forcing them to come here just to survive. And Gul'dan was their leader, their instigator, by far the most powerful, most cunning, and most selfish of them all. Doomhammer knew the warlocks' value to the Horde but he could not help but feel they would all be better off without them.

Perhaps Gul'dan saw this in his own eyes, for the anger vanished, replaced by caution and grudging respect. "Of course, mighty Doomhammer," the warlock said, dropping his head. "You are correct. The Horde must come first." He grinned, fully recovered from his fright, the anger apparently gone or at least buried deep once more. "And I have many new ideas to aid our conquest. But first I shall deliver the warriors I promised, unstoppable but fully under your control."

Doomhammer nodded slowly. "Very well," he

grated. "I will not ignore anything that could make our success more assured." He turned away, dismissing the warlock and his lieutenant, and Gul'dan took the hint, bowing and walking away, Cho'gall stomping along beside him. Doomhammer knew he would have to watch both of them very closely. Gul'dan was not one to take an insult lightly, or to allow anyone to control him for long. But until the warlock stepped out of line his magic would be useful, and Doomhammer would take full advantage of that. The sooner they crushed any opposition, the sooner his people could set aside their weapons and turn to building homes and families once more.

With that in mind, Doomhammer sought out another of his lieutenants, finding him at last in what had once been a great hall, feasting upon the food and drink they had found there.

"Zuluhed!" The orc shaman glanced up as Doomhammer shouted his name and quickly stood, pushing away the goblet and platter before him. Though old and thin and shriveled, Zuluhed's red-brown eyes were still sharp beneath his tattered gray braids.

"Doomhammer." Unlike Gul'dan, Zuluhed did not snivel or bow, and Doomhammer respected that. But then Zuluhed was a chieftain in his own right, the head of the Dragonmaw clan. He was also a shaman, the only shaman to have accompanied the Horde. And it was those abilities and what they might provide that interested Doomhammer.

"How goes the work?" Doomhammer did not bother with pleasantries, though he did accept the goblet Zuluhed offered him. The wine within it was fine indeed, and the traces of human blood that had spilled into it only enhanced the flavor.

"The same," the Dragonmaw leader replied, disgust written plainly across his features.

Months ago Zuluhed had approached, telling Doomhammer of strange visions that had plagued him. Visions of a particular mountain range, and of a mighty treasure buried deep beneath it—a treasure not of wealth but of power. Doomhammer respected the older chieftain and remembered the power of a shaman's visions from their own world. He had approved Zuluhed's request to lead his clan in search of that mountain and the power it concealed. It had taken weeks but at last the Dragonmaw clan had found a cavern deep in the earth, and within it a strange object, a golden disc they had named the Demon Soul. Though Doomhammer had not seen the artifact himself, Zuluhed had assured him that it radiated immense age and incredible power. Unfortunately, that power was proving difficult to obtain.

"You assured me you could trigger its power," Doomhammer reminded, tossing the empty goblet aside. It struck the far wall with a dull crunch.

"And I shall," Zuluhed assured him. "The Demon Soul contains immense resources, enough power to let us shatter mountains and tear open the sky!" He frowned. "But thus far it has resisted my magics." He shook his head. "But I will find the key! I know it! I have seen it in my dreams! And once we can tap its power, we shall use it to enslave our chosen servants! And with them beneath us we shall rule the skies, and rain fire down upon all those who stand against us!"

"Excellent." Doomhammer clapped the other orc on the shoulder. The shaman's fanaticism worried him from time to time, especially since Zuluhed did not seem to live entirely in this world, but he had no doubts of his loyalty. That was why he had supported the old orc's quest, when he had spurned Gul'dan's request to embark on a similarly vision-based search for power. Doomhammer knew that, whatever else happened, Zuluhed would not turn against him or against their people. And if this Demon Soul could do half what Zuluhed had promised, if it enabled the shaman to make his visions a reality, it would indeed ensure the Horde's superiority in battle. "Send word when all is ready."

"Of course." Zuluhed saluted him with his own goblet, which he refilled from a blood-smeared golden pitcher. Doomhammer left the shaman to his celebration and resumed his wanderings through the fallen city. He liked to see what his warriors were doing first-hand, and he knew that seeing their leader walking among them gave the others a sense of him as one of them, bonding them to him ever more tightly. Black-hand had known that as well, making sure his orcs saw him as a fellow warrior as well as a chieftain and later warchief, and it was one of the lessons Doomhammer had learned well from his predecessor. His meeting with Zuluhed had wiped away the sour taste Gul'dan had left in his mouth, and as he stalked through the streets Doomhammer found his spirits high. His people had achieved a great victory here and deserved to celebrate. He would let them enjoy themselves for a few days. Then they would move on to the next target.

Gul'dan watched Doomhammer from a few buildings away.

"What are he and Zuluhed planning?" he demanded, not turning away from glaring at the Warchief's retreating back.

"I do not know," Cho'gall admitted. "They have been secretive about it. I know it involves something the Dragonmaw found in the mountains. Half their clan is there now but I do not know what they are doing."

"Well, it does not matter." Gul'dan frowned, rubbing absently at one tusk as he thought. "Whatever it is, it serves to keep Doomhammer distracted, and that works to our advantage. It would not do for him to uncover our own plans before we can set them in motion." He grinned. "And then—then it will be too late for him."

"Will you replace him as warchief?" Cho'gall's other head asked as they moved away, returning to the quarters that had been set aside for them.

"Myself? No." Gul'dan laughed. "I have no desire to march through the streets with an axe or a hammer, meeting my foes in the flesh," he admitted. "My path is the far greater one. I shall meet them in spirit and crush them from afar, devouring them by the hundreds and the thousands." He smiled at the thought. "Soon all that was promised me shall be mine, and then Doomhammer will be as nothing against me. Even the might of the Horde will pale before me, and I shall stretch out my hand and wipe this world clean, to remake it in my own image!" He laughed again, and the sound came back to him from the tumbled walls and torn buildings, as if the dying city were laughing with him.

CHAPTER THREE

K hadgar watched quietly from one side of the throneroom. Lothar had wanted him present both as a witness and, Khadgar suspected, as a familiar face in this strange land, and Khadgar's own curiosity had compelled him to accept the invitation. But he knew better than to present himself to these men as an equal—despite the power he now wielded personally, every one of them was a ruler and capable of having him killed in seconds. Besides, Khadgar felt he had been in the center of things too much of late. As a youth he had been more accustomed to watching and waiting and studying before he acted. It was nice to return to old habits again, if only for the moment.

He recognized many of the men present, at least by description. The large, bearish man with the thick features, the heavy black beard, and the black and gray armor was Genn Graymane. He ruled the southern nation of Gilneas, and Khadgar had heard he was far more clever than his appearance suggested. The tall, slender man with the weathered skin and the green naval uniform was of course Admiral Daelin Proud-moore. He ruled Kul Tiras, but it was his position as commander of the world's largest, fiercest navy that made even Terenas treat him as an equal. The quiet, cultured-looking man with the graying brown hair and hazel eyes was Lord Aiden Perenolde, master of Al-terac. He was glaring at Thoras Trollbane, king of neighboring Stromgarde, but the tall, gruff Trollbane was ignoring him, his leathers and furs apparently shielding him as well from Perenolde's anger as they did from his mountain home's fierce weather. Instead Trollbane's craggy features were turned toward a short, stout man with a snow-white beard and a friendly face. He needed no introduction anywhere on the continent, even without his ceremonial robes and staff—Alonsus Faol was the archbishop of the Church of Light and revered by humans everywhere. Khadgar could see why—he had never met Faol himself but just watching him created a sense of peace and wisdom.

A violet flicker from the corner of his eye distracted Khadgar, and he turned—and struggled not to gape. Striding into the throneroom was a legend. Tall and ca-daverously thin, with a long, gray-streaked brown beard and mustache and matching bushy eyebrows, his bald head covered by a gold-edged skullcap, was the Arch-mage Antonidas. In all his years in Dalaran Khadgar had seen the Kirin Tor leader only twice, once in passing and once when they informed Khadgar they were sending him to Medivh. To see the master wizard now, openly taking his place beside the other rulers, looking every inch as regal as any monarch, filled Khadgar with awe and a surprising wave of homesickness. He missed Dalaran, and found himself wondering if he would ever be able to return to the wizard city. Perhaps after the wars were over. Assuming they survived.

Antonidas had been the last to arrive, and when he reached the area just before the dais Terenas stood and clapped his hands—the sound reverberated and conversations died away, as everyone turned their attention toward their royal host.

"Thank you all for coming," Terenas began, his voice carrying easily across the room. "I know the request seemed sudden, but we have matters of grave import to discuss and time seems to be of the essence." He paused, then turned to the man standing on the dais beside him. "I present to you Anduin Lothar, Champion of Stormwind. He has come here as a messenger and more, perhaps a savior. I think it best if I let him tell you himself what he has seen and what we may expect soon ourselves."

Lothar stepped forward. Terenas had provided him with fresh clothing, of course, but Lothar had insisted on keeping his armor rather than trading it for undamaged Lordaeron gear. His greatsword still rose above one shoulder, a fact Khadgar was sure many of the monarchs had noticed, but it was the Champion's face and words that caught their attention right from the start. For once Lothar's inability to hide his emotions worked to his advantage, letting the assembled kings see the truth in his words.

"Your Majesties," Lothar began, "I thank you for attending this meeting, and for listening to what I have to say. I am no poet or diplomat but a warrior, so I will keep my words brief and blunt." He took a deep breath. "I must tell you that my home, Stormwind, is no more." Several of the monarchs gasped. Others paled. "It fell before a Horde of creatures known as orcs," Lothar explained. "They are terrible foes, as tall as a man and far stronger, with bestial features, green skin, and red eyes." This time no one laughed. "This Horde appeared recently and began harassing our patrols," Lothar continued, "but those were just their raiding parties. When their full force marched we were astounded. They literally have thousands, tens of thousands, of warriors—enough to cover the land like a foul shadow. And they are implacable foes, strong and cruel and merciless." He sighed. "We fought them as best we could. But it was not enough. They besieged our city, after wreaking havoc across the land itself, and though we held them back for a time they finally breached our defenses. King Llane died at their hands." Khadgar noticed Lothar did not say how. Perhaps mentioning the half-orc assassin they had trusted as a scout and ally would weaken his recounting. Or perhaps Lothar simply did not want to think about it. Khadgar could understand that. He didn't want to dwell on the matter either—he had considered Garona a friend, and had been saddened by her betrayal, even though he had been with her when they saw a vision of it, back in Medivh's tower. "As did most of our nobles," Lothar was continuing. "I was charged with seeing his son and as many people to safety as possible, and with warning the rest of the world what had happened. For this Horde is not native to our land, not even to our world. And they will not be content to control a single continent. They will want the rest of the world as well."

"You are saying they are coming here," Proudmoore commented, more a statement than a question, when Lothar paused.

"Yes." Lothar's simple response sent a ripple of surprise—and perhaps fear—through the room. But Proudmoore nodded.

"Do they have ships?" he asked.

"I do not know," Lothar replied. "We had not seen any before now, but then we had not seen the Horde itself until this past year." He frowned. "And if they did not have ships before, they certainly have them now—they raided all along our coastline, and while they sank many vessels others are simply missing."

"We can assume, then, that they have the means to cross the ocean." Proudmoore did not look surprised by this, and Khadgar guessed the admiral had already assumed the worst. "They could be sailing toward us even now."

"They can march over land as well," Trollbane growled. "Don't forget that."

"Aye, they can indeed," Lothar agreed. "We first encountered them to the east, near the Swamp of Sorrows, and they crossed all Azeroth to reach Stormwind. If they turn north they can cross the Burning Steppes and the mountains and come upon Lordaeron from the south."

"The south?" That was Genn Graymane. "They shall not pass us! I will crush any who attempt landfall on my southern coast!"

"You do not understand." Lothar looked and sounded weary. "You have not faced them, and so their numbers and strength are difficult to comprehend. But I tell you now, you cannot stand against them." He faced the assembled monarchs, pride and grief clear on his face. "Stormwind's armies were great," he assured them softly. "My warriors were trained and seasoned. We had faced the orcs before and defeated them. But that was merely their vanguard. Before the Horde itself we fell like addled children, like old men, like wheat." His voice was flat, his words carrying a ring of grim certainty. "They will sweep across the mountains and across your lands and across you."

"What do you propose we do, then?" That was Archbishop Faol, and his calm voice soothed the tempers Khadgar saw ready to erupt. No one liked being called a fool, especially a king, and especially not in front of his peers.

"We need to band together," Lothar insisted. "None of you alone can withstand them. But all of us together . . . might."

"You say this threat is coming, and I would not dispute it," Perenolde commented, his smooth voice cutting across the other kings. "And you say we must band together to end the threat. Yet I wonder, have you tried other methods to resolve the matter? Surely these . . . orcs . . . are rational beings? Surely they have some goal in mind? Perhaps we can negotiate with them?"

Lothar shook his head, his pained expression showing just how foolish he found this discussion. "They want this world, our world," he answered slowly, as if talking to a child. "They will not settle for less. We did send messengers, envoys, ambassadors." He smiled, a grim, hard smile. "Most of them came back in pieces. If they came back at all."

Khadgar saw several of the kings murmuring to each other, and from their tone suspected they still did not understand the danger they all faced. He sighed and began to step forward, wondering even as he did why they would listen to him any more than they had to Lothar. Yet he had to try.

Fortunately, another moved forward as well, and though he also wore robes rather than armor this new figure carried more authority by far.

"Hear me," Antonidas cried, his voice thin but still powerful. He raised his carved staff high and light burst from its tip, dazzling the other men present. "Hear me!"

he demanded again, and this time all turned and quieted to listen. "I have received reports before now of this new menace," the archmage admitted. "The wizards of Azeroth were first intrigued and then terrified by the orcs' appearance, and sent many letters with information and a request for aid." He frowned. "I fear we did not listen as well as we might have. We appreciated their danger but thought the orcs little more than a local nuisance, confined to that continent. It seems we were wrong. But I tell you that they are dangerous—many I respect have confirmed this. We disregard the Champion's words at our own peril."

"If they are so dangerous, why did the wizards there not deal with them?" Graymane demanded. "Why did they not use their magic to end the threat?"

"Because the orcs possess magic of their own," Antonidas countered. "Potent magic. Most of their warlocks are weaker than our own wizards, at least from what my fellows reported, yet they have far greater numbers and can work in unison, something my own brethren have never found easy." Khadgar was sure he heard some bitterness in the old archmage's voice, and understood it well. If there was one thing every member of the Kirin Tor valued, it was his independence. Getting even two wizards to work together was difficult enough—the thought of managing more than that was almost beyond imagining.

"Our wizards did fight back," Lothar explained. "They helped turn the tide of several battles. But the archmage is correct. We lacked the numbers to stand against them, magically as well as physically. For every orc spellcaster killed, another rose to take his place, and two more beside him. And they traveled with raiding parties and smaller armies to protect them from more mundane dangers, lending their magic to increase the power of the warriors around them." He frowned. "Our greatest wizard, Medivh, fell to the Horde's darkness. Most of our other wizards were lost as well. I do not think magic alone will turn them back." Khadgar noticed that Lothar did not mention how or why Medivh had died and appreciated the warrior's tact. This was not the place for such revelations. He did not miss the sharp glance Antonidas directed his way, however, and suppressed a sigh. At some point soon, the ruling council of the Kirin Tor would demand a full explanation. Khadgar knew they would not be satisfied with less than the truth. And he suspected withholding anything could prove deadly to them all, since it tied so closely to the Horde's presence and early activities.

"I find it strange," Perenolde's soft purr cut through the conversation again, "that a stranger to our shores should be so concerned for our survival." He glanced at Lothar with what looked suspiciously like a smirk and Khadgar resisted the urge to set the oily king's beard alight. "Forgive me for treading upon fresh wounds, sir, but your own kingdom is gone, your king dead, your prince little more than a boy, your lands overrun. Is this not so?" Lothar nodded, grinding his teeth—presumably to keep from snapping the arrogant king's head off. "You have brought word of this threat to us, for which we are grateful. Yet you speak repeatedly of what we must do, how we must unite." He made a great show of looking around the chamber. Varian was not there—Terenas had taken him in, treating the still shaken prince as a member of his own household, and both he and Lothar had agreed that the boy should not have to deal with additional scrutiny right now. "I do not see anyone else from your kingdom here, and you have said yourself that the prince is but a boy and the lands a conquered territory. If we were to consider your suggestion and unite, what could you possibly add to the assembly? Beyond your own martial prowess, of course."

Lothar opened his mouth to respond, fury evident in every feature, but he was cut off again. By King Terenas, surprisingly enough.

"I will not have my guest insulted so," Lordaeron's ruler announced, the steel plain in his voice. "He has brought us this news at great personal peril and has shown nothing but honor and compassion despite his own personal grief!" Perenolde nodded and half-bowed a silent if mocking apology. "Further, you are wrong to think him alone or invaluable," Terenas continued. "Prince Varian Wrynn is now my honored guest, and will be so until such time as he chooses to depart. I have pledged myself to aiding him in regaining his kingdom." Several of the other monarchs murmured at that, and Khadgar knew what they were thinking. Terenas had just renounced any claims he might make to Stormwind and warned the other kings that Varian had his support, all in a single statement. It was a clever move, and his respect for Lordaeron's king rose still higher. "Sir Lothar has brought with him others from his kingdom," Terenas continued, "including some soldiers. While their numbers are not significant when compared to the threat we face, their experience in dealing with the orcs firsthand could be invaluable. Many more still wander what was Stormwind, confused and unguided. These may rally upon hearing their Champion's call, giving us additional numbers. Lothar himself is a seasoned commander and tactician, and I have nothing but the utmost respect for his personal abilities." He paused, and glanced at Lothar in what looked curiously like a question. Khadgar was intrigued to see his companion nod. The Champion and the king had met several times while waiting for the other monarchs to arrive and Khadgar had not been privy to all their discussions, but now he wondered what exactly he had missed.

"Finally, there is the question of his being a stranger." Terenas smiled. "Though Lothar himself has not graced this continent with his presence before now, he is far from a stranger, for he has strong ties to this land and to our own kingdoms. For he is of the Arathi bloodline, indeed the last of their noble line, and thus has as much right to speak at this council as any of us!"

The revelation caused a stir among the other kings, and Khadgar also looked at his companion with new eyes. An Arathi! He had heard of Arathor, of course, as had everyone in Lordaeron—it had been the first nation on the continent, long ago, and the people there had formed strong ties with the elves. Together the two races had fought against a massive troll army at the foot of the Alterac Mountains, and together the two races broke the troll threat and shattered the troll nation forever. The Arathorian Empire had prospered and expanded before finally, years later, collapsing into the smaller nations that covered the continent today. The Arathor capital, Strom, had been abandoned for the lusher northern lands, and the last of the Arathi had disappeared. Some stories claimed they had gone south, past Khaz Modan, into the wilderness of Azeroth. Strom had become the center of Stromgarde, Trollbane's domain.

"It is true," Lothar announced in ringing tones, his eyes daring any man to call him a liar. "I descend from King Thoradin, the founder of Arathor. My family settled in Azeroth after the empire collapsed, and founded a new nation there, which became known as Stormwind."

"So you have come to claim sovereignty over us?" Graymane demanded, though his face showed he did not believe it.

"No," Lothar assured him. "My ancestors surrendered any claim upon Lordaeron long ago, when they chose to depart. But I still have ties to this land, which my people helped conquer and civilize."

"And he can still call upon ancient pacts for aid," Terenas pointed out. "The elves swore to support Thoradin and his line in times of need. They will still honor that commitment."

That drew appreciative glances and whispers from several, and Khadgar nodded. Suddenly Lothar was more than just a warrior or even a commander in their eyes. Now he was a potential ambassador to the elves. And if that ancient, magic-wielding race chose to ally with them, suddenly the Horde did not seem nearly as unstoppable.

"This is a great deal to take in," Perenolde commented dryly. "Perhaps we should give ourselves time to consider all we have heard, and all that must be done to protect our lands from this new threat."

"Agreed," Terenas said, not even bothering to ask the others their opinion. "Food has been set out in the dining hall, and I invite all of you to join me, not as kings but as neighbors and friends. Let us not discuss this matter over our food, but mull it to ourselves, that we may approach it more clearly after we have digested both the food and the danger that lay before us."

Khadgar shook his head as the monarchs nodded and began moving toward the door. Perenolde was a wily one, that was certain. He had seen that his fellow rulers' support was swinging toward Lothar and had found a way to regroup. Khadgar suspected the Alterac king would announce after lunch that he had reconsidered and that clearly Lothar's idea had merit. That way he could avoid losing face or being forced into a junior position in the upcoming alliance, which it seemed the kings would likely agree upon soon.

As he followed the monarchs from the room, Khadgar noticed a movement above and off to one side. Turning he caught a brief glimpse of two heads peeking out from one of the upper balconies. One was dark-haired and solemn, and he recognized Prince Varian. Of course the Stormwind heir would want to know what took place in this meeting. The second head was fair-haired and younger, a mere boy, standing back far enough that Varian probably did not realize he had a shadow. The boy saw him looking and grinned before disappearing behind the balcony's back curtain. So, Khadgar thought to himself. Young Prince Arthas also wants to know what his father and the others are planning. And why not? All Lordaeron would be his one day—provided they could keep the Horde from overrunning it.

CHAPTER FOUR

Doomhammer was speaking with one of his lieutenants, Rend Blackhand of the Black Tooth Grin clan, when a scout came running up. Though the orc warrior clearly had news to import, he stopped several paces from them and waited, catching his breath, until Doomhammer glanced in his direction and nodded.

"Trolls!" the orc scout announced, still gasping. "Forest trolls, a full war party, by the looks of it!"

"Trolls?" Rend laughed. "What, are they attacking us? I'd thought they were smarter than ogres, not dumber!"

Doomhammer had to agree. The one time he had encountered forest trolls he had been impressed and a little disquieted by their cunning. Though the trolls were taller than orcs they were leaner and more agile, particularly in the forests, which made them a significant threat within such places. Crossing the waters to reach this island, however, did not match what he had seen of their behavior.

But the scout was shaking his head. "Not attacking. They're on the mainland and they've been captured." He grinned. "By humans."

That got Doomhammer's attention. "Where?" he demanded.

"Not far from the shore, along the hills just within the forests," the scout answered promptly. "They were marching west, though it was slow going for them."

"How many?"

"Close to forty humans," the scout replied. "Ten trolls."

Doomhammer nodded and turned back to Rend. "Gather your strongest warriors," he instructed. "And quickly. You leave at once." He glowered at the Black Tooth Grin leader. "Be clear, however," he warned, "that this is a raiding party only. You are to rescue the trolls and bring them back here with you. Avoid being seen as much as possible, and kill any who do spy you. I will not have our battle plans ruined because you were careless."

The chieftain nodded and departed without a word, moving quickly toward a warrior lounging nearby. Rend began barking orders even before he had reached the other orc, and the warrior quickly straightened, nodded, and ran off, no doubt seeking his fellows. Doomhammer waited impatiently, signaling the scout to wait as well. His hands flexed in anticipation but his mind was far away, back many months to his previous encounter with the trolls.

★   ★   ★

Blackhand had shocked the other orc clans, back on their homeworld, by declaring his intent to ally with the ogres. It had proven a useful partnership, the monstrous creatures lending considerable strength to their Horde, but it still went against the grain. Thus many had been skeptical when they had heard reports of similar creatures here on this new, lush world—and Blackhand had announced they would win these creatures to their war banner as well.

He had sent Doomhammer and a handful of other Blackrock warriors to make contact, a sign of the trust he placed in his young Second. Even now Doomhammer felt guilty about that, for he had betrayed his warchief's trust and turned on him, killing him and taking his place as leader. Still, it was the way of the clans, and Blackhand had been leading their people to their own death and destruction. Doomhammer had been forced to act in order to save them. He reached back and down, running his fingers along the smooth stone head of his hammer where it hung across his back, the handle high over his shoulder and the head down beside his thigh. Long ago shaman had prophesied that the mighty weapon would one day see the salvation of their people. They had also said, however, that the wielder who saved them would also doom them. And that he would be the last of the Doomhammer line. Doomhammer had wondered about that many times, and even more since he had become warchief and leader of the Horde. Had his taking control meant their people's salvation? He certainly felt that to be the case. But did that mean he was also destined to doom them afterward? And that his line would end with him? He hoped not.

At that time, however, Doomhammer had not been as concerned with such matters. He still trusted Blackhand, at least the orc leader's loyalty to their people and intent to see them masters of this world, and still followed the warchief's orders, though he did his best to moderate Blackhand's love of unnecessary violence. Not that Doomhammer shrank from combat, and as with most orc warriors he delighted in the exertions and the thrill of battle, but there were times when too much force could actually reduce the value of a victory. This mission, however, had involved communication rather than warfare, and Doomhammer had been intrigued and honored. And perhaps, deep down, even a little frightened. Thus far they had encountered only humans on this new world, and one or two of the diminutive but mighty creatures called dwarves. If this world had ogres, however, the Horde could find itself with a more powerful enemy than they had yet seen.

It took two weeks before Doomhammer finally encountered a troll. He and his warriors wandered through the forest where a scout had seen one, making no effort to conceal themselves. As the time passed they had become more convinced the scout had lied or simply been mistaken, jumping at shadows and then concocting a story to cover his own cowardice. Then one night, just as twilight stretched across the land and threw long shadows under the trees, a figure swung down from the branches high above, dropping silently to the ground just beyond the orcs' campfire. Another appeared an instant later, than another, until the orcs found themselves surrounded by six of the silent, shadowy figures.

At first Doomhammer thought the scout had been correct and they were facing ogres, though these were slightly smaller and moved with a silence and a grace he had never seen the behemoths possess before. But then a ray of fading sunlight struck one of the creatures as it stalked forward and Doomhammer saw that its skin was green, as green as his own, as green as the leaves on the trees. That explained why they had not noticed the creatures before—their coloration allowed them to blend into the foliage, especially if they moved through the branches as these evidently had. He also saw that the creature was taller than he was and leaner than an ogre, and more proportioned, lacking the overlong arms and oversized hands and massive head of those creatures. And the look the approaching figure gave him, firelight glinting in its dark eyes as it extended a spear to prod at Doomhammer, showed a certain intelligence as well.

"We are not your foes!" Doomhammer shouted, his cry splitting the quiet night. He batted the spear aside with one hand, noting as he did that the head was chipped stone and looked very sharp. "I seek your leader!"

A rumble came from the creatures then, and after an instant Doomhammer realized it was laughter.

"What you be wantin' with our leader, morsel?" the lead creature replied, its mouth splitting in a monstrous grin. They had tusks as well, Doomhammer saw, though longer and thicker than his own, and more blunt from the look of them. He also noticed the creature's hair, which rose in a dark crest above its head. Surely that look was not natural, meaning these creatures groomed themselves. Definitely not mere beasts, then.

"I would speak with him, on behalf of my own leader," Doomhammer replied. He kept his hands at his side, open to show he carried no weapon, yet he was wary. He would be a fool not to be.

That was fortunate, for the creature laughed again. "We no be speakin' with morsels," it replied. "We be eatin' them!" And it thrust its spear, no longer a questioning prod but a hard, swift motion that would have gutted Doomhammer as easily as he might have speared a fish. If he had stood still for the blow. Instead he twisted away, pulling his hammer free from his back, and bellowed a warcry. The shout seemed to startle the creature, which paused in the act of withdrawing its weapon for a second attack. Doomhammer did not give it time to recover. He leaped forward, hammer swinging hard, and smashed one of the creature's legs full in the knee. The creature toppled with a howl of pain, clutching the shattered limb, and Doomhammer swung again, a mighty overhand blow that crushed the creature's skull.

"I say again, I seek your leader!" he shouted, turning to face the other creatures, who had not moved during the quick fight. "Take me to him or I shall kill the rest of you and seek others more willing!" He raised his hammer for emphasis, knowing from long experience the sight of its black stone head dripping with fresh blood and matted hair and bone was enough to unnerve most foes.

The gesture worked. The other creatures backed away a step, raising their weapons high to show they were not attacking. And then one stepped around the others and approached him. This one's hair was braided rather than cut in a stiff crest, and it wore a necklace of bones around its neck.

"You be wishin' ta speak with Zul'jin?" the creature asked. Doomhammer nodded, assuming that was either the name or the title of their leader. "I be bringin' him here," the creature offered. It turned away and disappeared into the shadows without a sound, leaving its four companions behind. They glanced at each other, and at the orcs, clearly not sure what to do now.

"We shall wait," Doomhammer announced calmly, both to them and to his own warriors. He set the head of his hammer on the ground and leaned on the long handle, alert but unconcerned. When they saw he was not attacking the creatures relaxed slightly, lowering their own weapons as well. One even sprawled on the ground, though his eyes tracked the orcs' every movement.

"What are you called?" Doomhammer asked that one after several minutes.

"I am Krul'tan," the creature replied.

"Orgrim Doomhammer." Doomhammer indicated himself with a thumb. "And we are orcs, of the Blackrock clan. What are your people?"

"We be forest trolls," came the surprised answer, as if Krul'tan could not believe they did not know. "Amani tribe."

Doomhammer nodded. Forest trolls. And they had tribes. Which meant they were civilized. Much, much more than ogres. For the first time he found himself thinking Blackhand's idea might be wise. These creatures seemed more like orcs than ogres, despite their size and strength. What allies they would make! And they were native to this world, which meant they would know its geography, its inhabitants, and its dangers.

An hour passed. Then, without warning, shadows separated from the trees and moved forward on large, silent feet, becoming the troll who had left and three others.

"You be wantin' Zul'jin?" one of them demanded, stepping close enough for Doomhammer to see the beads and bits of metal dangling from his long braids. "I am here!" Zul'jin was even taller than the other trolls and leaner. He wore some sort of heavy cloth wrapped around his waist and groin and an open vest of heavy leather. A thick scarf was wound about his neck and covered his face up to the nose, giving him a sinister appearance. This close Doomhammer could also see that the troll's skin was furred; after a second he realized it looked like moss. The trolls were green because they were covered in moss! What odd new creatures they were!

"I am Doomhammer, and yes, I would speak with you." Doomhammer looked up at the forest troll leader, refusing to show any fear. "My leader, Blackhand, rules the orc Horde. No doubt you have seen our people moving through the forest."

Zul'jin nodded. "We been seein' you crashing through the trees, ya. You be clumsier than the humans," he commented. "Stronger, though. An' armed for battle. What you be wantin' with us?" Even behind the scarf Doomhammer could see the troll grin and it was not a pleasant expression. "You want our forests, ya? You be fightin' us for them, then." His hands dropped to his sides, and to the twin axes that hung there. "And you be losin'." Doomhammer suspected the troll leader was right, too. The Horde significantly outnumbered them, of course, but if all forest trolls were as strong and silent as these they could strike from anywhere and disappear again. They could cut down any orcs entering this place, and the Horde would not be able to move a large force through the trees to combat the attacks.

Fortunately, that was not their goal.

"We do not want your forests," Doomhammer assured the troll leader. "We want your strength. We plan to conquer this world, and we would have you beside us as allies."

Zul'jin frowned. "Allies? Why? What would we gain?"

"What would you want?"

One of the other trolls said something in a strange, hissing language and Zul'jin cut him off with a sharp reply. "We need nothing, ya" he answered finally, decisively. "We have our forest. None dare intrude here, save only the accursed elves, and those we be handlin' ourselves."

"Are you sure?" Doomhammer asked, sensing a possible opening. "These elves, they are a race unto themselves? A mighty one?"

"Mighty, ya," the troll agreed grudgingly. "But we been killin' them since ancient times, when they first came to this land. We needin' no help with them."

"Why pick them off one by one, though?" Doomhammer asked. "Why not march on their homes and destroy them utterly? We could aid you! With the Horde behind you, you could crush the elves once and for all and truly hold the forest without contest!"

Zul'jin seemed to consider that, and for a moment Doomhammer dared to hope the lean forest troll would agree. But finally he shook his head. "We fight the elves ourselves," he explained. "We needin' no help. And we're not wantin' the rest of the world, not any more. So fighting others will not be givin' us anything."

Doomhammer sighed. He could see the forest troll's mind was set. And he guessed that pushing the point would only antagonize him. "I understand," he said at last. "My leader will be disappointed, as am I. But I respect your decision."

Zul'jin nodded. "Go in peace, orc," he whispered, already stepping backward toward the shadows. "No troll will hinder you, ya." And then he was gone, and the other forest trolls with him.

Blackhand had indeed been disappointed, and the warchief had bellowed at Doomhammer and the others about failing in their mission. But he had calmed down soon enough, and agreed with Doomhammer's own assessment that pushing the trolls might have made them enemies instead of neutral parties. And that they did not wish to do.

Doomhammer still regretted the troll leader's decision, however, and he had instructed his scouts to watch for trolls any time they entered or even passed near the forest. And now that watching had perhaps paid off.

Doomhammer watched as the two boats beached upon the island's north shore. Rend leaped ashore at once, followed more slowly by a troll whose hair was knotted into braids. A long scarf was wrapped around the troll's neck and lower face, and Doomhammer grinned with delight. It was Zul'jin himself!

"They were penned and chained," Rend reported, stopping only a few feet from where Doomhammer stood. "The humans were careless, assuming the only threat in the forest was the one they had already captured." The Black Tooth Grin chieftain laughed. "No one who saw us lived."

"Good." They watched as the troll leader approached. He looked the same as the last time they had met, and Doomhammer could tell from the troll's expression that he remembered their encounter as well.

"Your warriors saved us," the forest troll acknowledged, stepping up beside Doomhammer and giving him a nod, a greeting among equals. "They were too many, ya, an' used torches ta hold us at bay."

Doomhammer nodded. "I am pleased to aid a fellow warrior," he said. "When I heard you had been captured I sent my warriors at once."

Zul'jin grinned. "Your leader be sendin' you?"

"I am leader now," Doomhammer replied, his own grin widening.

The troll considered this. "Your Horde still seekin' to conquer the world, ya?" he asked finally.

Doomhammer nodded, not daring to speak.

"We be aidin' you, then," Zul'jin announced after a moment. "As you aided us. Allies." He extended his hand.

"Allies." Doomhammer clasped it. His mind was already awhirl with possibilities. Between the trolls and the Horde and the new forces Zuluhed was binding to the Horde's will, nothing would stand in their way.

CHAPTER FIVE

Two days after the first meeting, Lothar found himself back in the Lordaeron throne room with the continent's rulers. Khadgar had accompanied him again, and Lothar was glad of the lad's presence. Terenas was a kindly host and a good man, as were some of the other monarchs, but the young wizard was the only one Lothar had known from Azeroth. Even though the young man was not native to Stormwind his presence reminded Lothar of home.

Home. A place that no longer existed. Lothar knew he would have to accept that at some point. It still seemed unreal for now. He kept expecting to turn and see Llane laughing, or look up and watch a pair of gryphons gliding by, or hear the sound of his men martialling in the courtyard. But all that was gone now. Their friends were dead. Their home had fallen. And he vowed to keep this land from following it into darkness, even if it cost his life.

Right now he thought it more likely to cost him his sanity. Lothar had never had much patience for politics, and had watched amazed over the years as Llane placated this noble and that one, easing arguments, diffusing conflicts, settling disputes, all the while never favoring any one over the other or letting personal interests interfere with affairs of state. It was all a game, Llane had told him over and over again, a game of positioning and influence and subtle maneuvering. No one ever really won, not for long, and the goal was simply to maintain the strongest position possible for as long as possible.

From what Lothar had seen, this continent's monarchs were experts at the game. And being forced to deal with them, supposedly as an equal, was driving him to his wit's end.

After lunch that first day, they had returned to the throne room for more discussions. Everyone seemed to accept the idea that the Horde would come, even that too-smooth Perenolde. Now the question was what to do about it.

It had taken the rest of the day to convince everyone that a unified army was the only answer. Terenas had agreed at once, fortunately, as had Trollbane, and Proudmoore had taken little coaxing. But Perenolde and Graymane had been more difficult. Lothar wasn't surprised at Perenolde's reluctance. He'd known similar men back in Stormwind, smooth and silky and nasty and always out for themselves at any cost. More often than not they had turned out to be cowards. Perenolde was probably afraid of battle personally and extended that to his subjects, many of whom were no doubt braver than he was. Graymane was a surprise, however. The man certainly looked the warrior, with that powerful frame and his heavy armor. Nor had he stated that he would not fight. But he had been quick to suggest other options every time the talk had turned back toward war, and Perenolde of course had insisted on examining each suggestion in great detail. It was only after Proudmoore and Trollbane all but accused Graymane of cowardice that the burly man had agreed an army was their own recourse.

The second day had been more of the same. They had settled on the idea of war, at least, but now there were the logistics of cooperation to consider. Which armies would supply what troops, where they would be stationed, how they would be supplied—details Lothar had dealt with himself for years but only for one nation's military. Now they were dealing with five, not counting any Stormwind survivors he could muster, and each king had his own ideas and his own methods.

And of course the biggest question was the one of command.

Each king seemed to feel he should have command of the unified army. Terenas pointed out that Lordaeron was the largest kingdom with the most troops, and also that he was the one who had summoned the rest of them. Trollbane claimed to have the most actual fighting experience, at looking at the gruff mountain king Lothar believed him. Proudmoore mentioned the power of his navy, and the importance of ships for troop transport and supplies. Graymane's was the most southern of the kingdoms, and he seemed to feel that meant he should have command because his lands would be the first overrun if the Horde approached on foot—even though that wasn't true, since Stromgarde actually was foremost along the path the Horde would take from Khaz Modan to Dun Modr and on. Perenolde suggested that brute force alone was not enough but that the commander should have intelligence, wisdom, and vision, all of which he felt he possessed in abundance.

And then there were the two non-kings, each a leader in his own right. Archbishop Faol, whose followers included most of the people from all the kingdoms combined, and Archmage Antonidas, who essentially ruled a single city but whose people's powers likely matched the strength of any army they could muster. Fortunately the two men, the one short and friendly and the other tall and stern, were not interested in control of the army. They had both played a moderating influence, keeping the kings focused on the fact that the Horde would come whether an army was ready to face them or not, and reminding the monarchs frequently that an army without a single leader was useless no matter its size.

Lothar had watched the discussions with a mixture of amusement and horror, leaning more toward the latter as he himself was drawn more frequently into the conversations. At times he was called upon as the resident orc expert. Other times they wanted his opinion as an outsider. A few times they had even left a deciding voice to him, pointing out slyly that his family had been the original rulers of this land and thus in some sense he should have some ancestral rights to that effect. Half the time Lothar couldn't tell if they were mocking him or admiring him, and he knew several of the kings wanted something from him but that something seemed to change from moment to moment. He would be much happier when these discussions were over and done and he could return to the rest of the Stormwind refugees and try to assemble at least a small force to add to the army's might.

As he waited for King Terenas to call the morning council to order, however, Lothar realized the other monarchs were watching him closely. Some, like Trollbane, were doing so openly. Others, like Perenolde and Graymane, were more subtle about it, sneaking glances now and again. Lothar wasn't sure what was going on but he didn't like it.

"We are all here, then?" Terenas asked, though of course he could see this was the case. Lordaeron's king did not miss much. "Good. Now then, we have all agreed that time is of the essence if we are to marshal our united forces and meet the Horde when it arrives.

And we have all agreed upon our course of action?" Each of the other monarchs nodded, which surprised and further worried Lothar. They had still been arguing when he had given up and returned to his rooms late last night. When had they reached an agreement, and what was it about? But the king's next words told him clearly, and Lothar's blood ran cold as he heard the announcement clearly: "Then I hereby declare the founding of the Alliance of Lordaeron! We shall stand together as one, as our ancestors did long ago, in the Arathi Empire." The others nodded and Terenas continued. "And it is only fitting, then, that our commander should hail from that ancient ruling stock. We the kings of the Alliance do hereby appoint Lord Anduin Lothar, Champion of Stormwind, as our Supreme Commander!"

Lothar stared at Terenas, who winked at him. "It was the only way, really," the Lordaeron monarch explained quietly, his voice soft enough Lothar knew he was the only one to hear. "Each of them wanted to be in charge, and they were deadset against seeing another king in their place. You aren't a king so they don't feel anyone has gotten special treatment, but your bloodline makes you noble enough they don't feel slighted by being passed over." The king leaned forward. "I know it is a great deal to ask of you, and I apologize. I would not ask if it were not for our very survival, as you yourself warned us. Will you accept this charge?" The last words were spoken more loudly, Terenas's voice shifting back to formality, and silence crept across the room as the others all waited for Lothar's answer.

It did not take him long. He did not really have a choice, and Terenas knew it. He could not walk away from this, not now, not after all that had happened. "I accept the charge," he replied, his voice ringing through the chamber. "I will lead the Alliance army against the Horde."

"Very good!" Terenas clapped his hands. "We shall each go now to assemble our own troops, gear, and supplies. I suggest we meet again in one week to present our rosters and inventories to Lord Lothar, so that he may see what forces he has at his disposal and begin his planning."

The other kings muttered or nodded their agreement. Each one in turn came up to Lothar to congratulate him on his appointment and to pledge their full support, though from Perenolde and Graymane the statements seemed less sincere. Then the kings were gone, leaving only four in the room. Lothar glanced at Khadgar, who actually grinned at him.

"Out of the frying pan, eh?" the young-old mage asked, shaking his head. "And you let them talk you into that. Those clever bastards! They'd sell their own children if they thought it would win them even a single acre more to their domains! I particularly liked the way they just assumed you'd accept. But that's what happens when you have authority over others—you stop realizing that anyone else matters, much less has a say in events."

"Ahem!" The cough cut off whatever else the young wizard meant to say, and he looked up at one of the other men present, embarrassment plain on his face for once. "Not all authority is corrupt and self-serving, young man," Archbishop Faol pointed out, his normally jovial face stern. "There are those of us called to serve by leading, just as your friend here was."

"Of course, Father. Please forgive me. I did not mean to imply . . . I was referring to those of temporal authority only . . . of course you . . ." It was the first time Lothar had ever seen the normally smooth Khadgar too flustered for words, and he couldn't help chuckling at his young companion's predicament. Faol was laughing as well, in such a good-natured way Khadgar himself soon joined in.

"Enough, lad," Faol said at last, raising one palm. "I do not blame you for your outburst. And Lord Lothar was certainly maneuvered neatly into that trap. I must confess, however, that I too lent my weight to that decision. You are a good man, sir, and I believe you are our best possible choice for the Alliance commander. I, for one, feel better knowing you will be planning our battles and leading our forces."

"Thank you, Father." Lothar had never been a religious man but he had a great deal of respect for the Church of Light, and everything he had seen of Faol thus far had impressed him. To hear the archbishop praising him so warmly left him uncomfortable but proud.

"You will both be tested during the course of this conflict," Faol warned, his voice somehow deeper and richer than before, as if casting a pronouncement from some great height. "You will be pushed to the very limits, not just of your talents but of your courage and of your resolve. I believe you both capable of enduring such challenges, however, and of emerging victorious. I pray the Holy Light fills you with strength and purity, and that you find within it the joy and unity you need to survive and conquer." His hand rose in a benediction, and Lothar thought he saw a faint glow around the limb, a glow that spread to Khadgar and to him. He felt a sense of peace and serenity, and a surge of inexplicable happiness.

"Now, on to other matters." Suddenly Faol was just a man again, if an old and wise one. "First, what can you tell me of Northshire, particularly the abbey there? Did it survive?"

"I am afraid not, Father," Lothar replied. "The abbey is gone, torn to pieces. A few of the clerics survived and are in Southshore with the rest of our people. The rest—" He shook his head.

"I see." Faol had turned pale, but retained his composure. "I will pray for them." He fell silent, clearly lost in thought, and Lothar and Khadgar waited respectfully. After a moment the archbishop glanced up at them, and there was a new resolve in his gaze.

"You will need lieutenants for your army, sir," he announced, "and I think it best if some of those come not from the kingdoms but from the Church. I have several in mind, and a new order that I believe will prove valuable to the Alliance. I will require a few days to work out the details and select appropriate candidates. Shall we say four days from now, in the main courtyard, after the noon meal? I believe you will not be disappointed." He nodded pleasantly and then walked away without hurrying but with a steady stride.

That left one other. Antonidas had been watching them without a word, and now the elderly archmage approached them. "The might and wisdom of the Kirin Tor are at your disposal, sir," he told Lothar. "I know you were acquainted with our fellow wizards in Stormwind, so you have some sense of our capabilities. I shall appoint one of our number to assist you and serve as our liaison." The powerful wizard paused, his eyes flickering to Lothar's side so quickly he almost missed it, and Lothar suppressed a smile.

"I would ask for Khadgar to fill that role, sir," Lothar stated, catching the smile that touched the archmage's lips for just an instant. "He is already a trusted companion and has faced the orcs with me more than once."

"Of course." Antonidas turned to the younger man. Then, surprisingly, he reached out, cupping Khadgar's chin with one hand and raising his head to study his face. "You have suffered much," the archmage said softly, and Lothar could see the sorrow and sympathy in the older man's eyes. "Your experience has marked you, and far more than in your appearance."

Khadgar pulled his head away, but gently. "I did what had to be done," he replied quietly, rubbing absently at his chin, where Antonidas's touch had irritated the white beard hairs beginning to sprout there.

Antonidas frowned. "As we all must." He sighed, then seemed to shake off whatever heavy thoughts had burdened him, and returned to the matter at hand. "You shall keep us apprised of the situation on the field, young Khadgar, and communicate Lord Lothar's needs and requests as quickly as possible. You shall also coordinate the efforts of any other magi present. I trust this is within your capabilities?" Khadgar nodded. "Good. I shall expect you at Dalaran at your earliest convenience, that we may discuss other important matters and consider how we may best help the Alliance." The gem at the top of the archmage's staff flared to light, an answering gleam dancing from the gem at the crest of his skullcap, right between his eyes. Then Antonidas seemed to blur and fade and suddenly he was gone.

"He wants to know about Medivh," Khadgar said several seconds after the archmage had vanished.

"Of course." Lothar turned and led the younger man out of the throneroom, back into the rest of the palace. There he turned and began walking in the direction of the dining hall.

"What should I tell him?" The young wizard fell into step beside him.

"Tell him the truth," Lothar replied, shrugging and

hoping the gesture looked casual. Inside, his stomach churned. "They need to know what happened."

Khadgar nodded, though he did not look pleased. "I will tell them," he said finally. "But that can wait until after lunch." He grinned, an expression that showed his true age despite the hair and wrinkles. "The Horde itself could not keep me from food right now."

Lothar laughed. "Let us hope it does not come to that."

A few days later Lothar and Khadgar returned to the main courtyard. They had eaten and drunk their fill and were now waiting for Archbishop Faol to arrive. He appeared after a few minutes and walked calmly out to meet them.

"Thank you for indulging me," the archbishop said as he reached them. "I would not take up your time but I believe this may prove of great help to you and to the Alliance. But first," he announced, "I would tell you, Sir Lothar, that the Church has pledged itself to Stormwind's aid. We shall gather funds to help you rebuild your kingdom, once the immediate crisis has passed."

Lothar smiled, one of the first genuine smiles Khadgar had seen from him since Stormwind had fallen. "Thank you, Father," he said, his voice husky with gratitude. "That means a great deal to me, and will to Prince Varian as well."

Faol nodded. "The Holy Light will fill your home

once more," he promised gently. Then he paused and studied both of them in turn. "When we spoke last," Faol began, pacing before them, "you told me of the Northshire abbey's destruction. I was dismayed, and wondered how the rest of my clergy could possibly survive this war that approaches so rapidly. Clearly these orcs are a threat even to sturdy warriors like yourself—how, then, can a mere priest defend himself, much less his congregation?" He smiled, a truly beatific expression. "And as I felt these concerns, an idea appeared to me, as if brought by the Holy Light itself. There had to be a way to ensure that warriors fought for the Light and with the Light, using both its gifts and their own martial prowess, and still behaved in a manner appropriate to the Church's teachings."

"And you found a way?" Lothar asked.

"I have," Faol agreed. "I will establish a new branch of the Church, the paladins. I have already selected the first candidates for this order. Some were knights before but others were priests. I chose these men for both their piety and their martial prowess. They will be trained, not only in war but in prayer and in healing. And each of these valiant fighters will possess both martial and spiritual power, particularly in blessing themselves and others with the strength of the Holy Light."

He turned and beckoned, and four men emerged from a nearby passage, walking briskly over to Faol. They each wore a gleaming plate with the symbol of the Church emblazoned upon their chest, upon their shield, and upon the crest of their helm. Each man carried a sword and Lothar could see from the way they walked that these men knew how to handle themselves. But the armor and the weapons were still new and utterly unstained and undented. They had the knowledge and the training but Lothar wondered if any of these men had ever faced real combat. Those who had been warriors before must have, though perhaps only against human foes, but the former priests were most likely experienced only in sparring with their fellows. And they would be going up against orcs almost immediately.

"May I present Uther, Saidan Dathrohan, Tirion Fordring, and Turalyon." Faol was beaming like a proud father. "These will be the Knights of the Silver Hand." He introduced Lothar and Khadgar as well. "This is Lord Anduin Lothar, Champion of Stormwind and Commander of the Alliance. And his companion, the wizard Khadgar of Dalaran." Faol smiled. "I shall leave you six to discuss matters."

And he did, leaving Lothar and Khadgar surrounded by the Paladin candidates. Some of them, like the lad Turalyon, seemed overwhelmed. Others, like Uther and Tirion, were more relaxed.

Uther took the lead, speaking while Lothar was still wondering what to say to them. "My lord, the archbishop has told us of the upcoming battle, and of the Horde's approach. We are at your service, and at the service of the people. Use us as you see fit, for we would smite our enemies and drive them forth, shielding this land with the Holy Light." He was a tall, powerfully built man, with strong, vaguely familiar features and stern eyes the color of the ocean. Lothar could feel the man's piety as an almost physical presence, very much like Faol's own but lacking the archbishop's warmth.

"You were a knight before?" he asked.

"Aye, my lord," the Paladin candidate replied. "But I have been a follower of the church and a devout believer in the Holy Light since my youth. I first met the Archbishop when he was merely Bishop Faol, and he was kind enough to serve as my spiritual advisor and mentor. I was honored when he told me of his plans for a new order, and offered me a place among them." Uther's jaw tightened. "With the coming of these foul creatures, I know we will need the Light's blessing to defeat them and protect our lands, our homes, and our people."

Lothar nodded. He could understand why the man had turned to faith as an answer, or at least part of an answer. And he had no doubt Uther would be a powerful force on the battlefield. But something about the man's zeal unnerved him. He suspected Uther was too focused upon honor and faith to use less noble methods of success, and that would not hold well here. Lothar himself had learned from bitter experience that, when dealing with the orcs, honor alone was not enough. To survive against the Horde they would have to use every means necessary.

He and Khadgar spent the next hour or more speaking with the four potential paladins, and Lothar was pleased to see that his young friend was also sounding them out. After the holy warriors had left to attend afternoon prayers Lothar turned to the old-seeming wizard.

"Well?" he asked. "What did you think of them?"

Khadgar frowned. "I doubt they will be much use to us," he said after a moment.

"Oh? And why is that?"

"They have no time to prepare," the wizard explained. "We anticipate the Horde will reach Lordaeron in a matter of weeks, if not less, and none of these men have seen battle—not as paladins, at least. I have no doubt they can fight, but we have warriors aplenty. If the Archbishop expects them to perform miracles I am afraid he will be disappointed."

Lothar nodded. "I agree," he admitted. "But Faol has faith in them, and perhaps we must as well." He grinned. "Assuming they are ready somehow, what is your opinion of them then?"

"Uther will be dangerous to the Horde, that's certain," Khadgar replied, "but I do not think he can command men other than fellow Paladins. His piety is too strong, too abrasive, for most soldiers to endure." Lothar nodded for his companion to continue. "Saidan and Tirion are much the same. Saidan was a knight first, and Tirion a warrior, but they have since found faith. That may make them hesitate to use tactics they might have appreciated as simple fighters."

Lothar smiled. "And Turalyon?"

"The least of them in faith, and thus the highest in my eyes," Khadgar admitted with a grin. "He was trained for the priesthood and is a loyal Church follower but lacks the blinding zeal of the others. He also sees farther than them, and has more wit."

"I agree." The young man had impressed Lothar as well. Turalyon had been hesitant to speak at first, and after a few minutes the reason became clear. He had heard of Lothar and his deeds in Stormwind and seemed awed, a fact that made Lothar uncomfortable though it was not the first time he had faced it—many youths back home had worshipped him as well and begged him to train them and induct them into his guard. But after overcoming that initial reserve Turalyon had proven to be a bright young man with an agile mind and more appreciation for subtleties and shades than his fellows. Lothar had liked him right away, and the fact that Khadgar felt the same only confirmed his opinion.

"I will speak to Faol," Lothar said at last. "The Paladins will no doubt be valued assets, and I will take Uther as our liaison to them and to any other forces the Church can supply." Something else occurred to him. "I will propose an additional candidate, as well," he said. "Gavinrad. He was one of my knights in Azeroth, the most faithful of us, and a good man. I suspect he would make a fine Paladin." He smiled. "But Turalyon I will take to serve as one of my lieutenants."

Khadgar nodded. "A good choice, I'd say." He shook his head. "Now let us hope the Horde gives us time to prepare them and the rest of our forces."

"We will prepare what we can," Lothar answered pragmatically, already thinking on how to disposition whatever troops the kings supplied. "And we will face them when we must. There is little else we can do."

CHAPTER SIX

Gul'dan was furious.

"Why have you not succeeded yet?" he demanded. The other orcs cowered away from him. They had seen the chief warlock enraged before, and knew he might turn his fearsome powers upon them as well if he was not appeased.

"We are trying, Gul'dan," Rakmar replied. The oldest of the surviving orc necromancers after Gul'dan himself, Rakmar Sharpfang was the necrolytes' unofficial leader and often thrust into the role of conveying their accomplishments—or failures—to the high warlock. "We have been able to animate the bodies, yes, but not to give them consciousness. They are little more than shells. We can direct them as puppets, but their movements are sloppy and slow. They will pose little threat to anyone."

Gul'dan glared at the bodies beyond Rakmar. They were human, warriors slain here on the fields of Stormwind, and would make a powerful force for the

Horde, just as he had promised Doomhammer. But only if his worthless assistants could transform them into something more than the shambling wrecks he saw here!

"Find a way!" Gul'dan shouted, spit flying from his mouth. He clenched his fists, tempted to strike down the necrolytes where they stood, but what good would that do him? If they were dead they would hardly be able to help him—

A thought struck him, and Gul'dan rocked back on his heels, stunned by its brilliance. Of course! That was the answer!

"You are right, Rakmar," he said softly, opening his hands and smoothing them along the front of his robes. "You are trying. I understand. This is a new and different thing we are attempting, and would pose a great challenge to anyone. I have no right to be angry that you have not yet succeeded. Please, return to work. I will leave you in peace to experiment once more."

"Uh, thank you," Rakmar stammered, his eyes wide. Gul'dan could see that the lesser orc was surprised by his sudden change of heart, as were the other warlocks behind him. He suppressed a chuckle, simply nodding to them and turning away. Let them think he had thought better of his outburst, or even that he had become distracted by something else and forgotten why he had been so angry at them. Let them think whatever they liked.

Soon it would not matter.

As he walked, Gul'dan glanced around. Cho'gall was nearby, as always—the ogre mage had been crouched within a ruined building not far away, close enough to be ready if Gul'dan should need him but far enough away that the other necrolytes would not see him and become unnerved by his presence. Gul'dan beckoned and the two-headed ogre rose and approached, his long strides quickly covering the distance between them.

"The necrolytes have served their purpose," Gul'dan told his towering lieutenant. "Now they shall have a new one, an even greater one." He grinned, stroking his beard in anticipation. "Gather our implements. We shall make a sacrifice."

"We are summoning our fallen brethren?" Rakmar asked softly. He and the other necrolytes were standing around the altar Gul'dan and Cho'gall had built, as ordered, but Gul'dan could see they were trying to decipher its purpose. Let them. By the time they did, it would be too late.

"Yes," Gul'dan replied, concentrating on the incantation he was about to perform. "Doomhammer slaughtered the other warlocks but their souls linger. We will summon them and instill them in the human bodies." He grinned. "They will be eager to return to this world, and to serve the Horde once more."

Rakmar nodded. "That will animate them," he agreed, "but will it give them power? Or will they be little more than walking corpses?"

Gul'dan frowned, surprised and not pleased that the necrolyte had figured that out so quickly. "Silence!" he commanded, forestalling other questions. "We begin!"

He began the ritual, summoning his magic to him and feeling it fill him with power. Not enough power, but soon that would change. In the meantime he concentrated on his task, channeling his energies into the altar before them, priming it for the transformation he was about to evoke.

Rakmar and the other necrolytes joined in, lending their own necromantic magic to his incantation. Thus they were distracted and did not notice that Gul'dan had moved from his position until it was too late.

"Rrargh!" Gul'dan could not stop the growl from escaping his lips, but it did not matter. He was already positioned right behind Rakmar, curved dagger at the ready, and as the taller orc turned Gul'dan's blade lashed out, catching the necrolyte full across the throat. Blood arced out, spraying them both, and Rakmar toppled backward, clutching at the wound, gasping for air. He fell onto the altar, and gasped with horror as he tried to push himself away from it. But Gul'dan was on top of him, straddling the fading necrolyte, and batted his hands away. Then he plunged the dagger into Rakmar's chest, wrenching it about to create a gaping hole. Into this he reached and, with a sharp tug, removed Rakmar's still-beating heart. Before his former assistant's eyes Gul'dan cast the spell he had prepared, his magic enveloping the bloody organ and trapping Rakmar's spirit within. The magic of the altar surged up then, reshaping the heart, shrinking it and hardening it and granting it an unnatural luster. As the necrolyte collapsed, his body now an empty shell, Gul'dan grinned down at him and held up the glowing gem.

"Do not fear, Rakmar," he assured the dead orc. "This is not the end for you. On the contrary. You shall succeed at your task, with my help. You will fight again for the Horde. And Doomhammer will have his un-dead warriors." He laughed. "That is the good thing about necromancers—we never let anything go to waste."

He glanced up. Cho'gall had killed several more necrolytes already, preserving their hearts and souls as jewels in the same manner. The rest were cowering, their magic still caught up in the altar, unable to flee and too terrified to fight. Gul'dan snorted. Worthless! He would have fought. But this made matters easier for him, at least. He laughed as he rose and stalked toward the remaining warlocks, licking the blood from his tusks as he approached. Soon they would be warlike enough for even the most bloodthirsty commander.

"Well?" Doomhammer asked as he strode onto the field. "Have you succeeded?" It did not escape Gul'dan's notice that the warchief's words were similar to those he had shouted at his necrolytes mere days earlier. But this time the answer was very different.

"I have, noble Doomhammer," he responded, gesturing at the bodies behind him. Doomhammer shouldered past him to glare at the figures, which lay stretched out upon the ground.

"These are fallen Stormwind soldiers," Doomhammer snarled. "What of them? Or did you ask me here to show me you could line bodies up so neatly?" He sneered. "Is this the extent of your powers, then, Gul'dan? To prepare corpses for burial?"

Gul'dan longed to wipe the smirk from his leader's face, to show the arrogant warrior the true extent of his magic. But now was not the time.

"Of course not," he did reply, the words still sharp enough to make Doomhammer's gaze narrow. "Watch!" He nodded to Cho'gall, who knelt beside the first body and placed a jeweled truncheon in its cold, stiff hands. Those enchanted weapons had been the most time-consuming part of the process but Gul'dan knew without them his new force would be far less powerful, just as Rakmar had guessed. Fortunately he and Cho'gall had been experimenting with such items already for their own purposes, and so they had merely modified the spells they had planned and adapted the weapons to this new role.

As he and Doomhammer watched, the corpse stirred. Its fingers closed tightly around the truncheon, which began to glow. That light spread to the body's hand, then up along its arm, slowly infusing the entire form with a green aura. And then the corpse opened its eyes.

Doomhammer started slightly, though he made no sound, and this time it was Gul'dan's lips that pulled back in a sneer. Still, he could not blame the warchief for being startled. He found the sight almost unnerving himself, and he had created these creatures.

The corpse slowly rose to its feet, its movements stiff at first but becoming more fluid by the second. It turned glowing red eyes upon Gul'dan, and the orc warlock saw them widen in recognition.

"You have succeeded then, Gul'dan," the creature stated, its words slurred from using an unfamiliar jaw and strange, too-small teeth. It stared down at itself, at its limbs and torso, and raised its empty hand to feel its face. "You have returned my spirit to this world!" It laughed, a harsh sound that was far more orc-like than human. "Excellent!"

"Welcome back, Teron Gorefiend," Gul'dan replied, trying to keep the laughter from his voice. "Yes, I have brought you back, to further serve the Horde."

Doomhammer stepped forward, studying the strange creature before him. "Gorefiend? One of your warlocks from the Shadow Council? I killed him myself."

"We all give ourselves to the Horde," Gul'dan replied mockingly, bowing low so Doomhammer could not see his expression. "Gorefiend's soul had not departed this plane—I merely recalled it and found it a new home. Only now his very body is imbued with sorcery. He is more powerful now than ever, and the other warlocks with him." Cho'gall had continued his task and behind Gorefiend the other bodies were rising as well.

"This, then, is what you give me?" Doomhammer rumbled. "Corpses for warriors, powered by your dead acolytes?" His face twisted in disgust.

"You asked for warriors," Gul'dan reminded him sharply. "I have provided them. They will be a match for anything the humans have and more. And though their bodies may be rotted human flesh, they are still orcs in spirit and in allegiance. And they can still wield their magic as well! Think what they will do in battle!"

Doomhammer nodded slowly, clearly considering. "Will you serve me?" he asked Gorefiend, showing what Gul'dan considered a fatal weakness. Warchiefs did not ask, they commanded. Though perhaps with creatures such as these it was best not to anger them.

Gorefiend considered for a moment, glowing eyes studying the Warchief. At last he nodded. "Gul'dan is correct," he said finally, his voice raspy. "I am still an orc, despite this shell. I live for the Horde, and I will serve you and our people." It grinned, a horrible rictus. "You killed me but I do not hold that against you, for it has resulted in this powerful new form. I am well pleased with the trade." The other bodies nodded behind him.

"Good!" Doomhammer stepped forward and clapped the surprised Gorefiend on the shoulder, a gesture of respect to an equal rather than a subordinate. "You shall be my death knights, the forefront of our great Horde," he informed the reanimated creatures. "Together we will crush the humans and take their lands, making this world safe for our people!" Then he turned and nodded at Gul'dan, though it seemed grudging. "You have done as you promised, Gul'dan," Doomhammer admitted. "You have given me a powerful force against our foes. I thank you for that."

"Of course, noble Doomhammer," Gul'dan replied, hoping he sounded more sincere than he felt. "Anything for our people."

Fool, he thought as he watched Doomhammer stride off, the newly awakened death knights beside him. Take them and go, yes, and return to your war. I have other matters to attend, and now that you are satisfied I will have the freedom to concentrate on them properly. I will play the loyal warlock a while longer, he vowed, but not forever. Soon enough I will have what I seek, and then you and the Horde may crumble away for all I care. I will raise a new race to replace you all, one loyal to me alone, and we shall reshape this world in my image!

A week later Doomhammer addressed the assembled Horde. They were gathered before the fortress Zul'jin told him was called the Blackrock Spire, a massive structure built from the same glossy black stone that dominated the landscape. It stood atop Blackrock Mountain, the tallest of the Burning Steppes mountain range that rose up along the continent, dividing east from west.

Zuluhed had led them here, sensing the power within the mountains, and after defeating the handful of dwarves dwelling here, Doomhammer had claimed it. He had felt it was a good omen that this place, which he had selected as the Horde's base, bore the same name as his own clan.

Below him the orcs of every clan were gathered, waiting eagerly to hear what he had to say. They had conquered this land thoroughly, and while that gave them far better hunting and far richer lands than any left back home it was still not enough to contain their entire race comfortably. There was also the question of retaliation—they had driven the humans from this continent but there was no guarantee they would not return with reinforcements and perhaps allies. Doomhammer grinned. But now he had allies of his own.

"My people!" he shouted, raising his hammer high above him. "Hear me!" The crowd quieted, every face turning toward him. "We have taken this land, and it is good!" A cheer erupted, and Doomhammer waited for it to die down before speaking again. "This world is rich with life, and we can raise strong families here!" Another cheer. "Yet it is not without its defenders! The humans are strong and skilled, and fight hard to retain what was theirs." Murmurs of agreement rippled through the Horde. There was no weakness in acknowledging a powerful foe, and the humans were certainly that. Enough orcs had fought them now to agree.

"We must continue our conquest!" Doomhammer

told his people, gesturing to the north with his hammer. "Another land, Lordaeron, lies beyond this one, and once we control it our clans may claim territories, settle, craft homes, and raise families again. But first we must take it from the humans! And they will not surrender it lightly." The crowd growled as one, showing its willingness to fight on. Doomhammer quieted them with a raised hand.

"I know that you are strong," he assured them. "I know that you are warriors, and will not falter in battle. But the humans are many, and this time they will be ready for us." He leaned on his hammer. "But they will not be ready for our allies."

He gestured behind him, and Zul'jin stepped forward. The forest troll leader had brought a hundred of his people for this meeting, and they stood now arrayed behind him and Doomhammer, hefting their axes and short, curved swords and wicked broad-bladed spears. "These are the forest trolls," Doomhammer told the orcs below. "They are now part of the Horde, and will fight alongside us! They are as mighty as an ogre but as crafty as an orc, and in woodcraft they are unsurpassed! They will be our guides, our scouts, and our forest warriors!"

Zul'jin stepped forward, his long scarf waving in the wind. "We have pledged to the Horde," he declared, his voice carrying clearly despite the fabric covering his mouth. "We be fightin' with you, and together we be crushin' the humans, the elves, an' any others who stand against us!" The orcs cheered, as did the forest trolls, and Zul'jin nodded before stepping back.

"Nor are they our only allies," Doomhammer announced. He turned, and Gorefiend strode forward, the other death knights beside him. They had masked themselves to conceal their hideous features, with heavy cloth wrapped around their heads and faces so that only their glowing eyes were visible. But the Horde could see the breadth of their shoulders and the width of their chests, and Gorefiend raised his truncheon high, the weapon's jewels flaring into a brightness that rivaled the sun overhead.

"We are the death knights," Gorefiend intoned, his strange voice casting the words across the crowd like a chill over the land. "We have pledged ourselves to the Horde, and to Doomhammer. We will fight as one of you, and will drive the orcs' foes from this world!" He had requested that Doomhammer not reveal their true nature to the other orcs, and Doomhammer had agreed. Many might not be happy to learn these new warriors were orcs themselves, former warlocks he had slaughtered and Gul'dan had then trapped within rotting human bodies.

"The death knights will be our cavalry and our vanguard," Doomhammer announced. "They are strong and swift and possess a dark magic to strip away our foes' defenses."

He paused. "We may have other allies soon as well," he admitted. He had hoped those would be ready as well, but Zuluhed had said his clan needed more time to finish the preparations. Still, this was enough for now.

"We march north," Doomhammer told his people. "Across this land and into Khaz Modan, the home of the dwarves. Those lands are rich with metals and with fuel. We shall take those resources and use them to build a mighty fleet of ships. With those ships our forces will sail north to Lordaeron, for the humans will not expect us by water. We shall land to the west and march back, catching them from behind. We will crush them, and then we shall rule that land and all this world as our own!"

The Horde cheered again, a cheer that grew and grew until it echoed from the rocks around them. Doomhammer felt the echo beneath his feet, shaking the very peak, and glanced back at Zuluhed, who stood behind him. His people's shouts and war cries should not have been able to disturb the mountain itself! But the old shaman nodded.

"The volcano speaks," Zuluhed said softly, stepping forward so that only Doomhammer could hear his words. "The spirits within the mountain are pleased." He grinned, bearing his worn tusks. "They grant us their blessing!"

Doomhammer nodded. The rocks still trembled as he raised his hammer high again, swinging it about over his head. The crowd began chanting his name.

"Doomhammer!" They shouted, and a loud boom followed their cry. The sky itself turned dark.

"Doomhammer!" They shouted again, and the air turned thick.

"Doomhammer!" They bellowed a third time, and with a loud crack the mountain behind them exploded, lava and rock spewing forth. The Horde's shouts increased, and not out of fear. They, like Zuluhed, saw this as a blessing, the earth itself approving their actions.

Doomhammer allowed the tumult to continue for a moment, accepting this sign of respect and loyalty and building his people's fervor to even greater heights. Then he pointed north with his weapon. "We march!" he bellowed. "And let the humans tremble at our approach!"

CHAPTER SEVEN

"Tell us everything."

Khadgar nodded, not bothering to look around. It would be pointless. He had been summoned before the ruling council of the Kirin Tor and those leaders were only visible when they wished to be.

He had stood in this council chamber once before, upon being told he was to be apprenticed to Medivh. Then he had been awed by the room, which seemed to somehow hang in the air, only the floor faintly visible as the world around darkened, lightened, and stormed far more rapidly that ever happened in nature. The council members themselves had awed him just as much, appearing only as cloaked, hooded figures, their forms and faces and very genders obscured by both cloth and magic. That was both dramatic and practical, since the wizard community's leaders were chosen in secret to avoid any danger of bribery, blackmail, and other pressure. The council members knew each other's identities but no one else did. The disguises ensured that. But they also gave the council an air of mystery, and many of its members delighted in the confusion, making sure no one entered or exited the chamber without being bewildered as to where they had been and whom they had seen and often even what they had said and heard. It had certainly worked on Khadgar back then, and he had left the chamber with his head awhirl, amazed at the power his superiors wielded and unable to recount exactly what had happened during his audience.

Much had changed since then, however. Though it had been only a few short years, Khadgar had grown considerably in both knowledge and power. His appearance had changed as well, and he amused himself by thinking that for once some of the council members would be as bewildered by their visitor as he was by them. After all, he had left a young man and returned an old one, older than many of them though he had lived far less.

Regardless, Khadgar found he was unwilling to play games. He was tired. He had teleported himself to Dalaran, and while his magic was strong enough to handle the task it was still a daunting distance. Plus he had been up late discussing matters with Lothar, planning for their first official strategy session next week. Khadgar appreciated his former masters' interest in recent events, and felt they needed to know what had occurred in Azeroth, but he felt he could do without the posturing and the performances and the shadow-plays.

That was why, when he did finally lift his head, he looked straight at the cloaked figure to his left. "I would be happy to recount events, Prince Kael'thas," he said politely, "but I would find the telling far easier were I able to see my audience properly."

He heard a gasp off to the side, but the cloaked figure he had addressed chuckled instead. "You are correct, young Khadgar," the mage replied. "I would find it difficult to speak to such shadowy figures myself." With a quick gesture the elven prince dismissed his disguise, standing revealed in his ornate violet and gold robes, his long golden hair flowing past his shoulders, his sharp features alert with anticipation. "Is that better?"

"Much, thank you," Khadgar said. He glanced around at the other council members. "And what of the rest of you? May I not see your face, Lord Krasus? Lord Kel'Thuzad? Lord Antonidas has not bothered with a disguise, and Prince Kael'thas has been considerate enough to dispense with his. Will the rest of you do the same?"

Antonidas, seated before Khadgar on an invisible chair, laughed. "Indeed, youngling, indeed," he agreed. "This matter is far too serious for such parlor tricks, and you are no longer a whelp to be fooled and amazed by such sleights. Unveil yourself, my friends, and let us be to this matter before the night grows older."

The other magi obeyed, though a few grumbled, and seconds later Khadgar found himself facing six people clearly. He recognized Krasus at once by his slight build, delicate features, and silvery hair still streaked here and there with red. And Kel'Thuzad was familiar as well, an impressive, charismatic man with dark hair and a full beard and strangely glassy eyes, as if he were not really looking at the world around them. The other two, a pudgy man and a tall, statuesque woman, Khadgar did not know, though their faces seemed vaguely familiar. Most likely he had passed them in the halls of the Violet Citadel back when he had been a student here and had simply not been important enough for them to address him directly.

Now, however, they were all attention.

"We have done as you asked," Kel'Thuzad complained. "Now tell us what has happened!"

"What do you want to know?" Khadgar asked the older mage.

"Everything!" And from the look in his eyes, Kel'Thuzad meant it. He had always had a reputation as a dreamer and a researcher, constantly questing for information, particularly about magic, its sources, and its potential. Of all the Kirin Tor he had been the one most interested in gaining access to Medivh's arcane library, and Khadgar assumed one of the ones most upset about its destruction. He had not bothered to mention that he had taken the choicest tomes for himself before vacating the tower.

"Very well." And so he told them. Gratefully accepting a chair the pudgy man offered, Khadgar sat and described everything that had happened since he had left Dalaran more than two years before. He told them about his strange apprenticeship with Medivh, about the master wizard's mercurial moods and strange disappearances. He told them about the first encounters with the orcs. He told them about the wizard murders. He told them about Medivh's betrayal, and about how he and Lothar had ended the wizard's life. Then he went on to talk about the Horde and the battles that had occurred, about the siege of Stormwind, Llane's death, the city's conquest, and their subsequent flight.

The master magi remained quiet for much of the recitation. Occasionally one would ask a question, but they showed surprising consideration for someone so much their junior, and the few questions they did ask were short and to the point. When he had finished, ending with the Alliance and the Paladins, Khadgar leaned back to catch his breath and waited to see what the magi might ask next.

"You did not mention the Order of Tirisfal," Kel'Thuzad pointed out, eliciting a sharp cough from Antonidas. "What?" the mage-researcher demanded. "It is relevant, when discussing Medivh!"

"It is," Khadgar answered, "and I apologize for my lapse. But"—he glanced around, trying to judge the magi's knowledge by their faces, and opted for discretion—"I know little of the Order's true workings. Medivh was a member, and spoke once or twice of the

Order's existence, but he did not name any other members or discuss its activities."

"Of course," the woman agreed, and Khadgar saw the look of frustration and disappointment she and Kel'Thuzad exchanged. He had been right then, he realized. They knew nothing about the Order, and had merely hoped to trick him into revealing its secrets. That had failed and they would not press the issue. "But I am more concerned with Medivh himself, and with what happened to him," she continued. "You are certain it was Sargeras you saw within him?"

"Absolutely." Khadgar leaned forward. "I had already seen the titan in a vision, and recognized him at once."

"So it was Medivh—or Sargeras through him—who opened a rift for the orcs," the pudgy man mused. "And what did you say their world was called?"

"Draenor," Khadgar answered, shuddering slightly. His mind flashed back to another vision from Medivh's tower, that of himself as an old man—or at least, looking as he did now—leading a small force of warriors against a multitude of orcs. On a world with a blood-red sky. Garona had told him it sounded like Draenor, which meant he was destined to go there. And most likely not survive. He forced himself back to the conversation before him.

"What do we know of it?" Krasus was asking. "This world? You've told us of the sky, but can you tell us anything else?"

"I haven't been there myself," Khadgar replied, thinking *at least not yet*. "But a companion, a half-orc, told me a great deal about the world and about the orcs." He could see Garona in his mind's eye, and quickly turned away from that painful memory as well. "The orcs were considerably more peaceful at home—they squabbled but didn't fight one another. Their only real enemies were the ogres, and orcs are far smarter and considerably more numerous."

"What happened?" Kel'Thuzad asked.

"They were corrupted," Khadgar explained. "She didn't know all the details—the why and how of it—but gradually their skin changed from brown to green and they began practicing different magic from what they had known before. They turned more savage, more violent. There was a great ceremony and a chalice of some sort. The chieftains drank from it, and the warriors—most of them, anyway. Their skin changed to a vivid green then, and their eyes turned red. They grew more powerful, stronger and fiercer, and they all went blood-crazy. They killed any foe they encountered and then began turning on each other. Plus their magics had leeched the life from the soil and their crops would not grow. They were on the verge of killing themselves, or of dying from starvation. But Medivh approached Gul'dan, the Horde's chief warlock, and offered him access to this world. Our world. Gul'dan accepted and together they built the portal. They sent through a few clans at a time, and gradually increased their numbers. Then it was just a matter of waiting, building strength, scouting defenses, and finally attacking."

"And now we have them approaching us full force." Kael'thas frowned.

"Yes."

Khadgar waited, but no one else spoke and at last he stirred in his unseen chair. "If there is nothing more, noble gentlemen and lady, I will take my leave," he said. "It has been a long day and I am very tired."

"What are your plans now?" the woman asked him as he rose from his chair.

Khadgar frowned. He had been pondering the same question since their arrival in Lordaeron. A part of him wanted to beg the Kirin Tor for protection. Perhaps he could resume his old job as an assistant to the librarian? He would not cause any trouble, and he would be safe behind the strongest magical defenses in the world.

Another part of him, however, hated the idea of hiding from the upcoming conflict. He had faced a demon, after all! And he had survived. If he could handle that, surely he could handle an army of orcs.

Besides, friendship and respect still counted for something, at least to him.

"I will stand by Lord Lothar," Khadgar replied finally, deliberately keeping his voice casual. "I have promised him my support, and he richly deserves it. After the war, assuming we survive—" He shrugged.

"You are still a subject of Dalaran," the woman pointed out. "If we called you back here and assigned you necessary work, would you obey the summons?"

Khadgar thought about it for a few seconds. "No," he answered slowly. "I cannot return to that. After this war, if we survive, I will return to my studies, though whether I do that here or at Medivh's tower or at some other location is entirely uncertain."

The council members studied him and he them. It was Krasus who finally broke the silence. "You left here a mere boy, a fledgling apprentice," he said, and Khadgar could hear the approval in his voice. "But you have returned a master, and a man." Khadgar dipped his head to acknowledge the compliment but did not say anything.

"You will not be ordered to do anything," Antonidas assured him. "We shall respect your wishes, and your independence. Though we would like to be kept up-to-date, particularly for anything involving Medivh, the necromancers, the Order, and that portal."

Khadgar nodded. "Then I am free to go?"

That earned him a tight smile from Antonidas. "Yes, you may go," the archmage said. "May the Light protect you and grant you strength."

"Keep us informed," the pudgy man added. "The sooner we know what the orcs plan, the sooner we can send troops to that area, and of course we can provide magical assistance as well."

Khadgar nodded. "Of course." He left the room quickly, but as soon as the doors had shut he summoned a scrying sphere. The Kirin Tor met in a quiet room that he assumed had been magically shielded not only from attacks but also from prying eyes. But Khadgar had learned a great deal from Medivh during his short apprenticeship, and had learned more from the books he had appropriated after the master mage's death. He was also very close to his target subject. He concentrated, and the colors within the sphere swirled, from green to black and back again. Faces began to appear in the image, and a faint murmuring, and then he was looking at the Kirin Tor's council members in plain violet robes. Even the room's active mural had changed, slowing down and finally coming to a stop, leaving only a plain chamber with six people milling about.

"—don't know how far we can trust him," the pudgy man was saying. "He did not seem very eager to accede to our wishes."

"Of course not," Kael'thas replied shortly. "I doubt you would be any more open and trusting if you had been through as much as he had. We do not need to trust him, regardless. We only need him to provide us an introduction to Lothar, and to mediate between us and any others. I am sure we can trust him not to undermine our efforts, not to turn against us, and not to withhold any evidence and information we might need. I do not see where we would want or need any more than that."

"This other world, Draenor, that troubles me," Krasus muttered. "If the orcs could pass through that portal, so could others—from either side. We know they had ogres there but have no idea what else to expect. That means they could have even worse creatures waiting eagerly for their chance to enter and then devastate this world. Also, there is nothing to stop the orcs from retreating to their home whenever they feel it necessary. Fighting an enemy with an impregnable home base becomes considerably more difficult, as he can pop out, attack, and then disappear again. We should make finding and destroying that portal our first priority."

"Agreed," said Kael'thas. "Destroy the portal." The others nodded. "Good, that's settled. What else?"

They began talking about something more mundane, schedules for cleaning the Violet Citadel's laboratories, and Khadgar let the scrying sphere fade away, image and all. That had gone better than he had expected. Kael'thas was right, he had gone through a great deal in the past three years, and he had half-expected the Kirin Tor to grow furious with his lack of respect. But they had not said anything at all and seemed to believe his story without any prompting, which certainly made for a pleasant change.

Now he just needed to teleport himself back to Capital City and sleep so that he would be awake enough to be of any use tomorrow.

A week later, Lothar stood in a command tent in southern Lordaeron not far from Southshore where he and Khadgar had first arrived. They had chosen this area because it was central enough to reach any part of the continent quickly, particularly by boat. Outside, his troops marshaled and drilled and slept. Inside, he and the Lordaeron kings and the four men he had chosen for lieutenants clustered around a table and stared at the map laid across it. Lothar had made Uther his liaison to the Silver Hand and to the Church—the Paladins had made surprising progress in their fighting skills and in wielding the Light. Khadgar was both his contact with the magi and his most objective adviser. Proudmoore controlled the navy, of course—it hadn't even been a question. But Turalyon, young Turalyon Lothar had made his second in command. The youth had impressed both him and Khadgar, and had shown himself to be smart, focused, loyal, and hard-working, even if he did still treat Lothar as if he were some legendary figure. Lothar was sure the lad would grow out of that, however, and could not think of anyone better qualified to serve as his right hand. Turalyon was clearly still nervous about such a heavy responsibility, and Lothar had twice been forced to remind him not to jab absently at the map. At least, not with a knife.

They were discussing the same things they had been discussing for a week now—which way the Horde would most likely go, where they might attack, and how to bring the Alliance troops there as quickly as possible, at least without trampling the very fields and crops they had united to protect. Just as Graymane was insisting for the tenth time that the Alliance forces be stationed all around Gilneas's borders in case the orcs somehow appeared there first, a scout burst in.

"Sir, you have to see this, sir!" he shouted, trying to stop his forward momentum, bow, and salute, all at the same time. "They're here!"

"Who's here, soldier?" Lothar frowned. He was trying to read the scout's expression and having a hard time of it, the man was so flustered. He didn't look terrified, however, which meant Lothar could take a deep breath and try to get his own racing heart back under control. Because no terror meant it wasn't the Horde. There was fear on the scout's face, but it was mixed with respect, even awe. Lothar had never seen anything quite like it.

"The elves, sir!" the scout all but shouted. "The elves are here!"

"The elves?" Lothar stared at the scout, trying to process that fact, then turned and glared at the assembled kings. As he had suspected, one of them coughed and looked slightly guilty.

"We need allies," King Terenas explained. "And the elves are a mighty race. I thought it best to contact them immediately."

"Without consulting me?" Lothar was furious. "And what if they have sent an entire army, and suddenly announce they are in control? What if the Horde arrives while we are working to assimilate them into our own forces? You do not conceal details like this from your military commander! It could mean our deaths, or at the very least the deaths of many of our people!"

Terenas nodded soberly. "You are correct, of course," he answered, reminding Lothar once again why he liked the king. Most men were unwilling to accept fault, and often those with authority were even worse about it. But Terenas took full responsibility for his actions, good or bad. "I should have consulted you first. I felt time was of the essence, but that is no excuse. It will not happen again."

Lothar nodded gruffly. "Fine. Let's go and see what these elves look like, then." He marched out of the tent, the others following close behind him.

The first thing Lothar saw as he peeled back the tent flap and stepped outside were his own troops. Their army filled the valley and beyond, stretching across the landscape, and for an instant Lothar felt a rush of pride and confidence. How could anyone, anything, stand against so mighty a force? But then he saw again in his mind's eye the Horde washing over Stormwind, an unstoppable emerald sea, and grew somber again. Still, the Alliance army was many times larger than Stormwind's had been. They would at least give the Horde serious pause.

Glancing past his troops Lothar's gaze came to the shore, and the sea beyond. Proudmoore's ships were anchored all along the coastline, from small fast scout ships to massive destroyers, creating a forest of masts and sails across the waves. But many of them had pulled back from the docks, creating an open channel, and sailing up that space were a cluster of ships such as Lothar had never seen.

"Elven destroyers," Proudmoore whispered at his

elbow. "Faster than our own, and lighter—they carry less weaponry but make up for that with speed. An excellent, excellent addition to our forces." The navy admiral frowned. "But so few? I count only four, and eight smaller vessels. This is a single battle group."

"Perhaps more are following them," Turalyon suggested from Lothar's other side.

But Proudmoore shook his head. "That would not be their way," he answered. "They would all arrive together."

"A dozen ships is still a dozen more than we had before," Khadgar pointed out. "And whatever troops they carry as well."

Lothar nodded. "We should go and greet them," he said, and the others all agreed. Together they set out across the valley. Perenolde and Graymane were not used to such exertion and were gasping in minutes but the rest were fit and they moved briskly, reaching the docks just as the first ship glided to a stop beside it.

A tall, lithe figure leaped across, landing lightly on the rough wooden pier. Long golden hair caught the sunlight, and Lothar heard at least one of his companions gasp behind him. As the figure drew closer Lothar saw it was a woman, and a stunning one at that. Her slender features were delicate but strong, as was her lean, willowy body. She wore forest green and oak brown, a strange lightweight breastplate over shirt and breeches and a long cloak with the hood tossed back, and leather gloves covered her arms to the elbow just as boots protected her legs to the knees. A slim sword hung at one hip, a pouch and horn at the other, and across her back were slung a longbow and a quiver of arrows. Lothar had seen many women over the years, some of them as beautiful as this elf approaching them, but he had never seen one who so easily combined strength and grace. He could understand why several of his companions already seemed smitten.

"Milady," Lothar called out when she was still a few paces away. "Welcome. I am Anduin Lothar, commander of the Alliance of Lordaeron."

She nodded, covering the remaining distance and stopping only a handspan away. From here he could see the pointed ears poking up through her hair, and the wide, emerald-green eyes that slanted up at the corners. "I am Alleria Windrunner, and I bring you greetings from Anasterian Sunstrider and the Council of Silvermoon." Her voice was lovely, musical and rich, and Lothar suspected it was pleasant even in anger.

"Thank you." He turned and gestured to the men gathered around him. "Allow me to present the kings of the Alliance, as well as my lieutenants." After introductions had been made, he turned to more serious matters. "Forgive my bluntness, Lady Alleria," he said, drawing a smile from her at the title, "but I must ask—is this all the aid your people can muster?"

That brought a frown from her. "I will tell you straight, Lord Lothar," she replied, glancing around to make sure no others were listening. Several other elves, both men and women, had left the ship now and were clustered at the far end of the pier, clearly awaiting Alleria's permission to move closer. "Anasterian and the others were little concerned at the reports you sent. This Horde is far distant from us and seems intent upon conquering human lands, not our own forests. The council members feel it is better to leave this conflict to the younger races, and merely strengthen our own borders to prevent any additional incursions." Her eyes narrowed, showing what she thought of such a decision.

"Yet you are here," Khadgar pointed out. "Surely that means something?"

She nodded. "The missive from King Terenas"—she nodded in his direction—"informed us that you, Lord Lothar, were the last of the Arathi bloodline. Our ancestors pledged eternal support to your King Thoradin and all his kin. Anasterian could not deny that obligation. He has sent this battle group to acknowledge the debt."

"And you?" Lothar asked, noticing she had only mentioned the ships.

"I am here of my own accord," she announced proudly, tossing her head back in the same way he had seen spirited stallions do when challenged. "I am a ranger, and chose to bring my own detachment and offer our aid freely." She glanced beyond Lothar, her eyes roaming, and he knew she was studying the army spread out behind him. "I sensed this conflict was far more serious than my own rulers realized. Such a war could easily spread to us all, and if the Horde is as vicious as you say our forests will not remain inviolate for long." She turned back and met Lothar's gaze, and he could see that for all her beauty this was a strong woman used to battle. "We must stop them."

Lothar nodded. "I agree." He bowed. "Well, you are welcome here, milady, and I thank your lords for their token support. But I am far more grateful for your presence, and that of your rangers." He smiled. "We were just discussing our next move, and I would be pleased to hear your opinion. And once your people are settled I will ask you to send them scouting, that we may be sure the enemy is not yet upon us."

"We need no rest," Alleria assured him. "I will send them at once." She gestured, and the other elves approached. Each was garbed as she was, and moved as quietly, though to Lothar's eyes they lacked her singular grace. Alleria spoke with them, her words fluid and musical and completely foreign to Lothar, and the others nodded and then flitted past them with a brief nod, disappearing at a run off the docks and through the valley. Within minutes they had vanished from sight.

"They will scout and report back," Alleria explained. "If the Horde has come within two days' march of here, we will know of it."

"Excellent." Lothar ran a hand absently over his bare forehead. "If you would care to accompany us back to the command tent, then, milady, I will show you what we know thus far and we will hear your thoughts on the matter."

She laughed. "Of course. But you will have to stop calling me 'milady' if you want me to pay proper attention. It is Alleria, nothing more."

Lothar nodded and turned, leading her off the docks. As he did he caught a glimpse of Turalyon's face and suppressed a grin. Now he knew where the gasp had come from.

Two days later, Lothar found he had nothing to smile about. Alleria's scouts had returned, as had Proudmoore's, and both had the same news to share. The Horde had taken Khaz Modan and used the dwarven mines to craft ships of their own, massive ungainly vessels of iron and timber that moved awkwardly but could carry thousands of orcs in their deep holds. These ships had carried the Horde swiftly across the water, and they had indeed aimed at the southern coast of Lordaeron. Not as far as Graymane's domain, however. It looked as if the Horde would come ashore in the Hillsbrad region, halfway between here and Gilneas. If the Alliance moved quickly, they could be there waiting when the Horde arrived.

"Gather the troops!" Lothar bellowed. "Leave everything nonessential—we can send people back for it later, if we survive! Right now we need speed more than anything else. Go! Go!" He turned to Khadgar as his other lieutenants ran from the command tent to muster their own troops, the kings right beside them. "And so it begins," he told the young-old wizard.

Khadgar nodded. "I thought we would have more time," he admitted.

"So did I," Lothar agreed. "But these orcs are impatient to conquer. That may be their downfall." He sighed. "At least, I hope so." He stared at the maps of Hillsbrad a moment, trying to envision the coming battle, then shook his head. There were things to do, many of them. And the battle would come soon enough.

CHAPTER EIGHT

"**A**re we ready?"

Turalyon gulped and nodded. "Ready, sir."

Lothar nodded and turned away, frowning, and for a second Turalyon worried the expression was because of him. Had he given the wrong response? Had Lord Lothar wanted more detail? Was there something else he was supposed to say or do?

Stop it, he warned himself. *You're panicking. Again! Calm down. You're doing fine. He's frowning because we're about to go into battle, not because you've disappointed him.*

Forcing himself not to think about it any more, Turalyon gave his gear one more inspection. The straps of his armor were all good and tight, his shield was steady on his arm, his warhammer was slung from the saddle-horn. He was ready. As ready as he could be.

Looking around, he studied the other figures nearby. Lothar was talking to Uther, and Turalyon envied both men their poise. They looked slightly impatient but otherwise completely calm. Was that just something you picked up as you got more experience? Khadgar was looking out over the plain, and must have sensed Turalyon's gaze because he turned and gave him a weary smile.

"Nervous?" the mage asked.

Turalyon grinned despite himself. "Very," he admitted. He had been raised with the typical sense of respect but wariness toward magi but Khadgar was different. Perhaps it was because they were near the same age, though the mage looked decades older. Or perhaps it was simply that Khadgar didn't hold himself above non-magi the way Turalyon had seen other wizards do. They had struck up an easy conversation that first day, after Archbishop Faol had introduced all of them, and Turalyon had found himself liking Khadgar. He liked Lothar as well, but was in awe of the Champion's experience and martial skill. Khadgar was probably more powerful personally, but somehow he was more approachable, and he and Turalyon had become fast friends. He was the only one Turalyon felt safe telling about his fears.

"Don't worry about it," Khadgar advised. "Everyone is. The trick is just to work past that."

"You're nervous too?"

The mage grinned. "Scared spitless would be closer," he revealed. "I have been every time we've been in combat. And it was Lothar who told me, after one encounter, that you should be scared. Because the man who isn't afraid gets careless, and that's when he gets hurt."

Turalyon nodded. "My instructors said much the same thing." He shook his head. "It's one thing to say that, though, and another to believe it."

His friend patted him on the shoulder. "You'll do fine," he assured. "Once it starts you'll be too busy to think about it."

They both turned and looked out again. The Hillsbrad region was so named for its rolling foothills, and the Alliance army was spread across the last line of those hills, facing Lordaeron's Southshore and the Great Sea beyond. The Horde ships were approaching even as they watched, massive unwieldy vessels of dark metal and blackened wood, without sails but with row upon row of oars. Lothar intended to meet the Horde as it emerged from the water, before the orcs had a chance to find their footing. Proudmoore's navy had already assaulted the ships during their passage, destroying several vessels and sending thousands of orcs to the bottom of the ocean, but the Horde was so numerous they had merely picked off the outermost ships while the rest sailed on past. There would still be fighting aplenty when they landed.

"They are almost ashore," Alleria reported, her sharp elven eyes seeing farther than theirs. She turned toward Turalyon. "Best ready your men for the attack."

Turalyon nodded, not trusting himself to speak. He had seen women before, of course, and nothing about his Order forbade relationships or even marriage. But the elven ranger made every other woman he had ever met seem both weak and rough at the same time. She was so confident, so graceful, and so lovely his mouth ran dry every time he saw her, and he often found himself trembling and sweating like a horse that had just run a hard race. And judging by the glint in her eyes and the half-smile when she said anything to him, Turalyon suspected she knew and enjoyed his discomfort.

Now at least he had something to distract him. Signaling his unit leaders, Turalyon gave them the go-ahead gesture. They in turn gave an order to their heralds, who sounded the advance on their battle horns. Within minutes the entire Alliance force was in motion, marching and riding slowly but steadily down the hill and toward the shore.

As they closed the distance Turalyon made out more details. He saw the first of the ships beach itself, and dark figures swarm over its side, stomping up the rocky beach and toward the foothills. Even from here he could see they were broadly built, with thick chests and long, powerful arms, and bandy legs that ate up the distance. They brandished weapons, axes and hammers and swords and spears. And there were a lot of them.

"They have reached the land!" Lothar shouted, drawing his massive greatsword with a single sweep and holding it aloft, the gold runes along its blade catching the light. "Charge! For Lordaeron!" He spurred his horse and it leaped forward, past the Alliance ranks, the golden lion on his shield catching the light.

"Damn!" Turalyon kicked his own steed into a gallop and took off after his commander, snatching up his hammer and dropping his helm into place as he moved. He saw soldiers scrambling out of the way, and others hastening to catch up, and then he was past them and in the narrow stretch between the two armies. But soon enough that vanished and he crashed full-force into the orcs, reaching them just as Lothar's first swing took down several and others advanced toward his horse, determined to pull the Champion down and tear him apart.

"No!" Turalyon swung as soon as he was within reach, his hammer catching an orc full in the head. The creature dropped with barely a sound and Turalyon knocked a second one aside with his shield, battering the orc away long enough to bring his hammer back around and smash at that one as well.

By the Light, they were ugly! Lothar and Khadgar had described them but it was not the same as seeing them firsthand, with that vivid green skin and those glowing red eyes. And those tusks! He had seen such things on boars before, but never on anything that walked on two legs and carried a weapon! They were strong too, he saw, as an orc's warhammer clashed with his own and almost drove his weapon back into his helm, the creature struck with such force. Fortunately they seemed to rely more upon strength and aggression than skill—he was able to twist his weapon free and bring it back around, its haft catching the orc a glancing blow across the cheek and stunning it long enough for Turalyon to strike again properly.

Lothar had cleared the orcs from his side with a vicious sword swing, and Turalyon guided his horse beside the commander so they stood side by side, hammer and greatsword in constant motion. Uther was right behind them now, his own mighty hammer crushing orcs left and right, a visible glow surround him and his weapon and making the orcs turn away, shielding their eyes. A cheer arose from the Alliance forces as they saw the Paladins' prowess. Turalyon was not surprised. He had trained alongside Uther and knew the older Paladin's faith was incredibly strong, strong enough to manifest visibly. He wished his own was as solid.

Now was not the time to think of that, however. More orc warships were reaching the beach, and orcs were pouring from them by the thousands. Turalyon saw at once that they would be overwhelmed if they stayed. "Sir!" he shouted at Lothar. "We need to move back to the rest of the army!"

At first he thought the Champion had not heard him, but Lothar skewered another orc and then nodded. "Uther!" he shouted, and the Paladin turned. "Back to the others!" Uther raised his hammer in salute and wheeled his horse around at once, bludgeoning a path back through the gathering Horde. Lothar was right behind him and Turalyon brought up the rear, laying about him with hammer and shield to keep orc hands and weapons at bay. One orc reached for him, a massive axe held ready in its other hand, only to fall with an arrow through its throat. Turalyon risked a quick glance around and saw a slender figure back on the hill raise a longbow in salute. He could just make out the gleam of her hair from here.

Several times he thought they would fall but he, Uther, and Lothar all made it back to the front lines safely. The Horde was right behind them.

"Form up!" Lothar shouted. "Raise spears. Link shields! Repel them!" The soldiers hurried to obey— they had been standing ready but separately, individuals rather than a unified force, but that would not work against the Horde's superior numbers. Now they moved together, forming a solid shield wall that bristled with spears, and the Horde crashed into that. In several places the wall fell, a defender overpowered by an orc's charge, but much of it held as orcs fell back, clutching new wounds. Some dropped and did not rise again, though their fellows quickly swarmed over and past them.

A second wave struck the shield wall, collapsing more sections, but again the orcs took heavy casualties. Turalyon signaled the nearest unit leaders and was pleased to see them respond quickly, a second shield wall already forming behind the first. They could build wall after wall, and if each one cost the orcs as heavily they could whittle away the Horde until it was small enough to face the creatures directly.

But the orcs were clearly not stupid. After the third collision they held back, as if waiting for something. And Turalyon soon saw what. A handful of heavily cloaked figures advanced. Each wore a cowl low over its face, so only the eyes were visible deep within, and each carried a strange glowing truncheon. These creatures rode strange, heavily barded horses with glowing eyes, and charged forward, directly toward the shield wall, and raised their truncheons as they approached. Turalyon felt as much as heard a strange buzzing, and the soldiers directly in front of the creatures collapsed, clutching their heads as blood poured from their mouths, noses, and ears.

"By the Light!" Uther was standing near Turalyon and bristled at the sight. "The fiends! They wield dark magic against us!" He raised his hammer high, and its head glowed silver like the moon. "Stand fast, soldiers!" he shouted. "The Holy Light protects you!" The glow spread from the hammer, shining down upon the warriors and bathing them in its light, and when the cloaked figures raised their hands again the soldiers winced but did not fall. Then Uther came crashing down upon them, the shield wall opening long enough to allow him and the other Paladins—including Gavinrad, who Faol had happily inducted into the order—through. Again Alliance soldiers cheered, heartened by the Paladins' surprising skill and power. Turalyon felt torn. As a Paladin his place was beside them, but as Lothar's lieutenant his place was here, overseeing the men.

The Paladins and the cloaked figures were battling now, neither able to gain the upper hand. Turalyon saw one of the strange invaders clamp a hand on Gavinrad's arm, darkness radiating from the grip. But Gavinrad's holy aura shone brighter and drove the darkness away, causing his attacker to shrink back and duck a blow from the Paladin's hammer. Meanwhile the orcs continued to batter at the shield wall, tearing holes in the defense only to have another soldier step up and fill the gap.

Then a movement caught Turalyon's eye and he saw several new figures approach, towering above the orcs. Ogres! The massive creatures advanced, swinging rough clubs that were little more than uprooted trees, and whole sections of the shield wall collapsed, soldiers crushed by the powerful blows. The Horde poured forward through the gaps, sweeping in among the Alliance soldiers.

"Change tactics!" Turalyon shouted at the nearest herald, knowing the man would relay the orders with his horn. "Small shield units! Pull back to the hills and regroup!" The soldier nodded and raised his horn, blowing a short burst and then another. At the sound the unit leaders began shouting orders of their own, gathering their soldiers and retreating while keeping the orcs at bay. The Horde tried overrunning them but the Alliance soldiers were clumped too close together and kept their weapons up, jabbing at any orc that came too close. Each unit had its shields linked as well, forming a small shield wall all around. The orcs overwhelmed several units by sheer numbers, crashing into the warriors again and again until they faltered, but most of the Alliance soldiers were able to pull back successfully.

Turalyon rode along the ranks at the base of the hills, organizing them. He set up another shield wall there, and as each unit retreated to it the wall opened to allow them in, then closed behind them. Those soldiers then reinforced the wall themselves and helped bring other units through safely. Turalyon tasked the archers with keeping the orcs away from the wall as much as possible, harassing any creature that came too close to pulling down a defender. They were taking a heavy toll upon the orcs, but the Horde was still beaching ships and adding more to the battle with every minute.

"We cannot hold them for long!" Turalyon shouted to Khadgar, who had just done something to make a strange orc collapse near the boats. The orc had been dressed in robes rather than armor and had carried a staff instead of a sword, so Turalyon guessed it was a warlock, their equivalent to a mage. "We need to do something to keep them from reaching the hills! If they do get past us they'll advance straight north to Capital City!"

Khadgar nodded. "I will do what I can," he promised. The young-old wizard concentrated and the sky above them darkened. Within minutes it went from a clear day to ominous black clouds. The sudden storm centered upon Khadgar, the mage's white hair dancing about him. Lightning flickered in the sky, and an answering spark danced across his outstretched fingers. Then there was a shattering boom, and a lightning bolt leaped forth, not from the sky but from Khadgar's hands, its light splitting the darkness. It struck just shy of the shield wall, in a cluster of orcs, and they went flying, burnt to a crisp by the powerful bolt. A second one struck, and a third, and Turalyon used the magical attack to his advantage. He regrouped his men, shoring up the shield wall, and also sent soldiers forward with brush and tinder. They laid fires in the orc's path, creating a raging blaze that stopped the Horde from advancing to the west. That reduced the risk of their surrounding the Alliance forces, and made them easier to contain and block.

Nor were the orcs slow to notice. Several of the creatures stepped forward, trying to put out the fire, but elven archers shot them down before they could reach the flames. One fell into the fire instead, and screamed as it consumed him. That made the others shrink back again.

The ogres were a problem, however. One lumbered through the flames, burning its legs but otherwise not slowing down. Turalyon directed a full unit against it, and targeted it with ballistae as well. But the ogre downed many warriors before it finally fell, and others were approaching behind it.

"Target them!" Turalyon told Khadgar. "Take out the ogres!"

Khadgar glanced his way, and Turalyon saw that his friend looked truly exhausted. "I will try," the mage agreed. "But drawing forth the lightning is . . . taxing." An instant later a lightning bolt burst from his fingers and struck the lead ogre, killing it at once, but even as its massive, blackened corpse fell Khadgar shook his head. "That is all I can do," he warned.

Turalyon hoped it would be enough. The other ogres hesitated, even their small brains able to comprehend the danger, and that gave his men time to target them with arrows and more ballistae. The shield wall still held but the Horde was massing again, and before long it would be able to simply roll over the defenders, its losses barely diminishing its bulk. Uther and the other Paladins had not returned, and Turalyon could only assume they were still keeping those cloaked figures at bay.

He was still wondering what to do when Lothar appeared beside him. "Ready the cavalry!" the Champion shouted. "And sound the charge!"

Charge? Into that? Turalyon stared at his commander for an instant, then shrugged. Well, why not? Their defenses could not hold out forever. He signaled the herald, who blew a might blast. Then those warriors on horseback were forming up, and Turalyon swung in with them, placing himself just behind Lothar, who rode at their head. The shield wall parted for them, and they crashed into the Horde's front ranks, carving a path back through the orcs. After a minute Lothar signaled and they wheeled about, the archers providing cover as they swung clear. Then they struck again.

They were readying for a third charge when a drum beat from somewhere within the Horde—and the orcs fell back!

"We did it!" Turalyon shouted. "They're retreating!"

Lothar nodded but did not turn away, watching as the orcs turned and ran a short distance, then regrouped. Then the creatures turned and began moving again, at a fast march—to the right of the Alliance forces.

"They're heading east," Lothar said quietly. He made no move to chase them. "Into the Hinterlands."

"Are we going after them?" Turalyon asked. His blood was still racing from the charges and he wanted to run after the orcs and smash them all. "We have them on the run!"

But the Champion shook his head. "No," he corrected. "We blocked them, and held. But they are not running from us. They are going around us." Now he did turn to Turalyon, and smiled, a grim, weary smile. "Still," he said, "that is something."

"But we should go after them before they can find another place to stand," Turalyon urged. "Shouldn't we?"

"We should," Lothar agreed. "But look behind you." Turalyon turned and saw at once what the older warrior meant. Their forces were sagging now that the battle was over, and he saw men collapsing where they stood, both from wounds and from sheer fatigue. The battle had lasted for hours, though it had not felt like it at the time, and he found himself aching as well now that it was done. Plus they had destroyed many weapons, emptied most of their ballistae, and used up most of the army's firewood and tinder as well.

"We need to resupply," Turalyon admitted out loud. "We are in no shape to pursue them now."

"No." Lothar turned his horse back toward their own lines. "But we have tested their forces now, and our men have seen that they can stand against the Horde. That is good. And we have kept them from the capital. Also good." He glanced at Turalyon, and nodded finally. "You did well," he said quietly before nudging his horse back toward their troops and the command tent that lay beyond.

Turalyon watched him go for a moment. The simple praise had filled him with pride. And, he realized as he brought his own horse around to follow his commander, Khadgar had been right. He had not had time to be afraid.

CHAPTER NINE

"Nekros!"

Zuluhed, chieftain and shaman of the Dragonmaw clan, strode down the long corridor, glaring at every orc that dared get in his way. "Nekros!" he bellowed again.

"Here, I'm here!" Nekros Skullcrusher limped out of a nearby cavern, his wooden leg clanking against the rough stone floor, ducking to keep from bashing his head against the low doorway. "What?"

Zuluhed stopped beside his Second and glared at him.

"How goes the weapon?" Zuluhed demanded, leaning in close. "Is it ready?"

Nekros grinned at him, showing his yellowed tusks. "Come and see for yourself." He turned and limped back the way he had come, and Zuluhed followed, muttering to himself. He hated this place. It was called Grim Batol, or at least the dwarves had named it so, but it had been one of their fortresses then. Now it belonged to the Dragonmaw, and though its chambers were large enough he despised the low-ceilinged corridors and even lower doorways, tall enough for dwarves but barely enough for most orcs. They would have enlarged the openings but stone was difficult to work and they had little time for such frivolities. The fortress was sturdy, carved into the mountain itself, and easily defended, and that was the important thing.

Nekros led him down farther into the fortress, and finally into a vast underground chamber. And there, chained to the wall by heavy links of dark iron, was a sight that still made Zuluhed catch his breath. Filling the room end to end was a vast figure, coiled in about itself either for comfort of from despair, yet still its wingtips brushed the ceiling and its tail lashed at the far wall. Torches guttered along the walls, their light reflecting from scale after scale, gleaming red as blood, red as flame.

A dragon.

Not just any dragon, either. This was Alexstrasza, greatest of the red dragons, mother of her flight, the queen of her people. Perhaps the most powerful creature in this world, strong enough to destroy entire clans with a single sweep of her majestic claws and consume whole ogres with a snap of her mighty jaws.

Yet they had captured her.

Well, Nekros had. The entire clan had sought a dragon for weeks, any dragon, and had at last spied a lone red male flying low above the forest, nursing a wounded wing. Zuluhed had not wanted to think what could have injured such a majestic creature, but it had made their task easier. They had followed the dragon back to its family's lair, a high mountain peak around which dragons flew like birds, dancing upon the air. They had watched that peak for days, unsure what to do next, until Nekros announced that he had tamed the Demon Soul. Then they had slowly, cautiously crept up to the top, and there they had discovered Alexstrasza and her three mates. The Dragonqueen had noticed them immediately, and had killed four orcs in an instant, opening her mouth and dousing them with flames. But then Nekros had stepped forward and subdued her. By himself. He had ordered Alexstrasza and her kin to follow him here, and they had. The rest of the Dragonmaw had sung Nekros's praises that day, the orc who had single-handedly cowed an entire dragon flight.

But the maimed warrior-warlock would not have been able to do so without Zuluhed, or the artifact he had found. Zuluhed wished he were able to wield the item himself, but the Demon Soul had not responded to him or his shamanic magic. It had only answered to Nekros, and now the peg-legged orc was the only one capable of controlling it.

But that was acceptable. Because that meant it was Nekros who was trapped here in these caves, and Zuluhed who could fight with the rest of the Horde. Not that the peg-legged orc was fit for much else—he had become useless in combat the minute a human had severed his left leg below the knee. Most orcs would have killed themselves then, or at least leaped upon another foe and died in battle. Nekros had survived, though whether from cowardice or ill luck no one could say.

Zuluhed was glad Nekros had. Because though he had found the Demon Soul, Zuluhed had been unable to use it. He had been able to sense the power trapped within the disc, even before he had uncovered it in a small cave deep below the mountains. But that power had remained locked within the gleaming gold artifact. Clearly something other than shaman lore was needed here. Zuluhed had considered bringing the object—which he had named the Demon Soul because he could sense the demon-tainted energy within it, along with some other massive power he could not identify—to Doomhammer, but had decided against it. The Warchief was a powerful warrior and a noble orc but he had no experience with or understanding of magic. Gul'dan had been another possibility, but Zuluhed did not trust the wily chief warlock. He remembered when Gul'dan had been young and apprenticed to Ner'zhul. Now there had been a shaman! Wise and noble, revered by all, Ner'zhul had worked for the betterment of not only his own clan but all the orcs. It had been he who had first brought them strange gifts of knowledge and power from ancient spirits, and he who had encouraged and cemented stronger bonds between the different clans.

For a time, all had been good. Then it had all gone wrong. The spirits had proven false, and their own ancestor spirits stopped speaking to them, out of anger.

The shaman had lost their powers, leaving their clans defenseless from magical attack. And then Gul'dan had stepped forward. The former apprentice supplanted his master and claimed to have found a new way, a new source of magic. He offered to teach the other shaman. And many had accepted his offer, becoming warlocks.

Not Zuluhed, however. He had not trusted Gul'dan, who had always struck him as self-serving. And these strange powers smacked of the demonic. It was horror enough that the ancestors no longer spoke to him, and that the elements no longer answered his call. He would not sully himself further by consorting with such unnatural powers as Gul'dan offered.

Zuluhed had not been the only shaman to refuse, of course. But most had accepted. And then they had changed, growing larger and darker, as if their bodies reflected the taint within. Their world had suffered depredations as well, the land dying bit by bit and the skies turning red. The Horde was forced to come to this strange world instead, and they had to conquer it if they wanted their clans to ever know peace again.

Nekros had shown promise as an apprentice shaman, and Zuluhed had held hopes for him. But when Gul'dan had offered other magics Nekros had jumped at them. The young orc had learned the warlock skills well, but something had made him step away, leaving all that behind to become a warrior once more. It had renewed Zuluhed's faith in the younger orc. He had never asked what had caused the change, but knew it had something to do with loyalties—Gul'dan and his Shadow Council, or the Dragonmaw clan. Nekros had chosen his clan. After that Zuluhed had begun to confide in him again, and to ask the warrior for advice whenever forced to deal with the warlocks. It had been to Nekros that he had brought the disc, and though maimed the warrior-warlock had not failed him. It was thanks to Nekros that they stood here today, ready to see their plans set in motion.

"So," Zuluhed said, starting to walk closer to the great beast. "Have we—" He stopped as Nekros extended a thick arm, blocking his path.

"Wait," the grizzled orc warned. He pulled the Demon Soul from a pouch at his belt, holding the large, featureless gold disc aloft. "Come," he called.

As Zuluhed watched, a rush of tiny sparks appeared from throughout the chamber and flew together, coalescing into a shape. The shape gained dimension, depth, and detail, forming a tall, powerfully built humanoid wearing strange bone-like armor. Its head was shaped like a skull but rimmed in flame, and its eyes were balls of black fire. The creature towered over them, as tall as an orc but less oafish, radiating power and vigilance.

"We will enter," Nekros told it, holding the Demon Soul before him. The strange creature burst into a shower of sparks again, scattering through the room, and the maimed orc nodded for his chieftain to continue.

Zuluhed advanced again, cautiously at first in case the creature had not in fact left. But it had—whatever it was, Nekros's hold over it seemed absolute. Which was good, since they had both seen what could happen otherwise. One of their clan members had rushed into the chamber at one point, bearing a message from Doomhammer, and had not waited for Nekros to dismiss the warden. The creature had appeared from nowhere and its large, fiery skeletal hands had grasped the unwary orc's head on either side. Flames had sprung up then, consuming the hapless messenger. Within seconds his shrieking stopped, his body going limp as his head collapsed in on itself, a mere pile of cinders.

Now, however, the chieftain was able to walk into the cavern unmolested, and he approached the Dragonqueen, stopping just beyond the reach of her chains. Her massive triangular head swiveled to watch him, those great yellow orbs staring unblinking as he studied her in turn.

"Have you come to gloat then, little orc? Have you not tormented me and harmed my children enough?" Alexstrasza demanded. Her jaws snapped in fury, but the chains held her fast, their natural strength enhanced by the power of the artifact.

"Not to gloat," Zuluhed told her, still awed by her sheer size and power, "just to make sure all is arranged. You understand what will happen to you if you refuse us?"

"That has been made abundantly clear," she replied, her words sharp with anger and grief, and she turned to look pointedly toward the cavern's far corner. A handful of pale objects lay clustered there, and though he could not see them well from here Zuluhed knew they were paper-thin and mottled gold. They were the remains of an enormous egg, the size of a large orc's head. A dragon egg.

When they had first captured Alexstrasza she had refused to cooperate. Nekros had solved the problem by seizing one of her unhatched eggs, holding it before the captive queen's face, and smashing it with his fist, spattering himself and her with the yolk. Her shrieks had all but deafened them, and her thrashing had knocked several orcs to the ground, breaking limbs on two of them. But the chains had held, and after that she had cooperated, albeit reluctantly. Anything to avoid seeing more of her children destroyed unborn.

"You will not succeed," Alexstrasza informed him. "You have chained me but my children will defy you, and win their freedom."

"Not while we have this," Nekros replied, showing her the disc. He frowned, clearly concentrating, and the Dragonqueen's body arced in pain, a thin hiss escaping her clenched jaws.

"I . . . will . . . kill . . . you . . . someday," she warned, still writhing in agony, her eyes narrowed in both pain and hatred.

Nekros laughed. "Perhaps," he agreed. "But until then you and yours will serve the Horde." Zuluhed gestured and Nekros nodded, following him from the cavern. The queen snapped at air behind them, her act of defiance meaningless after their own show of power.

Zuluhed led the way down another corridor and into a second, even larger chamber. This one opened along the side of the mountain, and beyond it fiery shapes flew, flashes of color against the darkening sky.

"Release her!" one of them demanded, swooping close, claws outstretched, jaws open. "Release our mother!"

"Never!" Nekros held up the Demon Soul, and the approaching dragon screamed in pain, twisting to stay aloft as its body trembled and spasmed. The other dragons backed off slightly, though they continued to wheel about overhead.

"Your mother is our captive, as are her mates," Zuluhed shouted, knowing the dragons could hear him despite their altitude. "They will remain so. You and all their children will serve us, serve the Horde, or she will die screaming from the same pain you just felt. And with her your flight will die, for without Alexstrasza there will be no more red dragon hatchlings. You will be the last of your kind."

The dragons cried out in anger, but Zuluhed knew they would obey. He had seen the bond between mother and child and it was strong, strong enough to force them to obedience. As long as Alexstrasza thought there was hope for her children she would serve them by producing litter upon litter of dragon eggs. And as long as she and three of her mates were their captives her children would serve as well, in the hopes of one day freeing their mother.

Zuluhed grinned, watching the young dragons soaring above him. Even now his orcs were hard at work, fashioning leather straps and reins and seats. Soon they would bring the first red dragon down into this cave, and fit him with a harness and a saddle. He would hate that, of course—the dragons were fiercely independent, and no one had ever dared ride them before. But his clan would.

This was what he had promised Doomhammer, and the Warchief had been enthused about the project. This would be their secret weapon. The humans had troops and cavalry and ships, but they could not take to the air. With the dragons under his control, and loyal orcs astride them, Zuluhed could strike at the humans from above and then swoop back out of their reach. The dragons were powerful foes physically, with their claws and their jaws and their tails, but it was their fiery breath that would truly devastate the humans. Fire would rain down upon them, destroying them and their equipment, and there was nothing they could do to stop it. With the dragons on their side, the Horde would be invincible.

And he, Zuluhed of the Dragonmaw clan, was responsible. Without those visions he would never have found the Demon Soul, or sensed that it was somehow linked with the dragons, and without its powers—and Nekros to unlock them—they could not have enslaved Alexstrasza. But they had, and soon the first dragonriders would take to the air, joining the rest of the Horde and awaiting Doomhammer's commands.

Zuluhed grinned. All was going according to plan.

CHAPTER TEN

"There, Thane! Look there!"

Kurdran Wildhammer wheeled Sky'ree about and peered down where Farand pointed. Yes, there! His sharp eyes spotted movement, and he tapped Sky'ree lightly with his heels. His gryphon mount cawed softly in response before tucking in her wings and diving down, the wind tugging at them both as they descended.

Yes, now he could make out figures traipsing through the forest below. Trolls? They were as green as the forest trolls his people hated, certainly, their skin blending in among the foliage, but they walked the ground rather than skimming the branches. And their footsteps were too heavy, too careless, to be the trolls, who knew the ways of the forest almost as well as an elf might. No, these creatures were something different. Kurdran caught a clear view of one as it passed through a small clearing, and frowned. Heavily built but big, as big as a human, with thick muscles and long legs. And heavy weapons, massive axes and hammers and maces. Whatever the creatures were, they were equipped for war.

He pulled back on the reins and Sky'ree lashed her tail, reared back on her leonine haunches, spread her wings and leaped upward once more, clear of the trees and back into the sky. Farand and the others were circling, their weathered skin blending into the tawny pelts of their mounts, and Kurdran rose to join them, his braided beard and hair streaming behind him, enjoying the sensation of flight even under these grim circumstances. Off in the distance he could see the massive stone carving of an eagle at rest, peering alertly and confidently out at the world, which was his own home and the heart of his domain. Aerie Peak. Yet the sight did not fill him with the usual pride and joy, for it seemed far too close for comfort given the activities occurring below him.

"Ye see, Thane?" Farand asked. "I told ye! Uglies in our forest!"

"Aye, ye were right," Kurdran told the scout. "They are ugly, and they are intruding. There be a lot o' them, though. And they'll be hard to hit as long as they stay beneath the trees."

"Are we just to let them traipse across our lands, then?" one of the other scouts demanded.

"Oh no," Kurdran replied. He grinned at the other Wildhammer dwarves. "We'll just have to be scaring them out into the open. Come on, lads, let's get back home. I have a few ideas. But don't worry, we'll soon be making it clear to those greenskins that they're not welcome in the Hinterlands."

"You there! Paladin!"

Turalyon glanced up as the elf slowed to a stop beside him. He hadn't seen the ranger approach, but that didn't surprise him. In the past few weeks he had learned how quickly the elves could come and go, and how silently. Alleria, in particular, delighted in startling him by suddenly speaking in his ear when he hadn't even realized she was back in camp.

"Yes?" He had been cleaning his gear but he paused respectfully.

"The orcs are in the Hinterlands," the elf reported. "And they're meeting up with the trolls there." That last was said with utter disgust. Turalyon had learned that the elves hated the forest trolls, and apparently the feeling was mutual. It made sense—both were woodlands creatures, and the forests here were not big enough for two such races. They had been enemies for thousands of years, too, ever since the elves had driven the trolls from part of the forest and established their kingdom there on that conquered land.

"You're certain they're allies and not just crossing paths?" Turalyon asked, setting his armor off to the side. He rubbed absently at his chin. If the orcs and the trolls really had formed a partnership, that could be trouble.

The ranger snorted in reply. "Of course I'm sure! I heard them talking. They've got a pact of some sort." The elf actually looked concerned for the first time. "They're planning on striking at Aerie Peak—and then moving up into Quel'Thalas."

Ah, that explained his agitation. Quel'Thalas was the elves' own homeland, and the trolls hated them. If they'd joined the Horde it made sense they'd direct the orcs there.

"I'll let Lothar know," Turalyon assured him, standing up. "We'll stop them before they can get anywhere near your homeland." The elf nodded, though he didn't look convinced, and turned away, jogging back into the trees and disappearing once again. But Turalyon wasn't watching. He was already making his way toward the command tent.

He found Lothar inside, along with Khadgar, Terenas, and a few others.

"The orcs are targeting Aerie Peak," he announced as he entered. Everyone turned toward him, and Turalyon saw several eyebrows raise in surprise. "One of the rangers just told me," he explained. "The orcs have allied with the forest trolls and they're planning to strike Aerie Peak."

Terenas nodded and turned to the everpresent map covering the tent's large table. "Makes sense," he admitted, tapping Aerie Peak's location. "The Wildhammer dwarves are strong enough to put up a fight so they'd not want to risk an attack from behind. And if the trolls are with them, they'd want the dwarves out of the Hinterlands altogether."

Lothar was staring at the map as well. "It'll be tough taking the fight to them in the forest," he commented. "We can't deploy properly in there, and we'll be forced to leave our ballistae behind." He rubbed a hand over his forehead, thinking. "Then again, they'll not be able to marshal their forces well either. We can pick off smaller groups of orcs and not worry about them sending the full army to any one location."

"Plus the dwarves would make strong allies," Khadgar pointed out. "If we help them they may agree to help us in return. They'd make excellent scouts and first-strike units."

"We could certainly use them and their gryphons," Lothar agreed. He glanced up, caught Turalyon's eye, and nodded. "Rally the troops," he ordered. "We're heading into the forest to save the dwarves."

"By the ancestors, there are a lot of them! They're like fleas, only bigger and better-armed!" Kurdran cursed as he studied the scene below. He and a full hunting party were on the wing, wheeling high above to get a better view of these new greenskins. And what he saw wasn't good.

The creatures were marching fast and were already only a day's travel from Aerie Peak itself. At first he'd only seen a score or so, but then he'd noticed another group not far away, and a third beyond that. The others had reported much the same. Though these greenskins were spread out in groups of twenty or so, there were more groupings than they could count. Wildhammer dwarves were not afraid of anything, but if those creatures were half as tough as they looked they could crush the Peak by sheer numbers alone.

Not that they'd sit by and let that happen. Kurdran glanced around, and each of his dwarves nodded in turn. "Good," he told them, raising his horn to his lips. "Wildhammers, attack!" He blew a blast on the horn and then slung it back at his side, already guiding Sky'ree into position with his knees. She responded with a fierce cry of her own, spreading her wings and rising up before folding them back in for the exhilarating dive. They plummeted down, and as they did Kurdran unlimbered his stormhammer, raising the massive weapon high.

But for the moment his targets were not the greenskins themselves. Instead he struck out, pounding the nearest tree solidly across the trunk. The impact sent leaves and berries and needles raining down, which startled the bewildered greenskins. Kurdran struck out at two more trees, and those sent cones and nuts down on the creatures, hitting hard enough to leave welts. The greenskins ducked, raising their hands to protect their eyes, but the onslaught continued as the Wildhammers struck tree after tree, dropping foliage and fruits and nuts in a veritable shower. The greenskins did not know what to make of all this, but they didn't like it, and they responded by taking the simplest solution—since the trees weren't safe, they left them behind, jogging away from the threatening foliage and out into the nearest small clearing.

Which was exactly what the Wildhammers had been waiting for.

With a loud warcry Kurdran led the way, his hammer at the ready. The first greenskin had time to glance up and half-raise a large axe before Kurdran's hurled, lightning-wreathed stormhammer caught him full across the jaw, shattering the bone with a thunderclap and sending the creature flying. "Ye're too ugly to be in me forest, ye bastard!" he shouted as the creature fell. The hammer returned and Kurdran loosed it again, the blow smashing a second greenskin, and then Sky'ree's arc drove her back up and she raised her wings to carry them back out of range before wheeling about for a second pass. The rest of his lads were striking as well, and the forest was filled with hoots and hollers, curses and insults as the gryphons darted past.

Whatever these creatures were, they were not easily frightened. As he came around again Kurdran saw that the remaining greenskins had their weapons up and ready now, and they gathered into a tighter cluster so the dwarves could not strike as easily. They had not counted on the aerial advantage, however. Kurdran whirled his hammer overhead, and let it fly. The heavy stone had struck a greenskin right in the temple, toppling it with a loud crack like an Ironforge pistol, and as the creature fell it pushed against two others, who stepped forward to avoid being entangled.

"Ha! That's taken ye down a peg!" Kurdran crowed at the fallen creatures. He was on them before they could realize their mistake, his stormhammer back in his hand, but let Sky'ree finish the fallen creatures, her powerful front claws laying one low and her sharp hooked beak tearing apart a second even as her wings stunned a third.

The skirmish was over quickly. Whatever these greenskins were, they were slow and not used to facing an airborne attack. And Kurdran and his people were experts at striking those on the ground. The creatures had managed to land a few blows, and some of his dwarves had wounds to tend, but they had lost no one and left no one unharmed behind them. Only a few of the greenskins in this particular grouping had survived, and only then by fleeing back under the trees.

"That's taught them to look up," Kurdran pointed out, and his dwarves laughed. "Back to the Peak then, lads. We'll send out another team soon to take out another o' their little clusters. Mayhap then they'll learn to give Aerie Peak a wider berth."

"Get ready," Lothar whispered. He had slowed his horse to a mere walk, since anything faster risked running into trees or being unhorsed by low branches, and now he drew his greatsword and held it before him, his shield raised on his other arm. "They should be close by."

Turalyon nodded and hefted his warhammer, riding

to his commander's back left as usual. Khadgar rode beside him, the three of them forming a classic cavalry triangle, and though the mage's hands were empty Turalyon had learned to respect the magics his friend could wield in battle. Straining his eyes, Turalyon tried to pierce the gloom of the trees and see their quarry. Somewhere around here . . .

"There!" He pointed ahead and to the right, beyond Khadgar, and his two companions followed his gesture. After a moment Lothar nodded. It took the wizard a minute longer before he too had noticed the flicker of movement against the trees in that direction, a motion too low to be a bird and too steady to be a snake or insect or whatever else infested such forests. No, that flicker could only be from something the size of a man walking through the forest, and the fact that it kept repeating meant either the same figure was circling back repeatedly or it was a large group, The fact that it was barely visible meant the figures were the same color as their surroundings. All of which added up to one thing: orcs.

"Got them," Lothar agreed quietly. He glanced back at Khadgar. "Let the others know," he instructed, and the young-old mage nodded and backed his horse away quietly. "Meantime, we'll keep watch," the Champion told Turalyon, who nodded. "And if they look like they're getting away, well, we'll just have to make sure they've got reason to turn and come back this way again, eh?"

"Yes, sir!" Turalyon grinned and patted the haft of his warhammer. He was ready. He still got nervous going into battle, but he no longer worried about freezing up or turning tail. He'd faced the orcs once already, and he knew he could do it again.

"We've lost Tearlach," Iomhar reported. Kurdran stared at him in surprise. "Oengus as well," the Wildhammer fighter continued. "And two more are too winded to continue fighting."

"What happened?" Kurdran demanded. The other dwarf looked embarrassed for a second, then turned belligerent.

"The greenskins, tha's what!" he replied. "They were ready for us! When we dropped toward them they started throwing spears! Then they scattered so we couldn't target them amid the trees." He shook his head. "Your strike was lucky, and took them by surprise. They've learned, though, the ugly buggers, and fast."

Kurdran nodded. "Not stupid, these greenskins," he agreed. "And more o' them than we thought." He studied the map of the Hinterlands spread out before him, and the markers he'd been using to show where the greenskins were marching. The map was almost completely covered. "Well, we'll just have to hit them afore they can react. Tell the lads to come in fast and hard, and to stay beyond the greenskins' throws. They're working against gravity and we're working with it, so we've got the advantage."

Iomhar nodded, but before he could say anything Beathan burst in. "Trolls!" he shouted, collapsing onto a nearby stool. His left arm hung useless at his side, still bleeding from a deep cut near the shoulder. "We were diving on a party of those greenskins when a pack of forest trolls jumped us! Took out Moray and Seaghdh with their first blows and knocked Alpin and Lachtin from their gryphons." He indicated his wound. "I took a nasty cut from one's axe but managed to dodge the second blow, or it'd have taken me head off."

"Damn!" Kurdran growled. "They're teamed with the trolls then, greenskin and greenskin! And those trolls'll keep us from using the trees!" He tugged at his mustache in frustration. "We need something to even the odds, and fast, lads, or they'll be swarming us over like ants on a beetle."

As if to answer his statement a third dwarf appeared to report. But this one, a scout named Dermid, wasn't wounded. And he looked pleased rather than worried.

"Humans!" he announced happily. "A great mass o' them! They say they've come to help us fight off the orcs—that's what they call the greenskins."

"Ancestors be praised," Kurdran rumbled. "If they can keep these orcs busy enough to forget their new tactics, we can strike them down from above again." He grinned as he hefted his stormhammer. "Aye, and we'll be taking care of any trolls that get close, too. They may control the trees but we rule the skies, and our gryphons will tear them apart an' they come within reach." He turned and stalked toward the door, already whistling for Sky'ree. "Wildhammers, let's fly!" he shouted, and behind him the other dwarves cheered and hastened to obey.

"Now!" Lothar spurred his mount forward and charged across the clearing, bursting upon the pack of orcs. They whirled about, clearly surprised—they had been busy watching the skies, and many of them were holding spears instead of their usual axes and hammers. One thought to throw its spear at Lothar but the Champion was too close by then, and his massive sword swept out, shearing through spear and arm together, then looping back and removing the orc's head before its severed arm had even hit the ground.

Turalyon was right beside him, and his hammer struck an orc and shattered its chest. His second blow glanced off an orc's arm, which was enough to make the green-skinned creature drop its axe. He simply struck it in the head this time, and it crumpled without a sound.

But Turalyon did hear a strange noise, somewhere between a cough and a laugh, and glanced up. A tall figure, taller than an orc and more narrowly built, dropped from the trees in front of him, a spear held in its large, long-fingered hands. Its eyes were sharp and narrow, its features narrow as well, and it grinned at him as it jabbed with its spear, showing rows of pointed teeth. A troll!

Turalyon raised his shield, blocking the spear thrust even though it hammered his shield back against him hard enough to leave his arm weak. He responded with a fierce blow from his hammer, staggering the troll but not stopping it. The creature glided forward again, spear at the ready, and Turalyon spurred his horse forward, bracing his shield just before it smashed into the troll's face and chest. The troll had not expected that crude an attack and took the blow full-force, reeling back and shaking its head to clear it. Turalyon didn't give it time to recover, however. His hammer took it in the jaw and dropped the troll to the ground in a heap.

Pleased with himself, Turalyon glanced up just in time to see a second troll step out onto a nearby branch. Its eyes were narrowed in hate and its spear was pulled back to throw. Turalyon knew at once that the weapon was aimed at him, and that he was not strong enough to block it or fast enough to dodge it. He prepared himself for the worst, closing his eyes and listening for the sound of the flying spear against the rising wind.

Instead he heard a strange, shrill shriek, mingled with a deep bellow then a massive thunderclap, and behind that a cry of sudden pain. Opening his eyes again Turalyon saw an amazing sight. The troll was falling from its perch, hands still clutching at the side of its face, which appeared to be crushed. Above it hovered a majestic creature, one Turalyon had heard of but never seen before. It was built like a lion, with the same tawny fur, but instead of a feline head it had a fierce bird's visage, the beak wide and emitting the shriek he had already heard. Its front legs ended in deadly talons but its rear legs had thick cat-like pads and a long tail swayed behind it. Great wings were flared out along its sides, and feathers covered its head and trailed off along its shoulders. And a man rode it like a steed.

No, not a man, Turalyon saw, though of course he already knew. He had heard of the Wildhammer dwarves, though he had not met one before. Taller and leaner than their Bronzebeard cousins, the Wildhammers were still shorter and stouter than a man, with heavy chest and thick corded arms. They wielded stormhammers, like the massive weapon even now returning to this dwarf's hand, and clearly that had caused the troll's demise.

The dwarf saw Turalyon looking at him and grinned, raising his hammer in salute. Turalyon raised his own hammer in return, then spurred his horse forward and targeted another orc. With the dwarves circling overhead he no longer worried about an attack from above, leaving him free to concentrate on the Horde. The orcs, on the other hand, had to worry about attacks from every direction except beneath their feet, leaving them confused and unnerved. And as Lothar had hoped the trees forced the orcs to move in small groups instead of a single mass, allowing the Alliance soldiers to pick them off one cluster at a time.

Hours later, Kurdran welcomed the human leaders into his home. Their commander was a big man, even bigger than most, with a good dwarf-like beard and a long braid even if the top of his head was almost bare. He carried himself like a warrior born, and Kurdran could tell the man had seen more than his share of battles, yet those blue eyes remained alert and the golden lion head on his shield and breastplate still gleamed. The younger one, woefully unbearded, seemed less sure of himself, but Zoradan said he'd seen him use that big hammer almost as well as a dwarf. There was something else about the lad, a sense of calm, that reminded Kurdran of his shaman. Perhaps the lad was a shaman himself, or otherwise in touch with the elements or the spirits? Certainly the third one, the violet-robed man with the short, scruffy white beard but the young man's walk, he was a wizard, that was plain enough. And then there was the elven lass, lovely and strong and lithe, as they all were, with her green and her bow and her laughing eyes. Kurdran had rarely met such interesting people, and he would have been happy to do under any circumstances. Right now he was even more pleased to make their acquaintance.

"Greetings, laddies—and lass!" he told them, gesturing to the chairs and stools and cushions scattered around the room. "Ye are welcome indeed! We feared those greenskins—the ones you call orcs—would overrun our homes, they were so many! But your arrival put an end to that, and together we'll be driving them from the Hinterlands! I am in your debt."

The big warrior sat on a stool near Kurdran's own chair, idly adjusting the massive sword slung across his back. "You lead the Wildhammers?" he asked.

"I am Kurdran Wildhammer," Kurdran replied. "I

am chief thane, so aye, they will go where I lead."

"Good." The warrior nodded. "I am Anduin Lothar, former Knight of Stormwind and now commander of the Alliance forces." He explained about the Horde, and about Stormwind's fate. "Will you join us?"

Kurdran frowned and tugged at his moustache. "You say they be out to conquer all the land?" Lothar nodded. "And they came in great black iron boats?" Another nod. "Then they have been through Khaz Modan," he decided, shaking his head. "We've not heard from our kin in Ironforge for many weeks. I had wondered why. This explains it."

"They conquered the mines and used the iron ore to make those ships," the wizard said.

"Aye." Kurdran bared his teeth. "We Wildhammers have had many quarrels with the Bronzebeard clan over the years—it is why me people left Khaz Modan at all. But still they are our cousins, our kin. And these foul creatures, this Horde, attacked them. And now it has attacked us. Only your timely aid saved us from suffering our cousins' fate." He pounded his fist on the arm of his chair. "Aye, we will join you! We must be striking back at these orcs, until this Horde canna threaten anyone!" He stood and extended his hand. "Ye have the Wildhammers' aid."

Lothar stood as well, and gravely accepted the clasp. "Thank you," was all he said, but it was enough.

"At least we have driven them from the Hinterlands," the clean-faced youth pointed out. "Your home is safe."

"That it is," Kurdran agreed. "For now. But where will these orcs be going next? Will they turn back toward the Hillsbrad? Or up toward Capital City? Or be heading north to join the rest o' their foul kin?"

Perhaps that had been the wrong thing to say, for suddenly his new allies were all leaping to their feet. "What did you say?" the elven lass demanded. "About the north?"

"That they might join the rest o' their kind?" Kurdran asked, puzzled. She nodded quickly and he shrugged. "My scouts say we saw but a fraction of this Horde here. The rest turned north, skirting our forests, and continued on toward the mountains." He studied their faces. "Ye didna know this?"

The clean-faced youth and the mage were shaking their heads, but already the older warrior was cursing. "It was a feint!" he said, almost spitting the words. "And we fell for it!"

"A feint?" Kurdran frowned. "Me home was at risk! This was no mere ploy!"

But this Lothar shook his head. "No, the threat was real," he agreed. "But whoever commands the Horde is smart. He knew we would step in to aid you here. He took the rest of his forces north, and left a portion to slow us down. Now he's got distance on us."

"And he's heading for Quel'Thalas!" the elven lass cried. "We have to warn them!"

Lothar nodded. "We'll rally the troops at once and set off again. If we move fast—"

But the lass cut him off. "There's no time!" she insisted. "You said yourself the Horde has distance on us. We've lost days already! And gathering the troops will only slow us down further." She shook her head. "I'll go myself."

"No." The voice was quiet but the tone brooked no resistance. "You'll not go alone," Lothar told her, ignoring her glare. "Turalyon, take the rest of the cavalry and half the troops. You're in charge. Khadgar, you go with him. I want the Alliance present to help defend Quel'Thalas." He turned back toward Kurdran, who was impressed. This man knew how to lead! "There will still be orcs here in the forest," he warned, "and we can't risk letting them get behind us as well as before us. We'll stay and make sure the forest is completely clean, then we'll move forward and rejoin the others."

Kurdran nodded. "I thank ye for your aid," he replied formally. "And when the Hinterlands are once again secure, my warriors and I will be accompanying ye north to deal with the rest of this Horde."

"Thank you." Lothar bowed, then turned toward the elven lass, the clean-faced youth, and the wizard. "Are you still here? Get moving—every second you waste puts the Horde one second closer to Quel'Thalas." The three bowed and quickly exited the room. Kurdran didn't envy them their task, chasing an army and trying desperately to pass it and warn the elves of its approach. He just hoped they got there in time.

CHAPTER ELEVEN

"**K**eep them moving!" Doomhammer bellowed, turning to look back at the Horde marching behind him. "We need to get through these peaks quickly!"

"Why?" This was from Rend Blackhand. He and his brother Maim hated Doomhammer for killing their father and taking his place as Warchief. They were among the few who dared to question Doomhammer's orders. Doomhammer allowed it, both because he knew any explanations he gave would filter back to the rest of the Horde and because the Black Tooth Grin was a large, powerful clan and therefore useful. Besides, the brothers might question actions or decisions but they never disobeyed a direct order, even when they disagreed with it. Doomhammer appreciated that, and was willing to tolerate their questions, up to a point.

"Why what?" Doomhammer answered now. He

was negotiating the steep path up the mountains and most of his attention was on the rocks beneath his hands and feet. The forest trolls had already passed them by, scaling the cliffs as easily as they climbed trees, and had lowered ropes to aid the orc warriors in their climb, but Doomhammer refused to use them. He needed his troops to know he was still the strongest of them, and climbing the mountain un-aided was one way to accomplish that. Rend had no such compunctions, and was pacing Doomhammer with one of the stout ropes wrapped firmly around his left arm.

"Why are we climbing?" Rend asked. "We could have gone around these mountains instead. Why are we taking this way? It is shorter, true, but harder. Scaling these peaks will slow us down."

Doomhammer reached the top of the cliff and grunted, wiping his hands clean of rock dust by rub-bing them against his upper arms. He turned to face Rend as the other chieftain joined him at the peak, his brother and the other Horde leaders right behind them. They knew better than to reach the top before Doomhammer.

"The humans think us stupid," Doomhammer began, making sure all of them could hear him. He did not like having to repeat himself. "They imagine us as dumb brutes, just as we see the ogres." Several turned to look below, where the ogres were trailing behind even the orcs in their climb. They were strong enough to move past but too clumsy to manage easily. "I encourage that image." He grinned, showing his tusks. "Let them think us brainless! It makes our conquest easier, because they underestimate us."

He stooped and picked up a small rock, tossing it from hand to hand as he spoke. "We have already fooled them once, by splitting off a few clans when we reached the Hinterlands," he pointed out. "They busied themselves battling that portion of the Horde while we proceeded this way, toward the mountains. And they will still be busy while we cross here."

"But we are heading to Quel'Thalas, are we not?" Maim asked, the strange name causing him some difficulty. "Why not sail as close to it as possible, then, and be there long before the humans emerge from the Hinterlands?"

"Because the elves will never let our ships pass unmolested," Doomhammer pointed out. "Zul'jin says they are expert archers, and we would be trapped on the ships while they rained arrows down upon us. We would lose thousands, whole clans, before we could even reach the shore to fight them." Several of the chieftains murmured. That had not occurred to them. The Horde was still not accustomed to the idea of using ships, though a few, like the Stormreavers, and taken to it quickly enough.

"But we could have marched around the mountains," Rend pointed out. "A longer route but less difficult."

Doomhammer sneered at that. "Are you afraid of

a challenge, then?" Several of the other chieftains laughed, and Rend bristled.

"Of course not!" he snapped, raising his one fist, clearly ready to fight anyone who claimed otherwise. "I am up to the task! I was right behind you the entire climb!" No one dared point out that he had used a rope, while Doomhammer had not. The Blackhands were fearsome warriors and widely respected, another reason Doomhammer allowed them to ask so many questions.

"Then you do wish to challenge?" Doomhammer asked quietly, his voice dropping. Rend backed away quickly, paling as he realized what he had almost said. The Blackhands wanted to lead the Horde, but they would have to challenge and defeat Doomhammer in combat to do so. And they all knew he would kill them, even if they both attacked at once. A part of him kept hoping they would try. Then he could replace them with a more reasonable Black Tooth Grin chieftain. But so far they had always backed down.

"Going around might have been faster," Doomhammer said finally, when he saw Rend was not going to take the bait, "but our movements would have been more visible. This way we will come upon the elves with them unawares." He grinned again. "If the humans survive their battle in the Hinterlands and can march around the mountains, they may well reach Quel'Thalas before us. And then, if the elves allow them entry, they will all be gathered together when we attack." He laughed and crushed the rock in his hand, dust spraying from between his fingers. "They have nowhere to go from there. We will crush them and make that land our own." He opened his hand and let the dust and rock chips fall. "And if they are behind us, they will find us already established in Quel'Thalas when they arrive. And we will beat them back and smash them against the foothills behind them." He made a show of wiping his hands clean again. "Either way, we win."

The others all murmured, several of them grinning and laughing as well, and Rend nodded. "You are wise," he grudgingly admitted. "This is a good plan." Doomhammer nodded to accept the compliment

"Now we must continue," Doomhammer told the rest of them. "There are still several peaks to cover." He turned to Zuluhed first, however. "Where are they?" he asked.

"On their way," the Dragonmaw chieftain answered, grinning at the murmurs that rose behind him. None of the other orcs knew anything more than that the Dragonmaw were planning something, with Doomhammer's full approval. "They have a long way to travel, but they are swift. They will reach us soon, and the world will tremble at their arrival."

"Good." Then Doomhammer turned and glanced at the tall figure standing a short distance away, its long scarf blowing in the wind. "How far are we from Quel'Thalas?"

"Four days travel, at this pace," Zul'jin replied. "But we could be there sooner." The forest troll's eyes gleamed at the prospect, and his hands strayed to the axes at his side.

"No," Doomhammer ordered, ignoring the troll's obvious disappointment. "You will stay with us and continue lowering ropes for the troops." He grinned at the troll leader. "Do not worry, you will get your chance to attack the elven homeland. But not until the Horde is right behind you, ready to roll down upon them."

Zul'jin pondered this a moment, then nodded. "They'll be angry, ya," he commented, then laughed. "They'll emerge like wasps, ready ta sting. An' you will swarm them like ants, devourin' them whole."

"Yes." Doomhammer liked the image. Ants were industrious workers, and sturdy beyond all expectation. They could be nasty as well, gathering to overwhelm much larger creatures. Yes, ants would do nicely. And right now he signaled the march to continue, the Horde marching up the mountain behind him like an army of ants intent upon conquest.

Four days later, Doomhammer and his chieftains looked down from a foothill that stood between the last mountain peak and the start of the great forest. The rest of the Horde was massing behind them, weary from the climbing and marching but shaking off fatigue now that their next target lay before them. But none were as excited as the forest trolls.

"We be goin' now?" Zul'jin looked eagerly at Doomhammer, who nodded.

"Yes, go now," the Warchief agreed. "Bring the fight to the elves. Spare no one and nothing." The forest troll leader grinned and tilted his head back to let loose a strange warbling cry. Another forest troll appeared immediately, just beyond where the two leaders stood, moving as silently and suddenly as a ghost. A third dropped from the rocks overhead to stand beside him, and another beside that one, and more after them, until the small valley behind the hill was filled with the tall, lanky forest creatures. There were far more than Doomhammer remembered Zul'jin bringing with him, and his surprise must have shown because the forest troll leader grinned through his everpresent scarf.

"Found more," he explained, laughing. "Witherbark tribe. They be joinin' us."

Doomhammer nodded. He was not particularly afraid of them, though the trolls were taller than him. He had faced bigger and stronger foes before and always he had been the one to walk away. Besides, in the months since forging their alliance Zul'jin had impressed him. The forest troll was a clever one but he also had honor. He had promised his people's aid to the Horde and would not go back on that. Doomhammer was willing to risk his life on that belief.

Of course, the fact that the forest trolls apparently hated these high elves certainly helped. The trolls had been all in favor of turning north toward Quel'Thalas, and had been almost frantic to breach the elven forest and begin finding and attacking the elves themselves. Doomhammer had insisted they wait, however. He wanted the rest of the Horde properly in position before the trolls struck. And Zul'jin had managed to keep his brethren in line, even though he was just as eager to strike as they were.

But now the time for waiting was over. With a howl Zul'jin leaped forward and raced down the hills. He did not slow as he struck the edge of the forest but jumped up into the trees, springing easily from limb to limb. The rest of his people followed him, bounding into the trees and disappearing from view, with only the rustle of leaves and the occasional growl to mark their presence. But Doomhammer knew they would make their way deep into the massive forest, seeking elves and killing any they found. Soon the forest's defenders would know about the trolls' invasion and would rush to meet them.

And that would keep the elves busy, too busy to check their borders for other threats.

Doomhammer signaled, and the rest of the Horde swept over the hill as well, marching steadily across the narrow strip of grassland and at last reaching the first row of trees.

"Now, Warchief?" a nearby orc warrior asked, axe at the ready. Doomhammer nodded, and the warrior turned back to the tree beside him, its trunk thick from age and smooth as silk, its leaves rich and green and smelling of nature and life and bounty—and with a mighty swing the orc chipped a large splinter of bark and wood from its trunk. Then he swung again, expanding the chip.

"No no!" Doomhammer snatched the axe from the startled warrior, shoving him back. "Do not approach it at an angle, but straight on," he instructed. He pulled the axe back, bunching his muscles, and then swung with all his force, imbedding the axe partway through the trunk. Then with a mighty wrench he retrieved the weapon and struck again in the same spot, deepening the wound. A third blow saw the axe almost through to the other side, only a small portion of wood and bark remaining. Doomhammer pulled the axe back, angling it upward as he did so its head pushed upward on the trunk, and the tree tipped and fell, snapping that remaining section from its own weight and momentum. The ground shook as the tree hit, and leaves and berries flew everywhere.

"There, like that." He tossed the axe back to the warrior, who nodded and moved to the next tree in line. A second warrior was already stepping up to the felled tree, axe in hand, ready to begin the task of chopping the great tree into smaller segments.

Beyond him more warriors were about the same task. Carrying supplies for an army as large as the Horde was a hopeless task, so instead they took what they needed from the lands they had conquered. And the wood from these trees would keep the Horde's fires burning for weeks. Perhaps even months. The fact that every tree they cut down deprived the elves of additional protection only made the task sweeter.

Doomhammer was leaning upon his hammer, watching the work progress, when he saw motion from the corner of his eye. A short, heavy-set orc with a bristling beard was heading toward him, scarred face twisted in an expression Doomhammer wasn't sure he liked. Gul'dan was excited about something.

"What is it?" Doomhammer demanded before the chief warlock had reached him.

"Something you should see, mighty Doomhammer," Gul'dan replied, sweeping into a low bow. Cho'gall chuckled and aped the gesture behind him. "Something that could aid the Horde greatly."

Doomhammer nodded and swung his hammer up onto his shoulder, gesturing for Gul'dan to precede him. The warlock turned and led both Doomhammer and Cho'gall back around, perhaps a hundred feet from where he had stood. Here stood a massive stone, forcing a gap in the trees. Its rough surface was carved with runes and even Doomhammer, who had no gift at all for the supernatural or spiritual, could feel the power radiating off this crude monolith.

"What is it?" he demanded.

"I do not know exactly," Gul'dan answered, stroking his beard. "But it is very powerful. I believe these Rune-stones, for there are others spaced evenly around the forest's edge, serve as a mystic barrier."

"They did not stop us," Doomhammer pointed out.

"No, because we used nothing more than our own hands and feet and blades," Gul'dan replied. "I believe these Runestones restrict the use of magic within, most likely allowing only the elves' own magic to function. I have tried tapping my magic here and I cannot, but if I move ten paces away, toward the hills, my spells return."

Doomhammer eyed the large hunk of stone with a new appreciation. "So we take them and set them around our enemies and they cannot cast spells," he mused, wondering how many orcs it would take to move the monoliths, and how they would transport them.

"That is one approach, yes," Gul'dan agreed, his tone clearly saying what he thought of such an idea. "But I have another in mind, my warchief. If you will indulge me a moment." Doomhammer nodded. He did not trust Gul'dan, not at all, but the warlock had proven useful with the creation of the death knights. He was curious what the stocky orc had in mind now.

"These stones contain immense magic," Gul'dan explained. "I believe I can harness that power for our own purposes."

'What do you mean?" Doomhammer demanded. He knew better than to give Gul'dan free rein. No, he wanted specifics.

"I can use these to create an altar," Gul'dan replied. "An Altar of Storms. By channeling the energy from these stones, I can transform creatures. We will make them more powerful, more dangerous, though they may suffer some disfigurement."

"I doubt any orc will let you experiment upon him a second time," Doomhammer pointed out sharply. He still remembered quite clearly the night Gul'dan had offered the so-called Cup of Unity, the Chalice of Rebirth, to every chieftain in the Horde, and to any warriors they deemed worthy. Doomhammer had not trusted the warlock, even then, and when Blackhand had invited him to drink he had refused, saying he did not wish to take away from his chieftain by sharing such power with him. But he had seen what the liquid had done to his friends and clanmates. It had made them larger and stronger, yes. But it had also turned their eyes a glowing red and their already greenish skin a vivid green, signs of demonic taint. And it had driven them all mad with bloodlust, with rage, with hunger. It had turned the once-noble orcs into animals, crazed killers. Some of the orcs had regretted their transformation later, but by then it was of course too late.

Gul'dan smiled as if he knew what his warchief was thinking. And perhaps he did. Who knew what strange powers the warlock now possessed? But he only replied to Doomhammer's words, not the thoughts behind them.

"I will not use an orc to test these altars," Gul'dan assured him. "No, I will use a creature that can benefit from even more strength but will barely notice any reduction to intellect." He grinned. "I will use an ogre."

Doomhammer considered that. They did not have many ogres but the ones they did control were easily worth ten times their weight in other soldiers. To make them even stronger—that would definitely be worth the risk. "All right," he said at last. "You may build one of these Altars. Let us see what happens. If it works I will supply you with more ogres, or any other race you wish." Gul'dan bowed low and Doomhammer nodded, his mind already onto other logistics as he turned away.

CHAPTER TWELVE

"Faster, damn you! Move faster!" Alleria struck her thigh with one fist, as if that motion could somehow spur the troops to more speed. She paced them for a moment, then sped up, unable to move that slowly for long. Within minutes she had passed the long line of men and caught up with the cavalry again. Automatically she glanced around, searching for the short blond hair near the front. There!

"You need to pick up the pace," she snapped at Turalyon as she slid between the other horses and moved alongside him. The young Paladin started and flushed, but right now she could not take her normal pleasure in his reaction. There was no time for such foolishness!

"We're moving as fast as we can," he told her calmly, though she noticed he glanced behind him to gauge the troops' speed anyway. "You know our men cannot match you for speed. And armies always move more slowly than individuals."

"Then I'll go on myself, as I should have from the start," she insisted, tensing to sprint past the horses and deeper into the forest.

"No!" Something in his voice stopped her, and she cursed under her breath. Why couldn't she disobey him? He didn't have the same presence as Lothar, and she was cooperating with the Alliance army at her own volition, not from any orders. Yet when he did actually command her she found herself unable to resist. Which didn't mean she couldn't argue.

"Let me go!" she insisted. "I need to warn them!" Her heart twisted again at the thought of her sisters, her friends, her kin being caught unawares by the Horde.

"We will warn them," Turalyon assured her, and she could hear the certainty in his voice. "And we will help them stand against the Horde. But if you go by yourself you will be caught, and killed, and that . . . will not do anyone any good." It had sounded as if he'd meant to say something else, and she felt a sudden surge of—was that joy?—in her chest, but had no time to wonder about it.

"I am an elf, and a ranger!" she insisted hotly. "I can disappear into the trees! No one can find me!"

"Not even a forest troll?" She turned and glared at the wizard, who was riding on Turalyon's far side. "Because we know they're working with the Horde," he continued. "And we know they're almost your equal in woodcraft."

"Almost, perhaps," she conceded. "But I am still better."

"No one would deny that," Khadgar agreed diplomatically, though she could see the grin lurking behind his calm. "But we don't know how many of them are out there, between us and your home. And ten of them would more than make up for your superior skill."

Alleria cursed again. He was right, of course. She knew that. But that didn't stop her from wanting to run full-speed, not caring about potential obstacles. She had seen the Horde, seen what it could do. She knew the dangers it posed. And now it was heading for her home! And her people had no idea such a danger was approaching!

"Just get them moving!" she snapped at Turalyon, and sprinted ahead, scouting the path. She half-hoped she would come across a few trolls or orcs, but knew they were still too far ahead for her to see. The Horde had a significant lead on them right now, and if those human soldiers could not move beyond their current snail's pace it would only increase!

"She's worried," Khadgar said quietly as they watched Alleria disappear from view.

"I know," Turalyon replied. "I can't blame her. I'd be worried too, if the Horde was heading toward my home. I was when we thought they would march toward Capital City, and that's as close to a home as I've had these past ten years or more." He sighed. "Plus she's only got half the Alliance army at her back. And only me to command it."

"Stop selling yourself short," his friend warned. "You're a good commander and a noble Paladin, one of the Silver Hand, the finest in Lordaeron. She's lucky to have you."

Turalyon smiled at his friend, grateful for the reassurance. He only wished he believed it. Oh, he knew he was decent enough in combat—he'd had sufficient training, and their first clash with the Horde had proven he could translate that into real fighting skill. But a leader? Before this war he had never had to lead anything, not even prayers. What did he know about leading anything?

True, as a boy he had been forward enough, often devising the games he and his friends played or commanding one of their mock-armies when they played at war. But once he'd joined the priesthood all that had changed. He had taken orders from the senior priests, and then after they had brought him to Faol he'd followed the archbishop's instructions. Upon joining the ranks of the first Paladins in training, he had fallen under Uther's guidance, as had they all—Uther had a powerful personality that did not brook dispute. He was also the oldest of them, and the closest to the archbishop.

Turalyon had been surprised Lothar had not chosen Uther as his lieutenant, though perhaps he felt the older Paladin's faith might make it difficult for him to interact with less pious men. Turalyon had been honored and shocked to be granted such a rank, and kept wondering what he could have done to deserve it. If he did deserve it.

Lothar seemed to think so. And the Champion of Stormwind had enough experience and wisdom to know. He was an incredible warrior and an amazing leader, someone the men followed automatically, the kind of man who demanded respect and obedience from everyone who met him. Already Alliance warriors called him "the Lion of Azeroth," from the sight of his shield flashing through the orc ranks at Hillsbrad. Turalyon wondered if he'd ever have even a portion of that presence.

He also wondered if he'd ever have a fraction of Uther's piety. And of his faith, or the powers that bestowed.

Turalyon believed in the Holy Light, of course. He had since he was a small child, and serving in the priesthood had brought him closer to that glorious presence. But he had never felt it directly, not its full strength, just glimmers of its attention or the outpouring of its effect on another. And after seeing the Horde, and facing them in battle, he found his faith weaker than ever.

The Holy Light, after all, resided in every living being, in every heart and soul. It was everywhere, the energy that bound all sentient beings together as one. But the Horde was terrible, monstrous. They did things no rational being could do; depraved, horrible things. They were truly beyond redemption. And how could such creatures be part of the Holy Light? How could its brilliant illumination reside within such utter darkness? And if it did, what did that say about its strength, that its purity and love could be so overpowered? But if it did not, if the

Horde was not part of the Holy Light, then it was not universal, as Turalyon had been taught. And what did that mean about its presence and its strength, and about the relationship of every being to every other being?

He didn't know. And that was the problem. His faith had been severely shaken. He had tried praying since meeting the Horde, but it had been empty words. His heart was not in it. And without that commitment the words meant nothing, accomplished nothing. Turalyon knew the other paladins could cast their blessing upon soldiers, could sense evil, could even heal grievous wounds with but a touch. But he could not. He was not sure he had ever had such talents, and he certainly did not possess them now. He wondered if he ever would.

"You've gone quiet again." Khadgar leaned closer and nudged him with one hand. "Don't think too deeply or you'll fall right out of the saddle." His tone was friendly and only a little concerned, and Turalyon did his best to smile at the weak joke.

"I'm fine," he assured the old-seeming mage. "Just wondering what to do next."

"What do you mean?" Khadgar glanced around, and looked back at the troops marching behind them. "You're doing fine. Keep the men moving, make the best time we can, and hope we catch the Horde before they can do too much damage."

"I know." Turalyon frowned. "I just wish there was some way we could pass them and reach Quel'Thalas first. Perhaps Alleria's right—maybe I should let her go on ahead. But if she got caught, if anything happened to her . . ." he trailed off and glared at Khadgar, who was now grinning openly. "What?"

"Oh, nothing," his friend said, laughing. "But if you're this concerned about every soldier, we might as well give up now, because you won't be willing to send any of them into battle for fear they'll get hurt." Turalyon swatted at the mage, who ducked the blow, still laughing. And they rode on, the army stretching out behind them.

"Almost there," Turalyon assured Alleria, who was pacing around his horse as if he was standing still.

"I know that!" she snapped, barely looking up. "This is my home, remember? I know the distance better than you could!"

Turalyon sighed. It had been a long two weeks. Leading the army had been demanding, though he had already done much of the same work on previous marches. The difference was that, before, Lothar had been responsible for the final decisions. This time it was all up to Turalyon, and that had been an added weight, enough to make him lose sleep most nights. And then there had been Alleria. All the elves had been on edge the whole way, worrying what might be happening in Quel'Thalas. But the others had kept quiet, knowing voicing their concerns would only increase his stress and possibly slow them down further. Not Alleria. She had questioned every decision the whole way:

why they were taking one valley and not another, why they were lighting camp fires instead of eating and sleeping cold, why they were halting at twilight instead of marching on into the night. Turalyon had been nervous enough about taking command, but Alleria's constant badgering had made it ten times worse. He felt like he was under constant scrutiny, and like every decision earned her further disapproval.

"We'll reach the base of the foothills soon," he reminded her. "Once we have we should be able to see the borders of Quel'Thalas. Then we'll know how far the Horde has gotten. Perhaps they were slowed going over the mountains, and have not yet reached it." That had been one blessing, at least. Lothar had persuaded the Wildhammer dwarves to send one of their number down to Alterac. The dwarf had carried orders for Admiral Proudmoore, who had several ships stationed near Darrowmere Lake.

Upon receiving the orders Proudmoore had dispatched his ships down the river. They had met up with Turalyon and the army just below Stromgarde and ferried the soldiers on board. They had then sailed upriver past the mountains, instead of going over them as the Horde had done. It had saved them considerable time. Turalyon just hoped it would be enough. He would have preferred to sail straight to Quel'Thalas, but Alleria had assured him that would be impossible. Her kin would never allow human ships up their portion of the river. They had been forced to disembark near Stratholme and proceed on foot once again.

"Once I see the forest I'm going on ahead," Alleria warned. "Don't try to stop me."

"I don't want to stop you," Turalyon replied, pleased to see a momentary smile cross her face, followed by surprise. "I want you and your rangers to find your brethren and warn them," he reminded her. "I just didn't want you possibly running into the entire Horde on the way. But we're close enough now that, if the Horde did get here first, we'll be able to distract them. That'll give you time to slip past and rally your kin. Then you can hit them from behind while we attack from the front, and we'll catch the Horde between us."

Alleria nodded. She glanced up at him, silent for once, and then laid a hand along his leg. To Turalyon it felt like the touch radiated the heat of a small sun, setting his blood on fire and his limbs tingling. "Thank you," she said softly. He nodded, unable to speak.

One of her rangers broke the moment by dashing back toward them. "The end of the hills lies just ahead," he told them quickly. "I can see the trees beyond!"

Alleria glanced up at Turalyon, who nodded, pleased that for once she was asking permission. She turned and raced away, the other ranger right beside her. But she didn't get far. The two elves were still in sight when they stopped as if struck, and stared. Then Alleria wailed, a sound full of such grief as Turalyon had never heard.

"By the Light!" Kicking his steed into a full gallop, Turalyon raced to her side. And then froze, tugging his horse to a stop, as he too saw what had upset them so. The foothills had indeed ended, and the majestic forest of Quel'Thalas, home of the high elves, spread out before them. Its tall trees swayed gently, almost as if dancing to silent music, and their heavy boughs cast deep shadows upon the land, shadows that somehow seemed peaceful rather than ominous. It was a beautiful scene, full of calm and quiet majesty.

Broken only by the thick clouds of gray smoke billowing up from several spots, including one along the front edge but slightly west of their own position. Squinting, Turalyon could see dark figures swarming among the trees there, and great gaps in the leafy canopy alongside them. He could also just make out great tongues of flame licking over thick objects in the empty spaces, and the smell of green wood burning reached him, almost choking him.

The Horde had arrived first after all.

And they were burning Quel'Thalas.

"We have to stop them!" Alleria cried. She spun back toward Turalyon. "We need to stop them!"

"We will," he told her. He looked out a second time, making sure what he saw, then turned to the herald just behind him. "Inform the unit leaders," he announced. "We will ride north through the hills until we are level with the orcs. Then we will charge, taking them unawares. Warn the men to gather water as best they can, and detail several units to put out those fires. We don't want the forest burning down around us." The herald nodded, saluted, and wheeled his horse around, riding back to convey the new orders. Turalyon was already turning to Khadgar. "Can you do something to stop the fires?" he asked.

His friend grinned. "Will a thunderstorm suffice?"

"As long as the lightning does not find any more trees, yes." Turalyon turned to Alleria. "Alleria." She did not respond, but still stared at the smoke, her face pale. "Alleria!" That snapped her around to face him. "Take your rangers and go. Go! Your brethren are no doubt already fighting the Horde somewhere within the forest. Find them and let them know we are here. We need to coordinate our attacks or the Horde will crush your people within the trees and then smother us without." She stared at him, nodding but still in shock. "Now!" he snapped, hating to speak to her so harshly but knowing it was the only way. "Or are you too slow to make it to the trees safely?

That earned a sharp glare, as he'd hoped it would, and she snarled at him but turned away. With a few quick words to the other elves and a quick tug to adjust the bow slung across her back, she set off, moving fast as an arrow down the hill and toward the forest. The other rangers flanked her, and soon they had reached the cover of the trees and disappeared into the shadows.

"May the Holy Light protect you," Turalyon whispered, watching them go.

"May it protect us all," Khadgar said grimly. "We'll certainly need it."

CHAPTER THIRTEEN

"Quiet now. No noise," Zul'jin warned his brethren. They had made their way quickly through the trees, deep into Quel'Thalas, but now his sharp nose warned him that elves were somewhere nearby. Accordingly he slowed, setting each foot carefully on the branch he trod, axes held tightly in his hands to avoid any chance of their rattling as he moved. He did not want the elves to know they were there. Not yet.

All around him the other Amani trolls crept just as quietly, weapons at the ready. Most of them wore big grins, revealing their triangular teeth, and Zul'jin understood completely. They were within the elves' own homeland, preparing to attack them in the one place they assumed themselves safe. He could almost taste the anticipation.

The elves had plagued them far too long. Ever since the pale-skinned, pointy-eared interlopers had first appeared thousands of years ago, stealing territories from the vast Amani empire, they had claimed mastery of the lands' forests. As if they could match a troll for speed, stealth, and dexterity! But the elves had several strong advantages, the greatest of this had been their accursed magic. The trolls had never encountered such magic before, and had not had a way to counter the elves' mystical attacks or breach their arcane defenses.

Fortunately the trolls had significantly outnumbered them, and could overwhelm the hated elves by sheer numbers.

And then the elves had allied with the humans.

Together the two pale races had shattered the Amani empire. They had laid waste to troll fortresses and slaughtered thousands of his ancestors. Zul'jin snarled at the thought, the sound fortunately absorbed by his thick scarf. Before the war his people had been numerous and powerful, and had controlled much of the land. Afterward they had been scattered, a shadow of their former selves, and never possessed the sheer numbers to reclaim their stolen heritage.

Until now.

The Horde had promised them vengeance. And Zul'jin believed them. The orc leader, Doomhammer, had honor about him, the honor of a strong leader secure in his own power. He would not play Zul'jin false. And he had vowed to help them restore the Amani empire.

Already Zul'jin had started that task. He was the first forest troll since those terrible wars to reunite the tribes. One by one he had challenged the other tribe leaders and defeated them, whether at combat or at racing or at some other task. And all had bowed before him, pledging themselves and their tribes to his rule. The forest trolls were a single people once more. And with the Horde's help they would wipe the world clean of humans and elves alike, and rule the forests once more. The orcs showed no interest in trees and Zul'jin suspected they would occupy the valleys and plains of the world. Let them. All he wanted was the woods.

But first they had to take them from the elves. And that would be a pleasure.

Even now his nose twitched, warning him they were close. Zul'jin halted, raising one hand to signal a stop, and felt more than heard his brethren pausing as well. He peered down through the leaves, his sharp eyes piercing the gloom easily, and waited.

There! A flicker of movement appeared below, something passing into his range of vision on the forest floor. Whatever it was, it was cloaked in browns and greens like the trees but he caught a glimpse of paler color beneath. And it made no sound as it stepped, walking across leaves and brush as if they were smooth stone.

An elf!

Another emerged behind the first, and then a third and a fourth. Soon a full hunting party was passing below, ten in all. And they did not look up. Secure in their own forest, it did not occur to the elves to be wary.

Zul'jin grinned. This would be easier than he had thought.

Signaling his kin he returned his axes to their sheaths and dropped quietly to a lower branch, and swung from that one down to a third. Now he was less than twenty feet above the elves and could see them clearly, their cloaks streaming behind them. They carried the accursed bows and arrows of their kind slung across their backs, but their hands were empty. They did not suspect what lurked above them.

Zul'jin dropped down from the trees, drawing his axes as he moved. He landed easily on the balls of his feet, right between two elves, and slashed at both before they could react. His first blow took the one facing him in the throat, while his second blow bit deep into the skull of the one before him. Both fell, blood spraying the leaves.

The other elves turned, shouting in surprise, and reached for their own weapons. But now Zul'jin's brethren fell upon them, axes and daggers and clubs at the ready. The elves twisted and dodged, desperate to get enough space to draw their swords or string their bows, but the trolls did not give them the chance. The elves were quick but the trolls were taller and stronger, and grabbed the rangers before they could get away.

One elf did manage to twist free. He took two quick steps away and turned, using a tree for cover. Zul'jin expected the elf to go for his bow, but instead his hands fell to a long horn hanging from his belt. The ranger lifted the horn to his lips and blew a mighty blast—but it was cut short as one of the other trolls stabbed the elf in the stomach, and the blast turned to a faint wheeze as the ranger collapsed, blood spilling from his mouth as well as his gut.

The skirmish was over. Zul'jin reached down and cut an ear from the first elf he'd slain, adding it to the pouch at his waist. Later he would dry the ear and string it onto his necklace with the others, to show his prowess. But for now they had other tasks.

"Come," he told his kin, who were laughing and amusing themselves by tearing off ears and hair and other parts from the fallen elves. Several had appropriated the elves' long slender swords as trophies—such weapons were pretty enough but not sturdy enough for the trolls' powerful thrusts. "More elves be comin'," Zul'jin warned them. "Back ta the trees. We lead them on a chase, keep them busy." He grinned and his brethren answered with fierce expressions of their own. "Then we kill them all."

Quickly the forest trolls leaped up, grabbing low branches with their long-fingered hands and pulling themselves up into the cover of the leaves. They swung up and away, leaving the bodies and the blood behind, their eyes alert and noses sniffing for any hint of approaching elves.

Zul'jin was not worried. He knew the other elves would come soon. And they would be ready. It had been a long time since he had spilled elf blood, and the brief battle had renewed his thirst for more. His kin felt the same, and many were snapping their jaws and flexing their fingers, eager for another fight with the pale-skinned elves. Soon, Zul'jin assured himself quietly. Soon they would have a chance to kill as many elves as they wanted. The forest would run red with blood, and the elves would know the fall of their own empire, just as the trolls had felt theirs die so long ago. And he, Zul'jin, would be responsible. He would hold the elf king's head high so it could see its people's death, just before he devoured it whole.

He could hardly wait.

"Is it ready?" Gul'dan asked impatiently. A short distance away, Cho'gall shook both his heads. The massive ogre grunted and shoved, his enormous shoulder pushing the last Runestone fragment another foot across the thickly grassed clearing.

"Now it is ready," he called out, straightening and rubbing at the shoulder with one hand.

Gul'dan nodded. It had taken them several hours to dig out a single Runestone, shatter the monolith into several still enormous pieces, and carry five of them here to this clearing, and then several more hours to position the stones just right and inscribe the circle and the pentagram between them. Fortunately Doomhammer had given them the use of several regular ogres for the labor, and Cho'gall was able to communicate with his stupid one-headed kin more easily than any orc could. The Runestone fragments were large and dense but two ogres could lift them, whereas it would have taken dozens of orcs to budge each stone. Gul'dan wondered idly how the elves had gotten the original unbroken stones to their locations in the first place. Most likely magic. Or perhaps they had used slave labor as well. The forest trolls were nearly as powerful as the ogres and far smarter, so they would have been able to follow more detailed instructions.

At least the stones were in place now. Gul'dan gestured and three other orc warlocks took their places beside three of the Runestone pieces. It was a good thing Doomhammer had not killed all of them or this ritual would not have stood even a chance of working. As it was, Gul'dan thought it would succeed but he was not completely sure. Still, if it failed he was fairly certain he would survive unscathed.

He nodded to Cho'gall, who called out to the ogres clustered off to one side. After a moment of jostling and pushing and grunting one of them stepped forward. Cho'gall barked a command and the ogre, shrugging, slouched into the space between the stones. It stood at the center of the pentagram and waited, motionless. One good thing about ogres was that they could stand still when required. Indeed, when not given an order and not looking for food ogres could stand for hours, as motionless as statues. Gul'dan had often wondered if they had somehow evolved from rocks. It would explain their dense hides as well as their utter stupidity.

Returning his mind to the task at hand, Gul'dan raised his arms and called forth the dark energies his demon masters had granted him back on Draenor. The energy crackled about him, and he fed it into the Rune-stone fragment directly before him. Cho'gall had taken the final place and he and the other warlocks added their magic as well, each powering a single stone. When all five stones hummed with power, almost vi-brating from the energies they contained, Gul'dan spoke a short incantation and concentrated. More en-ergy arced from his fingertips into his Runestone, but this time the energy then flickered through his stone and on to the nearest stone on his left. Nor did the en-ergy stop there. It passed to the next stone, and then the next, and then the next, and finally back to his, link-ing all five in an array of dancing, bristling magic. The air itself seemed to darken above the altar, and it felt thick with energy, the way the sky did right before a massive storm. The ogre still stood unmoving, though Gul'dan thought he saw a glimmer of fear in its eyes. Oh good, Cho'gall had picked a smart one.

Now that the stones had power Gul'dan turned the energy toward their center, and toward the towering figure standing there. Bolts of dark energy shot from his stone and struck the ogre full in the chest, sur-rounding it with a blazing dark aura. The other Rune-stone fragments lent their strength and the ogre almost disappeared within the dark glow that filled the space between the stones. More energy danced within that sphere, somehow feeding on itself, and now they could make out only the faintest hint of the ogre's outline. Gul'dan was sure he could feel his arms trembling from fatigue and magical drain but excitement kept him quivering with energy.

After a few minutes the shadowy glow began to fade. Slowly it dimmed, and the figure within stood out in greater detail. Still the ogre towered above them all, except Cho'gall, but something about the creature had changed. Gul'dan waited impatiently for the glow to dissipate enough for him to see into the sphere. Finally it did so, winking out completely in an instant, and Gul'dan had his first real look at the creature his Alter of Storms had created.

It was still clearly an ogre, though even larger than before, and somehow its proportions had shifted. Its arms were not quite as long, its legs not quite so bowed, and it held itself different, more alert.

And of course there were the two heads.

Back on Draenor, two-headed ogres were incredibly rare. They were bigger and stronger than their kin and more coordinated. They were venerated, and Cho'gall was the first seen in generations. Even more rare, he had proven intelligent enough to become a mage. Gul'dan had found the two-headed ogre when he was still young and had trained him carefully. Cho'gall had proven a valuable assistant and a powerful warlock in his own right, and still remained with Gul'dan to this day. And now it seemed Cho'gall was not alone.

The new two-headed ogre turned and stared at Gul'dan, somehow realizing he was in charge.

"What am I?" it demanded, one head speaking while the other looked around. Its language skill was far greater than a normal ogre's as well.

"You are an ogre," Gul'dan replied. "Perhaps an ogre mage."

"An ogre mage," the new ogre's other head asked. "What does that mean?"

Gul'dan found himself explaining about magi and warlocks and shaman and other workers of magic.

"And I am one of these?" the new ogre asked.

"Possibly." Gul'dan's eyes narrowed. "There is a simple test." He stooped and lifted a single leaf from the ground, handing it to the two-headed creature. "Take this." The ogre took the leaf with surprising skill, showing that his dexterity had dramatically increased as well. "Now concentrate on the idea of fire, of heat and flame," Gul'dan told the ogre.

The ogre frowned with both faces, studying the leaf. Then it nodded slightly, first one head and then the other.

"Good." Gul'dan spoke softly, not wanting to break the creature's concentration. "Now bring that flame to life. Let it claim the leaf, the fire licking across it, the heat warming your skin, almost burning your fingers."

He watched as a spark appeared near the middle of the leaf and rapidly grew to a small flame that spread hungrily. The leaf shriveled, turning dark and brittle in seconds as the fire consumed it. The breeze carried it away, and the ogre glanced up, meeting Gul'dan's eyes with both its own pairs, its double gaze bright.

"I am an ogre mage then, yes?" It sounded pleased. One head grinned. The other smiled slightly, though it seemed puzzled.

"Yes," Gul'dan agreed, also pleased. "You are one of us."

"What does that mean, 'one of us'?" the creature asked next, its less exuberant head frowning. "What do I do with this gift?"

Gul'dan explained about the Horde. He also told the ogre about the need to conquer here, and about the other races they had already faced in their quest. The ogre mage listened quietly, absorbing every detail.

"You created me," the ogre said at last. It was not a question, but Gul'dan nodded. "I am your creature then," the ogre affirmed. "I will serve you. Your cause is my cause. Tell me what to do."

Inside, Gul'dan rejoiced. It was exactly as he'd hoped. By shaping the two-headed ogre with his own magic, he had formed a bond between them. The creature was completely loyal! Outwardly, however, he was careful not to show too much glee. Instead he simply gestured for Cho'gall to approach. "This is Cho'gall," Gul'dan explained. "He, like you, is a trusted assistant and an ogre mage. He will explain what we are doing here. And he will give you a name of your own."

The new ogre bowed its heads. "Thank you, master,"

the more somber head said before the creature followed Cho'gall away. Gul'dan knew his assistant would set the new ogre mage to work powering the Altar again. And with each use they would gain another two-headed ogre. He knew he could not expect most of them to be ogre magi—that was too much to hope for. But if even one in ten possessed the necessary intelligence he would be able to assemble a second Altar and power that one as well. Gul'dan chuckled. He would transform every ogre in the Horde if Doomhammer did not stop him. And why would he? As far as Doomhammer knew, he was getting bigger, stronger warriors. The Warchief would never suspect that these new creatures were completely loyal to Gul'dan and not him, and Gul'dan would make sure his new servants did not reveal their true loyalties too soon. Only when the time was right. And then Doomhammer would discover there was a new faction within the Horde, one he could not so easily destroy or cast aside.

Gul'dan laughed again and turned away. Cho'gall would handle the rest of the process here. He had other tasks to oversee, ones that would later lead to his finally claiming the power that lay waiting for him elsewhere.

CHAPTER FOURTEEN

"By Silvermoon, where are they?" Alleria raced through the forest, sword in hand, the leaves and branches whipping past her as a blur. The other rangers had fanned out to cover more ground, and Alleria hoped they hadn't run into any orcs or trolls. She wanted those miserable green-skinned intruders for herself.

Not for the first time since seeing the fires she wished she'd never left home. Why had she decided that the Alliance needed her help? Weren't Anasterian Sunstrider and the other council members far older and wiser than she was, and thus far better equipped to decide what aid they should offer the younger races? Then again, Anasterian had been convinced the Horde would never pose a threat to them here in Quel'Thalas. That was why he had felt the Alliance was not their concern, because they were safe from whatever was occurring in the outside world.

Clearly he had been wrong.

Still, if Alleria had listened to him and abided by his decision she would have been here, not sailing down-river and marching over hills. She would have been here when the orcs and trolls arrived, here with her family and her people when the Horde breached their borders.

Would it have made any difference? She didn't know. Perhaps not. What could one more ranger have done to stop an enemy she wouldn't even realize was approaching? But at least she wouldn't now feel like she had deserted them in their hour of need.

The thought spurred her to even greater speed, and she leaped over a low bush into a tiny clearing between two clusters of trees—

—and found herself staring down the tip of a hunting arrow aimed at her throat.

The figure holding the bow was nearly as tall as her and wearing similar garb, though far less travel-stained. Long hair streamed back from beneath the cloak's hood and seemed to gleam like ivory in the sunlight, a shining silvery white that Alleria knew too well to ever mistake it.

"Vereesa?"

The other figure lowered the bow, her blue eyes wide with surprise and relief. "Alleria?" Then the bow had been tossed aside, and Alleria's younger sister had caught her up in a rough embrace. "You're home!"

"Of course." Alleria squeezed Vereesa in return and patted her head, a gesture so familiar it was automatic. "Are you all right?" she asked after a minute. "Where's Sylvanas? Are Mother and Father safe?"

"They're fine," Vereesa answered, disengaging and bending to retrieve her weapons. "Sylvanas is with a hunting party near the riverbank. As for Mother and Father, they should be in Silvermoon by now. They went to consult with the elders." She paused, fitting the arrow back to her string. "Alleria, where have you been? And what's going on? There are fires! All over Quel'Thalas! And some of the other rangers—they haven't reported back."

Alleria felt her stomach twist at the news. If rangers were going missing, it meant the Horde had penetrated deep into the forest already. "We're being invaded, little sister," she told Vereesa bluntly, bringing her sword up and turning to put her back against her sister. Her ears twitched. "Now, quiet."

"Quiet? But why—" Vereesa's comments were cut off as a tall figure dropped from the trees above. It lunged forward, a short-hafted, long-bladed axe in one hand, but Alleria had heard it just before its descent and was ready for it. She brought her sword up, parrying the blow, and spun to the side, neatly sidestepping its secondary attack with a long curving dagger. Her sword arced about and removed the creature's head and it pitched forward, the weapons falling from its now-lifeless fingers.

"Quick!" Alleria warned, stooping quickly and then straightening again. "We need to move! Now!" Vereesa, wide-eyed at the sudden bloodshed, nodded and turned away, running as much from the violence as from her sister's order. She was young still, the youngest of the three sisters, and had never seen real combat before. Alleria had hoped it would be a long time before that would happen but it was too late to worry about that now.

They ran through the woods, and Alleria was sure she heard laughter above them somewhere. Trolls! The creatures were following them, keeping pace on the branches above. No doubt they planned to drop down on her and Vereesa and kill both of them before they could find help. But the trolls didn't know this wood. Alleria did.

She ran, leading both Vereesa and their unseen pursuers, twisting and turning and leaping, crossing streams and clearings, darting through groves, ducking under trees and vines. Vereesa kept pace, her bow still in her hands. And the laughter clung to them as well.

Then Alleria saw a ribbon of silver ahead. The river! She put on a spurt of additional speed, Vereesa matching her, and they burst from the trees onto the strip of open land beside the river. She felt the impact behind her as one and then several trolls dropped from the trees, knowing they would have to catch her before she could wade into the deep water and float or swim beyond their reach. Trolls did not like water.

"Nice chase, pale one," one of the creatures behind her growled. "But now you die!"

Hands reached for her, long claws scraped at her, catching at her hair, but Alleria twisted away, avoiding their grasp. She spun around, sword coming up, ready to fight as long as she could—

—and watched as the troll stiffened and toppled backward. A long shaft protruded from its neck.

Similar shafts struck the other trolls, felling them before they could retreat to the safety of the trees. And Alleria, turning back toward the river, glanced around and saw several rangers on the far bank, their bows still quivering from the recent archery. One of them wore a long green cloak and a more ornate tunic than the others. She had long blond hair, darker than Alleria's but otherwise similar, and eyes more gray than green or blue but the same shape as both hers and Vereesa's. The other rangers positioned themselves around her as she smiled and held up her bow in salute.

"Welcome home, Alleria!" Sylvanas called. "Now what is this trouble you have brought us?" Even from across the river she radiated intensity, as if she could will the answers to appear.

Alleria smiled at her sister's greeting—Sylvanas, Ranger General of all Quel'Thalas, was as forceful as ever—then shook her head. "I did not bring it, Sylvanas," she answered truthfully. "I had hoped to outrun it. But I do bring possible salvation." She glanced back at the dead trolls behind her, and at Vereesa, who stood swaying and pale and resolutely facing away from the recent corpses. "I must speak to the Council."

"I do not know if they will listen," Sylvanas warned. "They are too busy worrying about these fires to consider much else right now. As am I. They are appearing all across the forest, seemingly at random." She glanced pointedly at the dead trolls. "And now I must tend to this matter as well."

Alleria grimaced and looked down. "They will listen," she promised. "I will give them no choice."

"What is the meaning of this?" Anasterian Sunstrider demanded. He and the Council of Silvermoon were discussing matters in low, serious voices when Alleria walked in unannounced and uninvited. Several of the high elf rulers rose from their seats, surprised at her presence, but Alleria ignored them. She focused only on Anasterian.

The high elf king was old, old even for an elf, with hair that had long since turned white and skin thin as parchment and lined as a piece of old wood. He had gone from slender to frail but his blue eyes were still piercing and his voice, though thin as well, was still filled with authority. Alleria instinctively shrank back from his anger but then she remembered why she was here and straightened.

"I am Alleria Windrunner," she announced, though she knew most of the council members recognized her. "I have been beyond our borders, and have fought alongside the humans in their war. And I have returned to bring you grave tidings, not just for them but for us." She frowned and studied the men and women before her. "The Horde the humans warned of is real and vast and powerful. The bulk of their forces are orcs, but they have other creatures as well. Including the forest trolls." That got a reaction, gasps and angry mutterings. None of the other high elves knew what an orc was—she hadn't herself until she'd fought them in the Hillsbrad—but they all knew about trolls. Some here, including Anasterian himself, had even fought in the great Troll Wars long ago, some four thousand years after Quel'Thalas was founded.

"You say this Horde includes trolls," a lord stated loudly, "yet why should that concern us? Let the trolls follow these strange creatures you tell of, and hopefully march far away from here. Perhaps the humans will even do us a favor and kill them for us!" Several other elves laughed and nodded.

"You do not understand," Alleria told them angrily. "The Horde is not some distant problem we can ignore and laugh about! They intend to conquer all of Lordaeron, from coast to coast! And that includes us here in Quel'Thalas!"

"Let them come!" Another lord, an elven mage she thought was named Dar'Khan, scoffed. "Our lands are well-defended—none can pass the Runestones and survive."

"Oh no?" Alleria snarled at him. "Are you so sure? Because already the trolls have entered our forests. Already they stalk through our lands, killing our people. And the orcs will not be far behind. They are less powerful than trolls, individually, but they are as numerous as locusts, enough of them to cover the land. And they are here."

"Here?" Anasterian scoffed. "Impossible!"

In answer Alleria swung her arm and released the object she had been carrying since she and Vereesa had run. The troll's head flew through the air, its short dark hair waving about it, the sun catching on a tusk, and fell again, landing just before Anasterian's feet.

"This one attacked Vereesa and me," Alleria explained, "not an hour's run from the river crossing. Several more followed us to there, and their bodies still lie on the far bank unless Sylvanas and her party have moved them." She noticed that none of the lords were laughing at her anymore. "They are here," she insisted again. "The trolls are within our woods, killing our people. And the orcs are the ones burning the edges of Eversong Forest!" Though she admitted to herself she did not know how they could be causing the other fires both Vereesa and Sylvanas had mentioned.

"Outrageous!" This time Anasterian's outburst was not directed at her. The elf king kicked the troll head, causing it to roll away under another lord's chair. His eyes were sharp and his brow drawn, and when he turned back to Alleria she could see the energy and focus that had made him such a great king for so many years. All hints of frailty were gone, brushed aside in the current crisis. "They dare to invade our home?" Anasterian fumed. "They dare!" He looked up and his expression was like thunder. "We shall teach them to trespass here! Gather our warriors," he instructed the other lords. "Summon our rangers. We will attack the trolls and drive them from our forest so sternly they shall never dare encroach again."

Alleria was pleased to see her king so determined, and certainly agreed with the sentiment. But she shook her head anyway. "The trolls are only part of the danger," she reminded Anasterian and the others. "The Horde is numerous beyond belief and the orcs are strong, tough, and determined." She grinned. "Fortunately I did not come alone."

Turalyon was battling a pair of orcs and had just smashed one to the ground with his hammer, though he took a heavy blow on his shield from the other. A third orc leaped at him, almost knocking him from his horse, and since the creature was too close to strike with a weapon Turalyon headbutted him instead, his heavy helm striking the orc across the brow and the bridge of the nose and leaving him stunned. Turalyon shoved the dazed orc off his horse and onto his third foe, then used that opportunity to strike both of them good hard blows. Neither of those two would get up again.

He brushed water from the front of his helmet, taking a second to peer up at the thick gray clouds that hung above them. The rain showed no sign of letting up, though he supposed that was a good thing. At least the fires were out now, and unlikely to start again. He supposed he could stand fighting in such soggy, miserable weather if it helped keep the elven homeland from burning to the ground. Off to his side he caught a brief glimpse of Khadgar, who was laying about him with sword and staff. The wizard had exhausted his magic summoning the vast storm, which stretched across the entire front of Quel'Thalas, but he was proving formidable enough with mundane weapons that Turalyon knew he should not waste time worrying about his friend. Besides, he had enough foes that he should be focusing that worry on himself instead.

Turalyon was just turning to deal with a pair of orcs at his left flank when one of the two stiffened, twitched, and toppled over, an arrow through his throat. Turalyon recognized the fletching and grinned. Sure enough, a lithe young woman darted toward him a moment later, her travel cloak's hood tossed back despite the downpour, the tips of her long pointed ears piercing the golden mane that surrounded her lovely face. Somehow the rain was ignoring her, falling around her instead of on her, and Turalyon was not sure if it was elven magic or just the sheer power of her natural beauty.

"I can see I got here just in time," Alleria commented as she reached him, idly turning and putting an arrow in another orc's throat. "What do you do when I am not around to save you?"

"I manage," Turalyon replied, too caught up in battle to feel flustered by her presence. He blocked an attack and struck down the orc in question, already turning to find the next foe. "Did you find them?"

"I did," she confirmed. "And they have agreed. Already the warriors and rangers are mobilized. They can be here in ten minutes, if here is where you want them."

Turalyon nodded, using his hammer's long shaft to block an axe swing and then shortening his grip so the hammer's head struck the offending orc on the return swing. "Here is as good a place as any," he answered. "And as long as we are here to fight them the Horde isn't going anywhere."

Alleria nodded. "I will run back and inform them. You have only to hold fast until they arrive." Her voice sounded strange, and Turalyon risked a quick glance. By the Light! Was she crying? She certainly looked sad. No doubt the invasion of her homeland had taken a hard toll upon her.

"We will hold," he assured her grimly. "We must." And Alleria was gone again. Turalyon only hoped she and her kin retuned before the rest of the Horde overwhelmed their tiny defense. Already waves of orcs were pouring in from the sides, and Turalyon knew his forces could not stand against the entire orc army, especially not here on an open field where the orcs could surround them and swarm them under. They would need support, and quickly. He just hoped the elves were as ready and as capable as Alleria made them sound.

Ter'lij, one of Zul'jin's subordinates, grinned. He and his pack had smelled something unpleasant nearby and had followed their noses to a delicious sound, a single soft thump-thump on the forest floor below. A lone elf. Ter'lij had been charged with watching this path, which led toward the elven city, and keeping any elves from crossing it. Well, this was one elf who would go no farther.

Lowering himself silently through the foliage, Ter'lij caught sight of his prey. The elf was moving quickly enough for one of its kind, and most likely other creatures would have thought it quiet, but to Ter'lij its passage was as loud as the thunder he heard rumbling near the forest's edge and its pace was easily surpassed. The elf wore a long brown cloak, the hood raised, and was leaning upon a long staff. An elder, then. Even better.

Licking his lips with anticipation, Ter'lij motioned his pack to follow him down. Then he dropped from the trees, his curved blade in hand, and grinned at his victim and started in surprise as the elf tossed back his cloak and straightened with a grin of his own. The staff swung up and around, revealing a long blade at one end, and armor gleamed even in the shadows of the trees.

"Did you think we could not hear you rustling about above us?" the elf sneered, his narrow features pulled taut in a glower. "Did you think we could not sense you befouling our forest? You are not welcome here, creature, and you will not be suffered to live."

Ter'lij recovered from his surprise and laughed. "Very clever, little pale one," he agreed. "A fine trick you be playin' on Ter'lij. But there is only one of you, wi' your little stick, an' many of us." The rest of his pack landed behind him and ranged out, ready to surround the arrogant elf.

But the elf only grinned more widely, his expression nasty. "Do you think so, oaf?" he taunted. "You pride yourself on your woodcraft, yet you are blind in the forest compared to us. And deaf."

Suddenly a second elf emerged from behind a nearby tree. And then a third. And a fourth. Ter'lij frowned. There were more and more of them, until he and his pack were surrounded and thoroughly outnumbered. And all of them carried the same long spears and bore tall oblong shields. This was not what he had expected.

Nonetheless, Ter'lij was a seasoned hunter and warrior and was not so easily frightened. "Better!" he announced finally, rising to his full height. "A real fight, not just pickin' off an unarmed elf! I like it!" And he leaped upon the lead elf, his sword raised high—

—and died in mid-air, the elf commander's spear sliding through his chest and piercing his heart before emerging out his back. The elf stepped to one side, letting Ter'lij's body slide from his weapon, and pivoted, sweeping the spear around in a deadly arc to slice off the hand of a troll advancing upon him.

The battle was over quickly. The elf leader kicked at one of the bodies, which did not move, and nodded. He had faced forest trolls before, though never here in Quel'Thalas, and while they were talented forest hunters compared to most races they were clumsy when matched against an elf. Sylvanas had sent his patrol out, one of many, with orders to flush out and kill any trolls they could find. This was the second pack he had encountered, and he wondered how many more still crashed through their forest.

He was opening his mouth to rally his men when a slender figure burst into the clearing, golden hair streaming behind her. His ears had picked up her approach seconds before she arrived, and clearly she had placed speed over customary stealth.

"Halduron!" she called as she approached, slowing to a stop a few feet from him. "Good! I have spoken with the Alliance commander, and with Sylvanas as well. She needs all our forces along the southwest edge of the forest. That is where the Horde has gathered, and he cannot hold them for long."

Halduron Brightwing nodded. "I shall inform Lor'themar, for his band is near here as well," he assured her, "and we will come to the aid of your friends. Their fight is now ours, and we will not allow them to fall before these foul creatures." He paused, studying her a second. "Are you well, Alleria? You seem flushed."

Alleria shook her head, though a faint frown flitted across her face. "I am fine," she assured him. "Now go! Bring our warriors! I will return to my sister and to the Alliance and reassure them that aid is on the way." And she was gone again, turning on her heel and dashing back into the trees.

Halduron watched her go, then shook himself. He

had known Alleria Windrunner a long time, and could see that something had bothered or unsettled her. But they were all bothered this day, when strange creatures roamed their sacred woods. Not for long, however. Gesturing to his rangers, Halduron pulled his spear free of a troll and wiped it clean on the body, then turned. There would be time to rid the forest of their filth later. First they must deal with the foes still living.

Turalyon felt it had only been minutes since Alleria's departure when she appeared again, surfacing through the battle to stand beside him. Her bow was slung across her back now and she had her sword in hand instead, using it to cut down an orc that had been trying to stab his horse in the hindquarters.

"They will be here," she assured him, her eyes bright, and Turalyon nodded. He felt a surge of relief, though whether at the thought of reinforcements or the fact that she was still safe he was not sure. He frowned, unused to such thoughts, and pushed them aside for now. First he needed to worry about his and his troops' survival.

The rain had finally stopped, though the clouds remained, casting the battlefield into shadow. So when Turalyon saw a dark shape loom up off to one side, at first he thought it was simply a distorted shadow from some orc warrior. But the shape continued to grow, and to gain solidity, and he stared, almost getting skewered by an orc as a result.

"Stay focused!" Khadgar warned, riding up beside

him and kicking the orc away before it could strike again. "What are you staring at?"

"That," Turalyon replied, pointing with his hammer before returning his attention the fight raging around him.

Now it was Khadgar's turn to stare, and the young-old wizard let out a string of curses as he saw the massive figure that had emerged from the trees and joined the far edge of the battle. It was easily twice the size of even an orc, with skin the color of aged leather. It held a massive hammer, most likely an orc two-handed weapon but used in a single hand by the behemoth, and wore strange armor—Turalyon's jaw tightened as he risked a second glance and realized the armor was human, breastplates and greaves and bracers linked together by thick chains to cover most of the massive creature's flesh.

Its twin heads were bare, however, and glared down at the men and orcs milling before it. The hammer swept down as well, crushing two men in a single blow, and then swept to one side, knocking four more soldiers from their feet and tossing them several yards away.

"What the hell is that thing?" Turalyon demanded, smashing a charging orc in the face and driving it back against another, who staggered under the shared impact.

"An ogre," Khadgar replied. "A two-headed one."

Turalyon started to tell his friend that yes, he had seen ogres before, and he had realized this one had two heads, when the strange ogre raised its empty hand toward a cluster of Alliance soldiers. Turalyon blinked, thinking his eyes were playing tricks upon him. Had he just seen fire pour from the creature's outstretched hand toward the soldiers? He looked again. Yes, there were flames licking about the soldiers now, and the men were dropping their weapons to beat at themselves where the fires danced across their armor and clothes. Several were pulling off their cloaks, which had ignited, and others were rolling in the grass, trying to put out the flames that tormented them. How had the strange new ogre done that?

"Damn!" Khadgar had clearly seen it as well, if his increased cursing was any indication. "He's an ogre mage!"

"A what?"

"A wizard," Khadgar snapped. "A bloody ogre wizard!"

"Ah." Turalyon dispatched another foe and stared at the monstrous ogre again, trying to understand this. The largest, strongest creature he had ever seen, and it cast magic? Wonderful. What would it take to kill such a beast? He started to ask Khadgar this, and choked on his words as the ogre mage suddenly reeled and fell forward, the hair on the back of its head spiked straight up by the last of the rainfall. At first Turalyon thought it was leaning down to do something to the bodies before it, perhaps devour them with its twin mouths, but the creature did not get up again. And then he realized that what he had taken for hair was too solid for that. Those were shafts, too big to be arrows. Spears!

"Yes!" Alleria cheered, raising her bow high in salute. "My people have arrived!"

And she was right, Turalyon saw. From the forest emerged row upon row of elves. These wore more armor than Alleria and her rangers, and heavier gear, and carried shields and spears as well. Clearly it had been their weapons that had felled the ogre mage. Turalyon had never been so happy to see anyone in his life.

"They have excellent timing!" he told Alleria, having to shout to make himself heard over the chaos of combat. "Can you relay messages at all?"

She nodded. "We use gestures for hunting, and they can be read at a distance."

"Good." Turalyon nodded and pounded another orc into the ground as he marshaled his thoughts. "We need to crush the Horde between us. Tell them to advance toward us, but also to spread out along the edges and sweep in. We'll do the same. I don't want the orcs to just squeeze out the sides because then they could close in on us instead." Alleria nodded and began gesturing toward the forest, and Turalyon saw one of the elves in front nod and turn to his fellows. Khadgar had been close enough to hear the discussion and he was already turning toward a nearby unit leader, shouting orders and telling the man to pass them along as well.

Both armies began to fan out, the Alliance forces retreating slightly so they would have room to move. The Horde clearly took this as a sign of defeat, because a cheer went up among the orcs. Most of them had not yet seen the elves, who were still partially hidden beneath the trees. That was fine. Turalyon wanted them taken by surprise as much as possible, to reduce the chance of their getting away. He pulled his men back, detailing several units to hold the orcs at bay while the others got some distance between them, and then sent a third of his troops to each side and told them to sweep back in from there. The rest he kept with him, and he could see the Horde's puzzlement as he turned and led the charge straight back into their midst.

On the far side, the elves had arrayed themselves in a similar fashion. And as the Horde braced itself to meet Turalyon's attack, the elves stepped forward, sweeping down with their spears to slice into the rearmost row of orcs. Many fell without a sound, but enough gasped or sighed or groaned that others turned to see what had disturbed their comrades. And then a ragged shout went up as the orcs realized they were beset on both sides.

Several orc warriors turned and tried to run, realizing they were now trapped between two armies. But the arms of both human and elven forces curled around, blocking any escape. The orcs were forced to stand and fight, and most did so happily, losing themselves in rage and bloodlust. But with enemies on all sides, and elven bows and spears to complement human swords and axes and hammers, the orcs began to take heavy casualties.

Turalyon felt a surge of hope. They were winning!

The Horde still outnumbered his own soldiers and the elven warriors, but they were trapped and undisciplined. Each orc was fighting for himself or with a handful of others, most likely members of the same clan, and that left them vulnerable to the human and elven tactics. Particularly as his own men and the elves began working together more smoothly, the elven archers firing into a cluster of orcs to thin their ranks and cause confusion before the humans waded in, with the elven spearmen right behind them to stab and block and keep the orcs from ganging up on any soldiers. Already he could see visible gaps in the Horde, and as the Alliance and the elves moved in those gaps expanded, leaving only pockets of the orcs behind.

Then he heard a loud roar. Glancing to the east, Turalyon saw a sight that made his stomach clench. Another of those monstrous two-headed ogres was striding into the battle, laying about with a massive club that he realized was simply a tree trunk with the branches shorn clean. A second of the brutes was right behind the first, a similar club in its own gargantuan hands, and then a third and a fourth followed them. Where were all these creatures coming from?

The two-headed ogres waded into the Alliance troops, sweeping away whole units at a time. Turalyon quickly ordered his men to fall back and let the elves handle this new menace. But the first ogre had been taken by surprise. These were better prepared. They used their clubs to knock aside the flights of arrows and volleys of spears, and then crashed into the elves, sending the slender warriors flying. The Horde began to reform around these massive figures, and more orcs poured in behind them, filling their ranks back out and quickly shifting the numbers back in their favor.

"We have to do something fast!" Turalyon shouted to Khadgar, who was beside him again. "Otherwise they'll sweep us back toward the mountains or west toward the water and we'll be the ones trapped!"

Khadgar started to reply, but Alleria interrupted him. "Listen," she shouted. Her ears quivered.

Turalyon shook his head. "I can't hear anything except fighting," he told her. "What is it?"

She grinned up at him. "Help," she answered. "Help from above."

"There! I see them!"

"Aye, I see them as well, laddie," Kurdran Wildhammer snapped, privately annoyed that the young gryphon rider beside him had spotted the battle first. "Circle around, lads, and then aim for those monstrous brutes in the center. Mind the clubs, though." Tapping Sky'ree with his heels, the Wildhammer leader sent her screaming around and down toward the battlefield. One of the strange two-headed monsters glanced up and, seeing them, roared in reply, but Kurdran was moving too fast to evade, especially with orc warriors everywhere, hampering the giant's progress. As he dropped Kurdran raised his stormhammer, muscles tensing in anticipation. The beast roared again and swung at him with that massive club, but Sky'ree dodged the blow and flew so close her wing-tip brushed one of the creature's faces. Then Kurdran threw, putting all his considerable strength into the toss. The skies echoed with thunder and a lightning bolt struck the creature just as he did, lending its strength to the impact. The creature reeled back, its one head caved in, the other blackened, and toppled. It crushed three orcs when it fell, and its club smashed into several more.

"Yes!" Kurdran whooped, catching his hammer as it returned and nudging Sky'ree up for another diving charge. "That's showed 'em, my beauty! It don't matter how big they are, the Wildhammers can bring 'em low!" He raised his hammer high and let out a loud whoop as he rose into the sky, his gryphon easily slipping past another brute's clumsy overhand swipe.

"What are you lot waiting for?" he bellowed at his warriors, who grinned from their own circling mounts. "I've shown you how it's done! Now get down there and make sure the rest of these giants come crashing down as well!" They saluted mockingly, knowing his taunts were good-natured, and wheeled their gryphons around to begin their own attacks.

Kurdran grinned. He glanced down and spotted the mage, the elf, and the commander he had met back in Aerie Peak. "Ho down there!" he bellowed, raising his hammer and twirling it above him. The elf raised her bow in salute, and the commander and the mage both nodded greetings. "Your Lord Lothar sent us!" Kurdran shouted, not sure they could hear him from this altitude. "And just in time, looks like!" Then he brought his hammer back down, gripping it with both hands once again, and steered Sky'ree back down toward the next of the mammoth two-headed creatures. Several had fallen already and the Horde was scattering around them, realizing their protectors were now actually a danger to them. And the humans and the elves were using the chaos to slaughter the panicked orcs left and right.

Then something shifted in the wind, and Kurdran glanced up. Above him to the south he saw a dark shape gliding down At first he thought it might be one of his warriors, come to relay news or orders, but then realized it did not fly right for a gryphon. And it seemed to be coming from more to the east, past the Hinterlands and possibly below them. But what?

Breaking off his attack, Kurdran brought Sky'ree back up beyond the brutes' reach and circled slowly, watching the approaching shadow. Was it a bird? If so it was higher than most, and its outline was strange. Some new form of attack? He laughed. It was no bigger than an eagle! Were the Horde sending eagles after them now, perhaps with gnomes perched on their backs? As if any raptor could stand against his beauty, he thought, patting Sky'ree's neck affectionately and receiving a musical caw in return.

But the shape was closer now, and growing larger. And larger. And larger still.

"By the Aerie!" Kurdran muttered, awed by its size. What was this thing that it could stay aloft and be so large? It was already as big as his Sky'ree, and he had a suspicion it was still high above him. Now he could make out its shape more clearly—long and lean, with a long tail and neck and great wings spread high above it and flapping only occasionally. The thing was gliding! It had to be high indeed to be coasting on the winds that way, and Kurdran felt a chill as he reestimated its size again. He only knew of one airborne creature that large, and he couldn't imagine what one of them would want with this conflict.

But then the last of the clouds faded away, and the sun shone down upon them. And gleamed red all along the creature, turning it into a soaring crimson streak. And Kurdran knew he had been right.

It was a dragon.

"Dragon!" he shouted. Most of his warriors were still battling the two-headed brutes, but young Murkhad glanced up and looked where Kurdran was pointing. Then the fool actually kicked his gryphon into a rapid ascent, the mount flaring her wings out to gain altitude.

"What are ye doing, ye halfwit?" Kurdran shouted, but if Murkhad heard he gave no reply. Instead the youthful Wildhammer turned his mount toward the dragon, which was now angled in a steep dive, and raised his stormhammer high. Giving a fierce yell, Murkhad charged straight for the plummeting lizard—

—and vanished without a sound as the dragon opened its mouth, revealing great triangular teeth the size of a large dwarf and a long forked tongue the color of blood, and consumed the hapless dwarf and his gryphon in a single snap.

Murkhad never even saw the sorrow evident in the dragon's enormous golden eyes, or the burly green-skinned figure perched on the dragon's back, long leather reins wrapped around one hand.

"By the Light!" Turalyon had cheered with the others when the Wildhammers had arrived, and when Kurdran felled the first two-headed ogre. But he had glanced up again at a faint cry from the Wildhammer leader, and had looked in time to see the fiery dragon descend upon one of the gryphon riders and swallow him like he was a sausage.

And now the dragon was descending upon them. And more were right behind it, streaks of crimson dropping from the sky.

The red dragons were not just the color of flame. Smoke curled from their nostrils and sparks shot from their mouths as they breathed, brighter even than the sunlight gleaming off their claws and along their wings and tails. The smoke and sparks increased as Turalyon stared.

And he suddenly realized what was about to happen.

"Pull back!" he shouted, slapping Khadgar's arm with his shield to get the mage's attention. "Have everyone pull back!" He waved his hammer overhead, hoping that would get both his own people and the elves' attention. "Pull back, everyone! Away from the forest! Now!"

"Away from the forest?" Alleria asked sharply, glancing up at him. He hadn't even realized she was still beside him, which showed how stunned he had been. "Why? We're winning!"

Turalyon started to explain, then realized there probably wasn't time. "Just do it!" he shouted, seeing the surprise on her face. "Tell your people to fall back toward the hills. Hurry!"

Something in his voice or expression convinced her, and she nodded, raising her bow and trying to signal the other elven warriors. Turalyon left her to it and turned away, grabbing the first Alliance officer he found and relaying his orders again. The officer nodded and started shouting and shoving, turning his troops around while bellowing for other officers to do the same.

There was nothing else Turalyon could do. He wheeled his own horse around and kicked it into a gallop, racing for the hills. Then he heard a strange sound, like a sudden burst of wind or a loud exhalation from a big man, and glanced over his shoulder.

The first dragon had swooped down, wings outspread, and opened its mouth wide. And from that mouth poured flames, great waves of flame that spread across the forest's front edge. The heat was intense, sapping every bit of moisture instantly, and the forest seemed to waver like a mirage in the sun's glare. Trees blackened in an instant, crumbling to ash despite being soaked minutes before, and smoke rose from them, thick black smoke that threatened to block out the sun again. The flames did not die, either—in some places they had licked trees farther back, not enough to destroy them completely but enough to ignite them, and now the flames were spreading, dancing from tree to tree. It was almost hypnotic, and Turalyon had to force himself to turn back around and watch where his horse was going. But soon he had reached the foothills and swung his mount back around, watching the horrible devastation.

"Do something!" Alleria yelled, appearing beside him again as he sat on his horse and squinted against the light and the heat. She pounded on his leg with her fists. "Do something!"

"There's nothing I can do," Turalyon pointed out, his heart breaking at the grief throbbing in her voice. "I wish there was!"

"Then you do something," the elven ranger demanded, turning to Khadgar as he rode up beside them. "Use your magic! Put out the flames!"

But the old-seeming mage shook his head sadly. "There's too much fire for me to combat it all," he explained softly. "And I've already drained myself for the day summoning that storm earlier." He said the last part bitterly, and Turalyon felt for his friend. It wasn't Khadgar's fault that he'd put out the first wave of fires only to have these far worse blazes appear now.

"I need to get to Silvermoon," Alleria said, more to herself than to them. "My parents are there, and our elders. I need to help them!"

"And what will you do?" Turalyon asked, his words coming out harsher than he'd intended, though at least it snapped her out of her grief long enough to look up at him. "Do you have a way to combat these flames?" He gestured at the forest, where the dragons were now diving and wheeling like bats at play, spreading flames with every pass. As far as the eye could see now, Quel'Thalas was burning. The smoke seemed a solid wall of gray above the elven homeland, and its shadow reached them on the foothills and cast darkness behind them, across the mountains. Turalyon was sure they could see the conflagration in Capital City.

Alleria shook her head, and he saw tears streaming down her cheeks. "But I have to do something," she all but wailed, her normally lovely voice hoarse with anger and pain. "My home is dying!"

"I know. And I understand." Reaching down, Turalyon rested one hand on her shoulder, squeezing gently. "But going in there now would only spell your death. Even if you could get to the river, it must be boiling from all that heat. You'd die, and that would not help anyone."

She looked up at him. "My family, the lords—will they be all right?" He could hear the desperation in her voice. She wanted, perhaps needed, to believe they survive.

"They're powerful magi," Khadgar pointed out. "And

while I've never seen it, I understand the Sunwell is a source of immense power. They'll shield the city from harm. Even the dragons won't be able to touch them." He sounded completely certain, though Turalyon saw his friend quirk one eyebrow at him, as if to say, "at least I hope so."

Alleria nodded, though she was clearly still shaken. "Thank you," she said quietly. "You are right. My death now would accomplish nothing." Turalyon suspected she was trying to convince herself of that. She glared at the dragons fluttering and soaring beyond. "But theirs would. The entire Horde's would. Especially the orcs." Her green eyes narrowed, and Turalyon saw something there he had not seen in her before. Hatred. "They brought this destruction upon us," she spat. "And I will see them suffer for it."

"We all will." Turalyon looked up as another elf strode toward them. He was dressed in full war gear, his armor beautiful and graceful but clearly functional and covered in blood and gore. At his side hung a long sword and a deep green cloak fluttered behind him. He had removed his leaf-patterned helm and dark brown eyes shone beneath glossy hair the color of the cornsilk. And his expression mirrored Alleria's own.

"Lor'themar Theron," Alleria introduced him, "one of our finest rangers." Then she turned and smiled briefly as a second elf approached, this one a tall woman with a similar cloak and features much like Alleria's own, though her hair was a shade darker. "And this is my sis-

ter, Sylvanas Windrunner, ranger-general and commander of our forces. Sylvanas, Lord Theron, this is Sir
Turalyon of the Silver Hand, second in command of the
Alliance forces. And Khadgar of Dalaran, mage." Turalyon nodded and Theron returned the gesture, a show of
respect among equals.

"Most of my warriors escaped the inferno," Theron
told them brusquely. "We cannot breach the flames,
however. And so we are trapped without, while our
families are trapped within. Now we know how the fire
spread through the forest so quickly and from so many
directions." His hand tightened on the hilt of his sword.
"But we cannot linger on such thoughts," he announced, his words directed at Alleria and perhaps
himself as well. "We are here, and we must do what we
can to succor our people as quickly as possible. And
that means destroying the forces threatening them."

"Your commander, Anduin Lothar, sent word to us
once before, asking for our participation in this Alliance," Sylvanas stated, looking up at Turalyon. "My
leaders chose not to respond beyond a token show of
support." Her gaze flickered to Alleria, and something
like a smile crossed her face. "Though some of our
rangers took it upon themselves to lend aid to your
cause." Then she sobered again. "But my elders realized
their error when the trolls and orcs invaded our lands.
For if Quel'Thalas is not safe from incursion, what is?
They ordered me to assemble our warriors and march
to meet you, and to render such aid as we could." She

bowed. "We would be proud to join your alliance, Sir Turalyon, and I hope that our deeds henceforth will compensate for the tardiness of our involvement."

Turalyon nodded, wishing once again that Lothar was here. The Champion would know how to handle this situation properly. But he was not, and so Turalyon was forced to muddle through as best he could. "I thank you, and your people," he told Sylvanas finally. "We welcome you and all your kin into our Alliance. Together we will drive the Horde from this continent, from your lands and ours, that we may afterward live in peace and cooperation once again."

Anything else he had planned to say was interrupted by a squawk overhead and the sudden fluttering of wings. Turalyon ducked, as did Khadgar, and Theron reached for his sword, but the descending creature was far smaller than a dragon, and covered in feathers and fur rather than scales.

"Sorry, lad," Kurdran Wildhammer said as he landed Sky'ree just beyond them, causing the horses to shudder and stamp their feet in dismay. "We tried, but those dragons are simply too big and too powerful for the handful o' us to face. Give us time and we'll be finding a way to face them in the sky and beat them down, but right now they've got the upper hand."

Turalyon nodded. "Thank you for your efforts," he told the dwarf leader. "And for your aid earlier. It saved many lives." He glanced around him. Khadgar, Alleria, Sylvanas, Lor'themar Theron, and Kurdran Wildhammer. These were good people, and good lieutenants. He suddenly did not feel so alone, or so self-conscious. With them at his side, perhaps he could be a leader, at least until Lothar returned.

"We need to get our people out of here," he told them after a moment. "We will return and free Quel'Thalas from the Horde, but right now we need to regroup and wait. I suspect the Horde is not going to stay here for long. They have some other goal in mind."

But what, he wondered. They had taken the forest, and driven the elves from their home. They had attacked Aerie Peak, and crushed Khaz Modan. Where would they strike next?

He tried to think of it from the orcs' point of view. If he were them, and was handling their campaign, where would he go? What was the single biggest remaining threat?

Then it hit him. The biggest threat was the heart of the Alliance itself. The place where it had all started. He glanced at Khadgar, who nodded, clearly thinking the same thing.

"Capital City!" It made sense. From Silvermoon, which stood at the northern tip of Quel'Thalas, the orcs could march over the mountains and directly into Lordaeron, emerging not far from Lordamere Lake and Capital City itself. The city had few defenders left, King Terenas having sent most of his men with the Alliance. Fortunately marching over the mountains would mean making their way across Alterac first, and while Perenolde had not been the most stalwart member of the Alliance he would certainly rally his forces against an invasion of his own lands. But the orcs could overwhelm Alterac through sheer numbers and then swarm down out of the mountains to strike the city.

"From Lordaeron they could spread down across the rest of the continent," Alleria pointed out. "And if they left a force here they would have two points of origin. They could blanket the land with orcs in weeks."

Turalyon nodded. "Now we know what they are planning," he said, sure they were right. "Which means we need to find a way to stop them." He glanced at the raging fires beyond. "But not here. Get the men back into the hills proper, and we will meet and discuss this further." Then he wheeled his horse around and cantered away from the forest, trusting his lieutenants to see his orders carried out. And unwilling to look any more at the majestic woods burning behind him.

CHAPTER FIFTEEN

"Let's go!" Doomhammer shouted. "Get your gear and get moving!" He watched the warriors for a moment, as their chieftains shouted and shoved and punched to get them ready, then turned back to Gul'dan, who stood waiting patiently nearby. "What?" he demanded.

"My clan and I will remain here for a time," Gul'dan replied. "I have other plans for the Altars of Storms, plans that will aid the Horde in its conquest."

Doomhammer frowned. He still did not trust the short, ugly warlock. But he had to admit that the two-headed ogres had proven immensely useful in the battle to take Quel'Thalas. True, those cursed dwarves and their gryphons had interfered, and cost him several of the creatures, but without the ogres they might not have broken the Alliance lines and been able to regroup. Finally he nodded. "Do what you must," he told Gul'dan. "But do not take too long. We will need every advantage if we want to conquer Lordaeron quickly."

"I will not delay," Gul'dan assured him, grinning. "You are right—speed is of the essence." The way he said it troubled Doomhammer, but just then Zuluhed came running up and the chief warlock slipped away from Doomhammer's penetrating gaze while he was listening to the latest report about the forest's remaining defenders.

"We cannot breach their defenses," the Dragonmaw chieftain was saying. He looked more angry than apologetic. "Even the dragons can do nothing," he insisted, shaking his head. "Their fire washes over the city but does not touch it, and their claws are repelled by an invisible barrier they cannot break."

"It is the Sunwell," Gul'dan commented, turning back to take part in the conversation. "The elven source of magic. It gives them immense power."

Of course the warlock would know about such a thing, Doomhammer reasoned. "Is there any way to destroy it, or drain it, or tap it for ourselves?" he asked.

But Gul'dan shook his head. "I have tried," he admitted. "I can feel its power but it is of a kind unfamiliar to me, and I cannot touch it." He scratched at his bristly beard. "I suspect only the elves can gain its power, for it is tied to them and this land."

"Can you use the Altars to break their defenses?" was Doomhammer's next question.

Gul'dan grinned again. "That is one of the things I

am attempting," he replied. "I do not yet know if it will work, but the Altars are crafted from the elves' own Runestones, which were originally powered by the Sunwell. I may be able to use that link in reverse, sending my own magic into their power source and either destroying it or wresting it away from them." It was clear which one the warlock would prefer, and Doomhammer disliked the idea of placing such potency in his hands. But that would still be better than leaving it to these strange, silent, deadly elves.

"Do what you can," he told Gul'dan again. "But breaching the city is secondary. We cannot get in right now but they cannot get out, either." He turned back to Zuluhed, who stood waiting. "The same goes for your dragons. We may need them, particularly if the Alliance has more warriors waiting at Capital City. If you have not managed to break their barrier after a few more days, leave it and send your dragons to join the rest of the Horde." He glanced at Gul'dan, who had already walked beyond hearing range. "And make sure he and his warlocks accompany you."

Zuluhed grinned. "I will drag him with us if I have to order a dragon to snap him up and carry him in its belly," he promised.

Doomhammer nodded. Then he left the Dragonmaw chieftain to speak with his dragon riders, and went to make sure his own Blackrock warriors were ready to set out toward their next target.

* * *

It was another two hours before the Horde finally moved out. Gul'dan and Cho'gall watched as the waves of orc warriors marched from Quel'Thalas, tramping over the charred remains of the trees that had fallen to the dragons' flames. Fully a third of the forest had burned, and that stretch was littered with soot and ash and the stray leaf that had crisped but not yet crumbled. The warriors had camped there, feeling more comfortable in the open air than under the remaining trees even if the ground was littered with bits of bark and leaf and nut, and now clouds of soot rose from the many feet stomping back across and toward the foothills and the mountains beyond. Doomhammer strode at their head, his long legs eating up the distance, his weapon bouncing slightly against his back and legs as he walked. He did not look around, clearly confident that he was in no danger whatsoever.

Gul'dan waited until the last marching orc had vanished from view. Then he turned to Cho'gall. "Are we ready?"

Both of the Twilight's Hammer chieftain's heads grinned. "Ready," he replied.

Gul'dan nodded. "Good. Tell your warriors we march at once. It is a long way back to Southshore." He rubbed at his beard. "Zuluhed is occupied with that elven city, and will not even notice we have gone until it is too late."

"What if he sends his dragons after us?" Cho'gall asked, his normal disregard for danger faltering at the thought of those massive creatures hurtling down upon them.

"He will not," Gul'dan assured the ogre. "He would not dare do so without Doomhammer's orders, and that means first sending a messenger after the rest of the Horde and then waiting for a reply. We will be well beyond his reach by then, and Doomhammer will not be able to spare any of his remaining troops to come after us, not if he wants to take that human city." He laughed. For weeks he had been trying to think of a way to break free of Doomhammer and pursue his own agenda, and the Warchief had actually handed him the perfect solution! He had half-expected Doomhammer to insist he accompany the rest of the Horde on the march, but the elves' resistance had provided him with the perfect excuse to remain behind.

"I will see to the warriors," Cho'gall promised, and turned away, already bellowing orders. Gul'dan nodded and moved off to gather his own gear. He was looking forward to this march. Each step would take him farther from Doomhammer and his careful scrutiny, and bring him closer to his destiny.

Doomhammer crept down the narrow trail that cut into the mountain peak, heading toward the small valley below. It was night and the rest of the Horde was sleeping, but he had urgent business to attend. He moved silently, his boots finding solid purchase on the well-worn rock, one hand holding his hammer so that it did not bounce across his back and glance against the rock walls, the other in front of him to help him feel his way down the path. The moon was half-full overhead, providing him ample light, and he could hear the chirping of some insect nearby. Otherwise the mountains were silent.

He had nearly reached the valley when he heard different noises. The sound of someone—or something—roughly orc-sized moving clumsily toward the valley from the far side. Doomhammer crouched down, using the sides of the trail for cover, and tugged his hammer from his shoulder, holding it before him. He peered out cautiously, waiting as the sounds grew louder. Then he saw movement off to one side and watched as a cloaked figure pulled itself up the last incline and stepped into the valley.

It was not much of a valley, more of a nook, perhaps twenty feet wide and fifteen feet deep, but the rocks rose on every side, providing it with both some shelter and decent concealment. Presumably that was the reason it had been selected.

As Doomhammer watched unmoving the figure leaned against one of the rocks, gasping for breath, then straightened and looked around. "Hello?" the cloaked man called softly.

"I am here," Doomhammer replied, straightening and stepping between the rocks to leave the trail and enter the valley himself. The stranger straightened and gave a small gasp as he approached. Doomhammer could see a longsword at the man's side, well-made and unblemished, and knew this stranger had never used it. Why did he repeatedly find himself dealing with cowards and weaklings and schemers? he wondered. Why not warriors, who were far more direct in their desires and blunt about their intended methods? He had seen the man leading the Alliance armies at Quel'Thalas, and a different man leading them in the Hillsbrad, and had been impressed by both. They would be fighters, following a code of honor and respecting strength and honesty. But of course such men never would have requested a meeting such as this one.

"Y-you are Lord Doomhammer?" the man stammered, shrinking back from him slightly. "You speak Common?"

"I am Orgrim Doomhammer, chieftain of the Black-rock clan and warchief of the Horde and I know your tongue," Doomhammer confirmed. "And you, human? You sent me that message?"

"I am," the man replied, tugging at his hood as if to make sure it still concealed his face. It was of fine cloth, Doomhammer saw, and richly embroidered along the hems. "I thought it might be best if we met before any . . . unpleasantness occurred." He spoke slowly, as if to a child.

"Very well." Doomhammer glanced around, making sure the human had not brought assassins, but if so he was unable to scent or hear them. He had to take the risk that this human really had come alone, as his strange message had claimed.

"I had not expected a human to contact me," Doomhammer admitted quietly, crouching so he could study the man more easily. "Especially in such a manner. Is that how you humans communicate? By use of trained birds?"

"It is one method, yes," the man replied. "I knew none of my people would be able to get close enough to convey a message to you and was not sure how else to reach you, so I sent the bird. Did you kill it?"

Doomhammer nodded, unable to hold back the grin that crossed his face. The man started and broke into a sweat at the sight. "We did not realize it was a messenger until we found the parchment tied to its leg. By then it was too late. I hope you did not want it back."

His companion waved the apology aside with one slender gloved hand. His hand shook but his voice was almost steady. "It was only a bird," he pointed out. "I am more interested in preventing a much larger number of regrettable deaths."

Doomhammer nodded. "So your message said. What do you want from me?"

"Assurances," the man replied.

"Of what sort?"

"I want your word, as a warrior and a leader, that you will keep your warriors in check," the man answered. "No killing, raiding, razing, or other atrocities here in the mountains. Leave our cities and villages intact and do not hound or hunt our people."

Doomhammer considered this, idly rubbing his

hammer's head with one hand. "And what do we gain in return?"

Now the man smiled, a cold expression meant no doubt to be friendly but seeming only conniving. "Free passage," he answered slowly, letting the two words hang in the still night air.

"Oh?" Doomhammer tilted his head, indicating that the man should continue.

"You and your warriors seek to cross the mountains and invade Lordaeron," the man pointed out. "These peaks are treacherous, and it is easy for those who know them to combat much larger forces. Your Horde might still win through, but only with heavy losses. And then you would be weakened in your battle against Lordaeron and its defenders." He smiled again and leaned back against the rock, clearly pleased with his reading of the situation, and his ability to alter it. "I can make sure this region's defenders stay clear of your army," he said confidently. "I will even show you which paths to take to cross the distance more rapidly. Your Horde can pass through the mountains quickly and unopposed."

Doomhammer considered this. "You will clear the way for us," he said out loud, "in exchange for our leaving your lands unharmed in return?"

The man nodded. "That is correct."

Doomhammer stood and stepped forward, until he was less than two feet from the man. This close he could make out some of the stranger's features beneath the hood, and they were narrow and elegant and calculating despite his obvious fear. The man reminded him of Gul'dan in some ways, clever and out for his own gain, but most likely too cowardly to betray a stronger force. "Very well," he said finally. "I agree. Show me the quickest path through these mountains and I will lead my warriors through at speed, without stopping for plunder. When we conquer this land I will place my protection around these mountains, that none may violate them. You and yours shall be safe."

"Excellent." The cloaked man smiled and clapped his hands together like a child. "I knew you would be reasonable." He pulled a rolled-up parchment from his belt and handed it to Doomhammer. "Here is a map of this area," he explained. "I have marked this valley to help orient you."

Doomhammer unrolled the map and studied it. "Yes, this is very clear," he said after a moment.

"Good." The man watched him a second. "I will return to my own people, then," he said after a pause.

Doomhammer nodded but did not say anything, and after a moment the man turned and walked quickly away, ducking back between the rocks and carefully working his way down the cliff beyond the valley. For a moment Doomhammer considered going after him. A single quick blow would finish such a man, and he already had the map. But that would be dishonorable. One of the things he hated about his own people, about what they had become, was their lack of honor. Before, on Draenor, they had been a noble race.

But Gul'dan's treachery had changed all that, making them little more than bloodthirsty savages. Doomhammer was determined to restore his race's pride and purity, and that meant following a strict code of behavior. The man had treated with him in good faith, and Doomhammer would not betray that. He would follow the path the man had marked, and if it proved quick and the human troops did not block them he would honor his half of the agreement.

With a shake of his head Doomhammer rerolled the scroll and stuck it in his own belt, then turned back to toward the trail he had used to reach this valley. He would summon his lieutenants once he returned and show them the route they would take.

"You summoned us, your Majesty?" General Hath, the commander of Alterac's forces, stood at the half-opened door to the map room. Perenolde could see the other army commanders behind the stout general.

"Yes, come in, General, officers," Perenolde said, trying to keep his voice calm beckoning them in. "I have just received some new information about the Horde and its movements, and wished to share it with you."

He saw Hath and a few of the others exchange quick glances, but they said nothing as they followed him over to the impressive tapestry-map covering the far wall. It showed Alterac from edge to edge, with towns and forts picked out in silver thread and the castle itself in gold.

"I have it under good authority," Perenolde began, "that the Horde is indeed heading toward us." Several of the officers gasped. "They apparently plan to invade Lordaeron, and have chosen to cross the mountains and approach Capital City from the north side."

"How far away are they?" Colonel Kavdan asked urgently. "How many of them are there? What sort of weapons are they carrying?" Several of the others were murmuring behind him.

Perenolde held up a hand and the officers fell silent. "I do not know how far away they are," he answered, "though I suspect a day, perhaps two, no more. I have no idea of their numbers, but certainly from all reports they are a formidable force." He smiled, though he knew it was weak. "That, however, is no longer our concern."

General Hath straightened. "Not our concern, your Majesty?" he asked, his breath setting his thick graying mustache aflutter. "But we are part of the Alliance, and have pledged ourselves to battling the Horde together."

"The situation has changed," Perenolde informed him, aware that he was sweating heavily—and that his officers had noticed. "I have reconsidered our options, and have decided to realign ourselves in the conflict. Alterac is no longer a part of the Alliance, effective immediately." He took a deep breath. "Believe me, we are far better off this way."

The officers all looked surprised. "How do you mean, your Majesty?" Kavdan asked.

"I have formed a nonaggression treaty with the

Horde," Perenolde replied. "We will not hinder their progress through the mountains, and in return they will leave Alterac unharmed and untouched."

His officers looked troubled, a few of them even angry or ill. "You would have us conspire with the orcs, your Majesty?" Hath asked softly, disgust evident in his tone.

"Yes, I would have us conspire with them!" Perenolde snapped, losing his composure. "Because I would have us survive!" He let his anger, and his terror, boil over into his words. "Do you have any idea what we are facing? The Horde, the entire Horde, is planning to sweep through these mountains! Through our home! Do you have any idea how many of them there are? Thousands! Tens of thousands!" Hath nodded grudgingly, as did a few of the others—they had seen the same reports he had. "And do you have any idea what these orcs are like? I have seen one of them, no farther away from me than you are now. They are enormous! Nearly as tall as trolls, and twice as wide! Massively muscled, with tusks and fangs—this one carried a hammer it would take three men to lift, and he waved it about as if it were a child's toy! No man could stand against that! They'll kill us all, don't you understand? They've already destroyed Stormwind, and Alterac will be next!"

"But the Alliance—" Hath began. Perenolde laughed bitterly.

"The Alliance what?" he demanded. "Where are they

now? Not here, I'll tell you that! We formed the Alliance to protect our kingdoms against exactly this sort of attack, but here we are with the Horde breathing down our necks and the precious Alliance is nowhere in sight. They've abandoned us, don't you see?" He could hear his voice rising to near-hysteria, and sought to rein it back in. "It is every kingdom for itself now," he told them as calmly as he could manage. "I have to think about Alterac first. The other kings would do the same."

"Yes, but these brutes—" another officer, Trand, started.

"—are monstrous and deadly, yes," Perenolde cut him off. "But they are not incapable of reason. I met with their leader. He spoke Common! He listened, and he agreed to leave us in peace if we do not hinder their passage."

"Can we—can we trust them?" A junior officer named Verand asked, and Perenolde let out a small sigh as he saw a few others nod. If they were asking that, they had already accepted that such a treaty might be necessary—now they were only worried about whether it would be upheld.

"We have no choice," he replied slowly. "They can crush us with barely a thought. If they betray us, we are finished. But if they hold to their word—and I think they will—Alterac will survive. No matter the cost."

"I still do not like this," Hath said stubbornly. "We gave our word to the other nations." He looked uncertain, however, and Perenolde knew the general was considering the situation and realizing that this might in fact be their only hope for survival.

"You do not have to like it," Perenolde replied sharply. "You only have to obey. I am king here, and I have made my decision. You have sworn oaths to me, and you will abide by them." He knew that would not stop them if they disagreed, but he hoped he had managed to convince them, at least enough to let their fealty sway them the rest of the way.

Hath studied him for a moment. "As you say, your Majesty," he stated finally. "I will obey." The others nodded as well.

Perenolde smiled. "Good. And as for the Alliance, I will accept any and all consequences personally." He turned back toward the map. "Now then, the Horde will come through here, here, and here," he said, indicating the southern passes on the map. He was annoyed to discover that his hand was shaking. "We have merely to leave these passes unmanned and the Horde will pass by without our ever encountering a single orc."

Hath was studying the locations. "They must be planning to strike Lordaeron from the north," he mused, tracing a line across the edge of the tapestry to where the city would lay if the image continued. "I would not have taken that approach myself, but then I don't have their numbers—or their arrogance." He turned back to Perenolde, his expression dubious. "The men may object, your Majesty," he stated coldly. "They may feel this is a betrayal of our oaths, or worse." His tone left little doubt that he agreed with them. "If they revolt, we will be unable to stop them."

Perenolde considered that. "Very well," he said after a moment. "Tell the soldiers that the Horde is planning to use only the three northernmost passes. If any ask how you acquired this information, hint that we had scouts and spies discover it at the cost of their own lives." He nodded, pleased with his own cleverness. "That should keep everyone occupied and safely out of the way."

Hath nodded brusquely. "I will station our men there at once, your Majesty," he promised crisply.

"That's fine." Perenolde favored the general with the warmest smile he could manage, to show that all was forgiven. "Now you'd best get them moving. We don't want to risk the orcs arriving while our troops are still moving into position."

The officers saluted and filed out of the map room—all except Hath.

"What is it, General?" Perenolde asked, not having to fake the weariness in his voice.

"There's been a messenger, sire," the general answered. "From the Alliance. He arrived while you were . . . resting." Hath gave a pointed glance at the cloak that lay tossed on a chair in the corner, his look saying clearly that he knew Perenolde had been outside the castle, and why. "He's waiting outside, sire."

"Show him in at once," Perenolde replied, striding over to the chair and scooping up his cloak. "Did you speak with him?"

"Only to ascertain who sent him," Hath assured him. "I knew you would want to hear his news first." The general was already at the map room door when he said this, and he beckoned to someone waiting outside. A young man in travel-stained leathers entered, looking down at the floor nervously.

"Your Majesty," the young man said, glancing up briefly and then away again. "I bring you greetings and a message from Lord Anduin Lothar, Commander of the Alliance."

Perenolde nodded and crossed to stand near the youth, tugging his cloak around him as he moved. "Thank you, General, that will be all for now," he told Hath, who looked relieved as he obediently left the room, shutting the door behind him. "Now, young man," Perenolde continued, turning back to the messenger, "what is this message you carry?"

"Lord Lothar says you are to bring your troops to Lordaeron," the young man replied nervously. "The Horde is likely to attack the city there, and your forces must aid in its defense."

"I see." Perenolde nodded, rubbing at his chin with the fingers of one hand. He reached out and laid the other arm across the youth's shoulder. "And does he expect you to report back on our progress?" he asked.

The messenger nodded.

"I see," Perenolde said again. "That is a shame." He turned toward the youth, his arm tightening to tug him closer, and stabbed with the dagger in his other hand. The blade passed up below the ribs and into the young man's heart, and he jerked, blood spilling from his mouth, before collapsing. Perenolde caught him before he could hit the floor, and eased him down.

"It would have been far better if the message had been a written one," Perenolde said softly to the corpse, wiping his dagger on the body before resheathing it. Then he dragged the body across the room and to the garderobe in the corner, tipping it in and listening to the dull thuds as it bumped the walls on the way down. As an afterthought he removed his cloak, now blood-spattered beyond any hope of cleaning, and tossed it in as well. A shame—he'd quite liked the embroidery.

After waiting a minute, Perenolde closed the curtain over the garderobe and walked back across the room. If Hath was waiting outside he would tell the general that the messenger had needed to leave so urgently he had allowed the use of his private exit. Otherwise he would simply tell Hath next time they met that the young man had returned to the Alliance. And of course his message had been simply to hold fast against the Horde. Perenolde smiled. He could all but guarantee that no orc would force its way past their defenses. The other mountain paths were another matter entirely.

Bradok clutched to the reins but not out of fear. He had forgotten all that the first time his dragon had taken wing, carrying him high into the sky. It was amazing, soaring among the clouds, and Bradok, who had always been a dutiful warrior but never more than content, had suddenly discovered true happiness. He was meant for this, meant to sail the skies, his massive red dragon beating its wings, the wind rushing through the crest of his hair. He still remembered the thrill of seeing flames spew from his dragon's mouth, and watching the trees burst from the sudden heat that incinerated them as soon as it touched them.

Glancing down, Bradok saw a stretch of silver amid the greens and browns of this rich world. That was the sea, he knew, the same one they had crossed after sacking that other kingdom not long ago.

Tapping his dragon with his heels, Bradok urged his mount lower and the dragon responded, furling its wings and diving down in a steep, exhilarating rush. The sea swelled in Bradok's vision, stretching almost to the horizon, and now he could see the dark shapes strung out where the sea met the shore. Those would be their ships, the ones that had carried the Horde from the other continent to this one. Bradok hated ships. He wasn't overly fond of water, either. But the air, that was a wonderful thing.

Pulling his dragon out of the dive, Bradok coasted over the ships, seeing the poor orcs seated in the benches all down their lengths, pulling on the long oars that kept the boat moving. An ogre stood near the center of each ship, beating time on a massive drum, and the orcs pulled in time, their steady strokes sending the dark ships sliding back into the water.

Bradok paused abruptly, and wheeled his dragon around for a second look. Yes, he had been right the first time. The ships were leaving the shore and returning to the sea. But they were supposed to be sitting idle, in case the Horde needed them again. Why were they moving now?

Glancing around, Bradok spied a familiar figure on the lead boat. It was Gul'dan, the warlock. Bradok had feared him, as did most of the orcs, but not anymore. He was a dragon rider now. What could he possibly have to be afraid of?

Angling his dragon around, Bradok swooped toward the lead ship. Gul'dan turned toward him as he approached.

"Why are you taking the boats?" Bradok shouted, waving his free arm while his dragon kept pace with the ship. The warlock looked puzzled, and held up both hands in confusion. Bradok coaxed his dragon closer. "You need to turn the boats around! The Horde is in Lordaeron, not across the sea!" he shouted again. Still Gul'dan gestured that he could not hear him. This time Bradok managed to bring his dragon almost on top of the ship, so he was barely ten feet from the warlock. "I said—" Suddenly Gul'dan's hand shot forward, a green ray lancing from it to Bradok's chest. He felt a burst of intense pain, and sensed his lungs tighten and his heart falter, then gasped as both stopped working altogether. The world turned dark with a rush, and Bradok toppled from his saddle, narrowly missing the ship and plummeting toward the waves. His last thought was that at least he'd had a chance to fly.

Gul'dan sneered as he watched the dragon rider's body disappear beneath the water. He'd needed the fool to get close before his magic would work fast enough to prevent retaliation. He'd also worried what the dragon itself might do with its rider dead, and watched warily as the massive red beast reared up, tilting its head back to release a fierce cry, and then beat its wings hard and shot up into the sky. Gul'dan watched long enough to make sure the dragon was not circling around for an attack and then turned back to watching the water flow past the ship's prow.

He didn't see the second figure soaring high above. Torgus had been racing Bradok before his friend had spotted the ships, and had seen everything. Now he wheeled his dragon around and headed back toward Quel'Thalas at top speed. Zuluhed would want to know what had happened, and Torgus suspected he would be flying off to inform the rest of the Horde, and perhaps even Doomhammer himself, as well.

The passes were utterly deserted, as promised, and Doomhammer led his warriors through them at a fast run. He had thought the cloaked stranger would keep his word, and glad to see his guess had been correct, but still this route was dangerous. With such narrow stone passes it would only take a handful of warriors to block their way, and once a few bodies piled up each pass would be too choked to allow passage of any sort. So he hurried his troops along, knowing he would be happier once they had left this cold mountain region far behind.

It took them two days to cross the snow-covered mountains and descend into foothills on the far side. In that time the orcs did not see a single human. Some of the warriors even grumbled that they had missed the chance to kill anyone during their passage, but their chieftains assured them they would get their chance.

On the second day the front ranks of the Horde poured down from the mountains. Doomhammer was leading them as always, and he stopped to admire the scene before him. Beyond the foothills stretched an enormous lake, its waters glistening silvery green in the early light. On the far side rose more mountains, marching north-south on a slight angle. The mountains the orcs had just crossed were similar except they angled east as they rose. These new peaks angled west, and together the two ranges formed a gargantuan V, with the lake filling the center. And on the lake's northern shore was a majestic walled city.

"Capital City." Doomhammer studied it a moment, then raised his hammer high above him with both hands and bellowed a warcry. The warriors of the Horde took up the cry, and soon the hills around them were echoing with their rage and joy and bloodlust. Doomhammer laughed. The city would know he and his people were here, but after that cry they would be quaking in their boots. And the Horde would be upon them before they could recover.

"To the city!" Doomhammer shouted, raising his hammer again. "We will crush it, and with it the heart of the opposition! Onward, warriors! Let us bring the fight to them while our warcry still echoes in their ears!"

And Doomhammer charged down out of the foothills and onto the plain, angling up and across as he focused upon the massive walled city that was his target.

CHAPTER SIXTEEN

"Sire! Sire, the orcs are coming!"

King Terenas looked up, startled, as Morev the guard commander burst into his throneroom. "What?" He stood, ignoring the panicked cries from the nobles and commoners gathered there to seek audience with him, and beckoned the commander forward. "The orcs? Here?"

"Yes, sire," the man answered. Morev was a seasoned veteran, a warrior Terenas had known since his youth, and it was shocking to see him pale and shaking. "They must have come across the mountains—they are pouring onto the far side of the lake even as we speak!"

Terenas brushed past the commander and strode out of the throne room, moving rapidly down the hall and up a short flight of stairs to the nearest balcony, which stood off his wife's drawing room. Lianne was in there with their daughter, Calia, and her ladies in waiting, and looked up, surprised, as he entered and walked right past her, Morev trailing behind him.

Throwing up the windows beyond, Terenas stepped out onto the balcony—and stopped, stunned. Normally from here he had a breathtaking view of the mountains across the lake. Those were still the same, but the strip of green he usually saw between water and rock was now black and he could see it shifting as he watched, like ground being churned up from beneath. The Horde had indeed arrived.

"How did this happen?" he demanded of Morev, who had stepped out as well and was staring at the sight, his mouth open. "They must have come through Alterac—why did Perenolde not stop them cold?"

"They must have overwhelmed him, sire," Morev answered dismissively, even in his terror showing his opinion of Alterac's king and soldiers. "Those mountain passes are narrow and a competent troop could have held the Horde back, but not if they were following incompetent orders."

Terenas frowned and shook his head. He shared Morev's opinion—he had never liked Perenolde, who had always struck him as selfish and scheming. But Hath, Perenolde's general, was a competent commander and a solid warrior in his own right. He would have assembled a solid defense—although if Perenolde gave an order, even a foolish one, Hath would probably obey it.

"Send messengers to Alterac," he decided finally. "And to the Alliance army as well, letting them know our situation. We'll find out what happened later," Terenas decided, not bothering to point out that this would require them to survive until then. "First things first. Rally the guards, sound the alarm, and get everyone inside the gates. We don't have much time." He glanced again across the lake, where the darkness was already creeping down the far bank and around the water. No, not much time at all.

Pigeons were released to the other Alliance leaders and to the last known location of the Alliance army, in the Hinterlands. One of those pigeons flew straight to Stromgarde, and its message was quickly untied and brought straight to Thoras Trollbane, Stromgarde's gruff master.

"What?" Trollbane shouted when he had read the message. He had been drinking ale from a heavy wooden mug and now he hurled the mug at the far wall, where it shattered, leaving a streak of ale and wood splinters down to the floor. "That fool! What did he do, let them through?" Trollbane despised Perenolde—not only were they neighbors and thus rivals over borderlands but he personally disliked the man. He was too oily, too smooth by far. But even an arrogant, overdressed idiot like Perenolde should have been able to block an invading army! Perhaps not stop them completely—if the Horde was as numerous as Lothar had claimed, and as subsequent reports had confirmed, they could muscle their way through regardless—but at least slow them down significantly, inflict heavy damage, and warn Lordaeron early enough for them to prepare properly. With the orcs already on the plains by the lake, Terenas would not have time to do much more than close his gates and brace for the first assault.

Trollbane stood and began pacing, the message slip still clenched unnoticed in his fist. He wanted to go to his friend's aid, but wasn't sure that would be the best course of action. Terenas was a fine strategist, and his guards were among the finest in the land, his gates and walls strong and thick. They could hold out against the first wave, he was sure of that. The danger lay in letting the full Horde roll down from the mountains and swarm Capital City with sheer numbers.

"Damn him!" Trollbane beat his fist against the arm of his heavy chair as he passed it. "Perenolde should have held them! He should at least have warned us! Even he is not that incompetent!" He paused mid-stride as another thought struck him. Perenolde had never been enthusiastic about the Alliance. He and Graymane had been the only two to resist, Trollbane remembered. He thought back to the meetings in Capital City, with Lothar and Terenas and the others. Yes. Graymane had spurned the idea, but mainly because he boasted that Gilneas could crush anyone foolish enough to invade them. But Perenolde had disliked the idea of combat. Trollbane had always thought his neighbor a coward at heart, and something of a bully—he was perfectly willing to fight when he knew he held the upper hand, but hated to engage in combat if it put him at any risk. And Perenolde had been the one to suggest they try negotiating first.

"That fool! That traitorous little fool!" Trollbane kicked his chair hard enough to send it skittering across the granite floor. He had done it, hadn't he? He had negotiated with the Horde! Trollbane knew he was right. Perenolde cared nothing for others, only for his own hide. He would happily make a deal with demons if it kept him and his own lands safe. And that was exactly what he had done. It all made perfect sense now. The reason the Horde had made it through the mountains without anyone raising the alarm, the reason Perenolde had not responded or warned anyone. He had let them pass. Presumably for some promise of leniency or continued autonomy after the war.

"Rargh!' Infuriated beyond words, Trollbane snatched his axe from where it hung on the column beside his chair and hacked at the table in front of him, shattering it with a single blow. "I'll kill him!" he bellowed. His warriors and nobles shrank back, alarmed, and only their reaction reminded Trollbane that he was not alone. And that personal vengeance would have to wait. The war came first.

"Assemble the troops," he instructed his startled guards. "We are going to Alterac."

"But, sire," his guard captain replied, "we've already sent half our troops out with the main Alliance army!"

Trollbane frowned. "Well, there's nothing for it. Grab everyone you can find."

"Are we lending them aid, sire?" one of the nobles asked.

"In a manner of speaking," Trollbane replied, hefting his axe again and grinning at the man. "In a manner of speaking."

Anduin Lothar raised his visor and glanced around, wiping grit and sweat from his eyes with the back of his hand as he idly drew his sword across the body of a fallen orc, cleaning the blade of the blood and gore that coated its length.

"Is that the last of them, sir?" one of his soldiers asked.

"I don't know, son," Lothar replied honestly, his eyes still roving the trees. "I hope so, but I wouldn't count on it."

"How many of these things are there?" another soldier demanded, pulling his axe free of the orc at his feet. The small clearing was littered with bodies, not all of them orcish. It had been a nasty little skirmish, and the branches above were too close for the Wildhammers to bring their gryphons to bear so it had been entirely up to Lothar and his men. They had won, but only because the small band of orcs had apparently wandered away from the rest of the orc forces.

"Too many," Lothar replied absently. He grinned at his men then. "But fewer now, eh?" They smiled back and Lothar felt a surge of pride. Some of these men were from Lordaeron, some from Stromgarde, one or two from Gilneas and even Alterac, and a few had come with him from Stormwind. But over the past few weeks they had set their regional differences aside. They were now Alliance soldiers, and fought together as brothers, and he was proud of them. If the rest of the army meshed as well as this one group did, there was hope for them all, both in this war and in the peace he hoped would follow afterward.

Then he caught a flicker of movement off to one side. "Be ready," he warned, dropping his visor back down and sinking into a wary crouch, his sword rising to point toward the motion. But the figure that burst through the trees was not an orc but a human, one of his own soldiers.

"Sir!" the man gasped, clearly winded. He did not seem harmed, however, and his sword was still by his side. "Messages, sir!" Then Lothar realized the man had a scrap of parchment in one hand, and was holding it out to him.

"Thank you," he said, taking the message. A soldier handed the messenger a waterskin, which he gratefully accepted. But Lothar was busy reading the words scribed onto the small scrap, and the warriors around him tensed as they saw his jaw tighten beneath his helm.

"What is it, sir?" one of them asked finally, as Lothar glanced up, balling the parchment between finger and thumb and flicking it away like a troublesome insect. "Is there a problem?"

Lothar nodded, still digesting the information he had

just received. "The Horde has made its way to Lordaeron," he said softly, eliciting a gasp from several soldiers. "They are probably attacking the capital even now."

"What can we do?" One of the men—one of those from Lordaeron, Lothar remembered—asked urgently. "We need to set out right away!"

But Lothar shook his head. "There's too much distance between us," he told the soldier sadly. "We'd never reach it in time." He sighed. "No. We need to finish our work here, to make sure the orcs they left in the Hinterlands are dead or driven off. We cannot allow the Horde to retain a foothold here, where they could then sweep back up or down to anywhere else on the continent."

His men nodded, though they did not look pleased about the prospect of wandering the woods seeking strays while their friends and families faced the rest of the Horde alone. Lothar could hardly blame them. "Turalyon and the rest of the Alliance army are already on their way," he assured them, making several warriors look up hopefully. "He will come to the city's aid." He gripped his sword tightly. "And when we are done here we will march to Capital City and mop up any orcs that have fled his attack."

The men cheered at that, and Lothar smiled though he still felt cold. He knew they liked the idea both of helping after all and of the Alliance being so victorious all that was left was the cleanup. He hoped it would be that easy.

"Enough distractions," he warned his men after allowing them a few seconds. "Let's make sure there aren't any other orc bands near here, and then we'll head back to Aerie Peak to regroup." The soldiers obediently nodded and raised their weapons, falling into rough ranks. Lothar took the lead, and together they set off into the trees again, the messenger walking in their midst.

"Here they come!"

King Terenas glanced down and grimaced. The orc Horde had crossed the lake—sharp-sighted archers assured him they had built rough bridges but from here it had looked as if they'd simply swarmed across the water like ants—and were now rapidly approaching the city's walls. He was still amazed by their sheer numbers. And from what he could see up here on the ramparts, they were massive brutes as well, easily as big as the largest of men and broader, with powerful muscles and large bestial heads. He did not see any siege weapons, at least, other than a thick log that was clearly intended for a battering ram, but the orcs carried what he thought were large hammers, axes, and thick swords, and he was sure they had ropes and grapples as well.

Well, Capital City's walls were as sturdy as ever. No foe had ever breached its defenses, and Terenas was determined to maintain that record.

They had not been able to prepare fully, of course. The people had been easy enough to gather, since most lived within the walls already. Livestock had been more problematic and some animals had simply been abandoned to their fate, as had all but the smallest and most precious possessions. The guards had done their best to make sure everyone and everything was inside before closing and sealing the gates, but most people had fled with little more than the clothes on their backs and whatever tools and other possessions they'd had to hand. Their homes would surely be destroyed by the Horde, and Terenas knew it would take some time to rebuild them afterward. Assuming they drove the orcs back and were able to leave the city once more.

He glanced along the ramparts, where his guards and soldiers stood ready. So few men to defend such large walls! But most of his soldiers had marched off with Lothar and the rest of the Alliance. Nor did Terenas regret that decision. The Horde had needed to be stopped, and Lothar had needed every soldier that could be spared for his army. Of course, he had not expected the Horde to strike at them here, and certainly not without the Alliance forces either blocking their path or marching after them to aid in the city's defense. But even if Capital City fell, if the Alliance won in the end it would be a small price to pay.

That did not mean he was about to surrender the city, however. Terenas glanced down again, and judged the orcs close enough now. He could see their tusks from here, and the tassels and bones and medals that hung around many of their necks and arms and heads, clearly trophies of previous battles. Well, they would find this fight more challenging than their previous encounters. No matter what happened, the Horde would remember this fight.

"Hot oil!" Terenas shouted, and down the line Morev and others nodded. They tipped the large cauldrons over the ramparts, letting the boiling oil pour down in sheets just beyond the walls. The leading orcs had almost reached the walls by then, and the oil spilled across them, drenching them utterly. Many screamed in pain as it burned away their flesh, and the entire front rank crumpled, writhing and twitching. A few staggered away but most did not get up again.

"Prepare more oil!" Terenas ordered, and servants scurried to obey, using stout poles to lift the heavy cauldrons and carry them away. It would take time to refill the cauldrons and then reheat them and bring them back up to the ramparts, but he doubted the Horde was going anywhere. This would not be a quick skirmish or a fast conflict—it would most likely be a long siege, and he thanked the Holy Light they had sufficient stores of food and water for several weeks. Oil they would run out of after another dousing or two, but it was merely the opening move in their defense. Terenas had other tricks to show these unruly orcs who dared attack his home.

Thoras Trollbane stalked across the mountains as easily as if he were one of the region's sturdy rams, his heavy hob-nailed boots finding solid purchase on the rough gray granite. His men moved behind him, each one as well-versed in mountaineering as in combat. Strom-garde was a mountain kingdom, and its children grew up learning to climb the rock faces and scale the peaks.

Ahead of him lay the first of the Alterac mountain passes. Trollbane could already see figures moving through the falling snow, large heavy-set figures marching steadily but awkwardly. Clearly the orcs of the Horde were not accustomed to the altitude or the peaks. The passes themselves were chiseled carefully out of the mountain range for just such people, allow-ing trade and communication with both Alterac and Stromgarde's lower neighbors. For themselves Troll-bane and his people did not need such conveniences. They preferred to scale the heights wherever they wished, rather than being trapped in a long chute like the one before them. The passes were far too easy to blockade—and to ambush.

Gesturing to his men, Trollbane crouched, his axe at the ready. Not yet, not yet . . . now! Leaping over the edge he landed solidly in the pass between two orcs, taking them by surprise. His axe flashed, carving one's head from its body and then catching the other in the throat on the backswing. Both fell, and the orcs on either side of them stumbled and snarled, raising their own weapons. But four of Trollbane's warriors dove into the pass just then, two on either side of him, and hacked apart the next orcs in line. Then more of his men jumped down and attacked the orcs beyond those already falling, and so on. In a matter of minutes two dozen orcs lay dead and the pass was clogged with bodies.

Trollbane and his men pushed the dead orcs, already stiffening from the cold, into a single stack that rose to the top of the pass. Then he stationed ten of his men there to guard the makeshift blockade and climbed back out, taking the rest of his warriors with him.

"Good," Trollbane told them as they worked their way to the north. "That's one taken care of." The next pass was less than an hour's climb away.

They found that pass also crowded with marching orcs, and attacked it in the same way. Trollbane could see that the orcs were fearsome warriors, large and strong and tough, but they had no experience with cold or mountains and were not used to foes leaping down on them. The second pass was taken as easily as the first one, and so was the third. The fourth pass proved slightly more difficult because it was the widest of them—four men could walk abreast here, or three orcs, and so Trollbane and his soldiers jumped down four at a time. But soon enough it was blocked off as well, and they rolled boulders down to make sure it stayed impassable.

The fifth pass was clear, at least of orcs. Trollbane found warriors stationed there but they were human, dressed in the orange of Alterac, and they were stationed above the pass as well as within it.

"Hold!" one of the Alterac soldiers called out, spotting them and leveling his spear in their direction. "State your name and business here!" Several of his fellows rushed to support him.

"Thoras Trollbane, king of Stromgarde," Trollbane replied curtly. He glared at the soldiers, though he knew they were only following orders. "Where is Perenolde?"

"The king is in his castle," the same soldier replied haughtily. "And you are trespassing on our lands."

"And the orcs?" Trollbane asked. "Are they trespassers, or guests?"

"The orcs shall not pass us," another soldier declared. "We will defend this pass with our lives!"

"Good," Trollbane said, "only they're not at this pass. They're at the four south of here."

That startled the soldiers. "We were told to guard here," one of them said, looking confused. "This was where they said the orcs would try to pass."

"Well, they didn't," Trollbane snapped. "Fortunately my men are blocking the other passes now, but many already made it through. To Lordaeron." One of the soldiers was older, clearly a veteran, and his face paled as that statement sank in. It was to him that Trollbane addressed his next question. "Where is Hath?"

"General Hath is at the next pass, with the bulk of our forces," the soldier replied. He considered for a second before offering, "I can take you there."

Trollbane knew the way, but he also knew it would be easier to get to speak with Hath if he arrived with an escort. So he nodded, and gestured for his men to follow him and the Alterac soldier.

It took another hour to reach the next pass. This one was the widest path through Alterac, easily broad enough for two full carts to pass one another without brushing the walls, and it made good sense to station most of the soldiers to guard it. If the orcs were going north instead of south. Trollbane spotted Hath speaking with several junior officers but waited until the soldier who had brought them had hailed the stout general.

"General Hath, sir!" the man called. "Visitors from Stromgarde to see you, sir!"

Hath glanced up and frowned when he spotted Trollbane. "Thank you, sergeant," he said, moving to join them and returning the veteran's parting salute. "Your Majesty," he said gravely, nodding to Trollbane.

"General." Trollbane had always liked Hath. The man was a solid soldier and a good tactician, and a decent fellow. He had always disliked fighting him and hoped that wouldn't be necessary this time. "The orcs are pouring through your southern passes," he said bluntly. "We blocked them for you."

Hath paled. "Our southern passes? You're sure?" He waved away Trollbane's nod. "Of course you are. But why? The king told me personally they would passing to the north, not the south. That's why he set us to guard these passes instead."

Trollbane glanced around them. None of the Alterac soldiers were close enough to hear him as he lowered his voice. "You're a fine soldier and a good commander, Hath," he said softly, "but you've always been a terrible liar. You knew they were heading south, didn't you?"

The Alterac general sighed and nodded. "Perenolde made arrangements with the Horde somehow," he admitted. "Free passage in exchange for protection."

Trollbane nodded. That was what he had suspected. "And you went along with this?" he demanded.

Hath stiffened. "We were faced with annihilation!" he replied sharply. "They would have crushed us all, and slaughtered our people! And there was no one to aid us!" He shook his head. "Perenolde made the choice to protect Alterac first and foremost. What he did may not be decent, but it saved lives!"

"And what of the lives in Lordaeron?" Trollbane asked softly. "They will die because you allowed the Horde to pass unhindered."

Hath glared at him. "They are soldiers! They know the risk! The Horde would have killed our families, our children! It is not the same!"

Trollbane nodded, feeling some sympathy toward the older man. "No, it is not," he agreed. "And your loyalty to your people is commendable. But if the Horde conquers Lordaeron they will control the entire continent. What makes you think you will be safe?"

Hath sighed. "I do not know," he admitted. "Their leader gave Perenolde his word, but I do not know how far such a creature may be trusted." He shook his head. "I told Perenolde we should abide by our oaths to the other nations, but he countermanded that. I have sworn fealty to him, and I must obey. Plus I thought he might be right, that this might be our only chance for survival."

He frowned. "But survival of the race is more important than that of any one kingdom. And if we do not have our honor, we have nothing at all." He raised his chin, a stern expression settling over his features. "Well, I will reclaim our honor," he declared. Then he turned and shouted at his men. "Corporal! Gather the men! March everyone to the southern passes at top speed! We are going to assist our Stromgarde friends in defending those passes and pushing back the orc Horde!"

"But sir—" the officer started to object, but Hath shouted him down.

"Now, soldier!" he bellowed, and the officer saluted quickly and leaped to obey. Then Hath turned back to Trollbane. "He is in the castle," the general said shortly. He did not have to explain whom he meant. "His personal guard will still be there, but there are only twenty of them. I can draw him out."

But Trollbane shook his head. "We do not have time to worry about him now. Besides," he pointed out, "if I go there, it is an invasion. And if you go, it is treason." He frowned. "We will let the Alliance settle matters with Perenolde later. For now all that matters is blocking the Horde."

The general nodded. "Thank you." Then he turned and joined his officers in rallying the men.

"Damn it, we're too late!" Turalyon reined in and stared out over the valley below.

They had ridden hard, he and Khadgar and the other

cavalry members, with the troops marching along behind them. It had seemed best to pass west through the foothills of Hearthglen and then emerge north of Capital City so they could swing back down and come at the city from the wide plain behind it, where its main gates lay. Now he wasn't sure the better positioning had been worth the added travel time.

Turalyon had also hoped to gather additional troops from Thoras Trollbane, but Stromgarde was simply too far out of the way. Turalyon had considered detouring, but the news that the Horde had also cut through the mountains and had done so before them spurred him to keep moving instead. They had to reach Capital City in time!

But now he looked down from the trailing edge of the mountain range, across the valley that fed into Lordaeron and the lake below it, and saw that he had failed. The Horde was already there, spreading across the valley and around the proud city like a spray of leaves about an autumn tree.

"They haven't breached the walls," Alleria pointed out, standing beside him. She and the other elves, both warriors and rangers, had kept up with the horses easily, and both she and Lor'themar Theron had come forward with him to see what lay before them. "It is not too late to aid them."

"No, you're right," Turalyon admitted, shoving his disappointment aside and studying the situation more dispassionately. "This battle is not yet lost, and with our aid Capital City will not fall." He rubbed at his chin. "This may even work out to our advantage," he said softly, considering the matter more fully. "The Horde does not know we are here yet, and we can trap them between us." He frowned. "We should let Terenas know we're here, though, so we can coordinate our attacks and so he does not feel he has been abandoned."

Theron nodded, eyeing the mass of orcs teeming below and beyond them. "A good plan," he agreed. "But how would you suggest we reach the city? No one could get past those warriors unharmed, not even an elf."

Alleria nodded. "If this were a forest I might," she admitted, "but here on an open plain there is no chance for cover. It would be suicide to attempt it."

Khadgar, sitting his horse on Turalyon's other side, grinned at the three of them. "I can get across," he assured them, laughing at their expressions. "With a little help," he added, glancing at a short, tattooed figure who had alighted on the rocks beside them.

"Sire!"

Terenas glanced up and saw a soldier shouting and pointing beyond the walls. Thinking the orcs had massed for another attack, he glanced out, following the man's gesture, but the soldier was pointing up rather than down. Terenas looked, and almost gasped as he saw a dark figure soaring toward them.

"Ready archers," he called, staring at the shape, "but hold fire until my command." Something seemed strange about it. Why send a single flier of any sort, when there were thousands upon thousands of orcs smashing against the walls below? Was it a scout? A spy? Or something else?

The archers positioned themselves, longbows drawn and arrows nocked, and waiting patiently. The shape grew closer. Now Terenas could see that it was a gryphon, though far wilder and more beautiful than the heraldric symbols would have led him to believe. Its feathers glowed gold and violet and red in the sunlight, and its fierce head turned, birdlike, to glance around with wide golden eyes as it approached.

And a figure sat upon its back, holding reins and riding a saddle as if upon a horse.

The rider was big, but did not seem large enough to be an orc. And it was wearing clothing, far more than the green-skinned warriors below. Terenas stared, and then let out a breath of relief as he caught a glimpse of violet. That wasn't armor, it was robes, and that could only mean one thing.

"Lower your weapons!" he called to his archers. "It is a wizard of Dalaran!"

The gryphon swooped toward them, its mighty wings beating, and then it was overhead, circling back even as the archers turned back to watching the orcs below. The rider was clearly searching for a place to land, and finally settled on the nearby corner tower, which had a wide flat circle for cauldrons and ballistae and signal fires. Terenas strode in that direction, Morev right behind him, and reached the tower just as the gryphon touched down and folded its wings along its body.

"Well, it's good to know I haven't forgotten how," the rider announced as he swung one leg over and dropped from the saddle. "Thank you," Terenas heard him murmur to the gryphon, which cawed in reply. Then the wizard turned, his short white beard visible now, and Terenas recognized him.

"Khadgar!" he said, reaching out and clasping the mage's hand. "What are you doing here, and on such a creature?"

"I come bearing good news," the old-seeming mage replied, grinning. He looked tired but otherwise well. "Turalyon and his forces are just the other side of the northern valley," he informed Terenas, gratefully accepting a wineskin Morev offered and taking a quick swallow. "We will attack the Horde from behind and draw them away from you."

"Excellent!" Terenas clapped his hands together, pleased for the first time in days. "With the Alliance army here we can attack them from two fronts and batter the orcs between us!"

"That was Turalyon's plan," the mage agreed cheerfully. "Kurdran loaned me the use of this gryphon so I could reach you and coordinate. I am just grateful I still retain the knowledge Medivh gave me on how to handle one."

"Come," Terenas told him. "My servants will see to

the gryphon—they will get it water, and I am sure we can find something for it to eat. Let us talk about what Sir Turalyon thinks we should do next, and how we can make these foul orcs rue the day they dared raise arms against our city."

"Charge!" Turalyon led the way, hammer held before him like a lance, spurring his horse up out of the water and onto the bank and toward the massed orc army. Many of the orcs were still concentrating on the city walls, which they had yet to dent for all their ferocity, and only a few heard the sound of his horse's hooves and turned to look. One of those opened his mouth to shout a warning, but Turalyon's hammer caught him full across the jaw, shattering it and snapping his neck from the force of the blow. The orc dropped and Turalyon's horse trampled him.

Behind him rode the rest of the cavalry, and the foot soldiers were marching after them, having crossed the plain north of the city. Now they advanced upon the Horde, which turned to meet them.

And that was when the city's ballistae fired, raining arrows and rocks down upon the orcs' backs.

Turalyon led his mounted soldiers into the Horde's front ranks and through them, circling around and back again. And then the city's defenders struck a second time.

The orcs milled about now, unsure what to do. When they faced the city the Alliance soldiers struck them from behind. When they turned toward the soldiers the city guard attacked them. They had yet to breach the walls and so they couldn't retreat into Capital City, but they couldn't get to the lake on the plains and the mountains without first going through the Alliance soldiers. No matter which way they turned, orcs died.

Unfortunately, the Horde had bodies to spare. A row of massive orc warriors marched forward, weapons at the ready, and Turalyon was forced to pull his riders back. The elven archers released a volley of arrows that rained down upon the orcs, felling many, but new warriors took their place at once. The orcs began throwing themselves at the Alliance army, forcing them to backpedal or be crushed beneath heavy orc bodies, and step by step Turalyon found himself and his men pushed back toward the water. Once they were out of reach half the remaining Horde soldiers turned their attention back to Capital City itself. They hurled themselves at the walls, quickly exhausting the city's supply of oil and rocks and gravel and other items to drop on attackers.

The ballistae could not be aimed at anyone up against the walls, not without doing more damage to the city than the invaders could, and so the orcs were now safe to scale the walls and batter at the gates. Thus far the gates were holding, but they were taking a terrible beating. And orc warriors were reaching the ramparts and pulling themselves up and over, grinning. Most were blocked and stabbed or bashed as they reached the top but before they could climb over, but a few made it and began attacking the guards, throwing them into disarray and leaving gaps in the wall's defenders. The first wave to climb over all died, but more followed them, and now the bodies were piling up and providing the orcs with some cover as they scaled the walls, giving them room to plant their feet and ready their weapons before attacking the guards.

"This isn't working!" Khadgar shouted to Turalyon as they backed their horses across a rough bridge the orcs must have built to traverse the lake. "We don't have enough fighters to overwhelm them like this! We need to try something else!"

"I'm open to suggestions!" Turalyon replied, battering a lunging orc with his hammer. "Can't you use your magic against them?"

"Yes, but it won't do much good," Khadgar answered, stabbing his sword into an orc that came too close. "I can kill them but only a few at a time. I could summon a storm but it wouldn't help, and it would leave me too drained to work more magic later."

Turalyon nodded. "Let's get the men back across the lake, and hold this bridge!" he told his friend, brandishing his hammer again even as he used his shield to knock an orc into the water that flowed beneath them. "Then we can wait until they've lost interest in us and attack again while their back is turned."

Khadgar nodded, too busy defending himself to speak. He hoped this new plan would work. Because otherwise the Horde would simply burn the bridge and keep pounding on the city gates until they collapsed. And once the gates went they were inside the city and would be impossible to remove. Khadgar had seen the orcs take a city once before, at Stormwind. He did not want to see it happen again.

"The gates are starting to give way!"

Terenas shook his head as if that would make the cry go away. He was too busy to see for himself, however. An orc had climbed the wall not far from where he stood watching the battle below and was advancing on him now, grinning widely enough to show its sharp tusks and swinging its heavy warhammer in slow arcs. Terenas reluctantly picked up a fallen sword, painfully aware that he was no fighter.

Someone appeared at his side, and he recognized Morev with some relief. The guard commander carried a long spear, and jabbed at the orc, forcing him back. "You should go see the gates, sire," he said calmly, poking at the orc again. "I will handle this." On the orc's other side Terenas could see several other guards approaching, two of them also armed with spears.

Accepting that he was no longer needed here, Terenas gratefully laid down the sword and turned away. He ducked down a short flight of steps within the rampart, coming out near a small guard's armory, and from there took a narrow walkway along the wall. It ended at a short stairway, and he leaped up the steps and onto the ramparts again, but now just above the main gates.

He could feel the heavy pounding even before he reached the rampart's edge, rattling his teeth and making the stones shake. And looking down he saw them slamming a thick tree trunk against the front gates. Even from here Terenas could tell they were shuddering from each impact.

"Shore it up," he told a young lieutenant standing nearby. "Get some men and shore up the front gates."

"With what, sir?" the young officer asked.

"Anything you can find," Terenas replied. He gazed out past the walls, at the untold number of orcs gathered there against him and his city. Beyond them he saw the glitter of metal on the bridge, and knew Turalyon and his forces had retreated to that distance so they could plan their next move. Terenas just hoped it was a good one.

CHAPTER SEVENTEEN

"We have them!" an orc shouted, and Doomhammer grinned. Victory was within his grasp! The walls of the city still stood firm no matter how many warriors he hurled at it, but the gates were beginning to buckle from their constant ramming. And once those fell, his warriors would pour into Capital City, crushing its remaining defenders and sacking the city. With this and the elven forest as bases they could spread across the rest of the continent rapidly, driving the humans back to the shores and finally into the sea. And then the land would belong to the Horde, and they could end this war and start a new life at last.

If only the ogres were here, Doomhammer thought yet again, leaning on his hammer and watching his followers strike yet again at the city's sturdy wood and iron gates. They would have been able to scale the walls and perhaps even batter holes in the thick stone with their clubs. He wondered why Gul'dan and

Cho'gall and their clans had not yet arrived. He had moved quickly across the mountains, he knew, but still they should have been here by now.

"Doomhammer!" He glanced up and saw one of his warriors pointing toward the sky. More gryphons? he wondered with a grimace. The feathered mounts had proven deadly in the forests of the Hinterlands, and equally so at Quel'Thalas. He had only seen a handful here so far, and one had flown to the castle and back but had not otherwise participated in the battle. But still he was wary. The Wildhammer dwarves were strong and sturdy, their mounts fast, and their stormhammers as deadly as the warhammers of his own people. They were not a foe to be taken lightly, despite their small stature, and if more were arriving he would need to be ready.

But the dark shape silhouetted against the clouds grew larger and larger, too long and sinuous for a gryphon, and Doomhammer heard many of his warriors cheer as its shadow fell across them. A dragon! That was good news! The massive beast could use its flames against the gates, and to clear the castle walls of defenders. The city was as good as theirs!

The dragon landed well clear of the lake, a large orc dropping from the saddle on its back as soon as it had set down, and Doomhammer strode forward, slinging his hammer back on his back.

"Where is Doomhammer?" the dragon rider was demanding. "I must speak with him!"

"I am here," Doomhammer answered, his warriors parting to let him pass. "What is it?"

The rider turned to face him and Doomhammer realized he had seen the warrior before. He was one of Zuluhed's favorites, a powerful warrior, who according to reports, had been one of the first to dare ride the still-rebellious dragons. Torgus, yes, that was his name.

"I bring a message from Zuluhed," Torgus announced, a strange expression on his broad face—Doomhammer saw anger there, and confusion, and also possibly shame and even fear.

"Tell me, then," Doomhammer replied, stepping close enough that he was within the circle of the dragon's tail as it lay coiled upon the battlefield. The other orcs nearby, recognizing this warning, backed away to give them privacy.

"It is Gul'dan," Torgus said. He was a big orc, as tall as Doomhammer himself, but would not look him in the eye. "He has fled."

"What?" And now Doomhammer understood the fear on the dragon rider's face, as he felt his blood boil with rage and his hands grip his hammer tight enough to make the wooden handle groan in protest. "When? How?"

"Shortly after you left," Torgus admitted. "Cho'gall is with him. They have the Twilight's Hammer and Storm-reaver clans. They have launched the boats back into the Great Sea and are sailing south." Now he did look up, and the fear was dominated by rage. "One of my clansmen spotted them and flew down to ask why they were going the wrong way. Gul'dan killed him, used his foul magic on him. I saw it happen! I wanted to go after them but knew Zuluhed must be told. And he ordered me to come here at once."

Doomhammer nodded. "You did right," he assured the dragon rider. "If Gul'dan killed your clanmate he would not have hesitated to kill you as well, and then we would not have known of his treachery." His lips pulled back from his teeth in a snarl. "Damn him! I knew he could not be trusted! And now he has taken the ships with him!"

"We can fly after him," Torgus offered. "Zuluhed said he would have the other dragon riders ready. We could burn the ships to ash, and every orc on them."

Doomhammer frowned. "Yes, but only if you can get close enough. Gul'dan's magic is strong, and Cho'gall is powerful as well." He smashed his hammer into the ground. "I knew those Altars he created would be a problem! And I let him transform the ogres into new warriors to fill out his own ranks!" Doomhammer bit down hard on his lip, punishing himself for his own stupidity. He had been so excited about having new weapons for the war against the humans that he had ignored his own instincts, which had warned him the warlock would only do things for his own purposes.

Torgus was still awaiting an order, but both of them turned as another orc came running up. It was Tharbek, Doomhammer's young Blackrock second, and he stopped just beyond the dragon's tail, which was flicking in annoyance.

"Yes?"

"There is a problem," Tharbek informed him bluntly. "The mountains are closed."

"What?" Doomhammer turned and stared out past the dragon, toward the Alterac Mountains. Sure enough, he could see that the steady dark stream of orcs flowing from the southern passes had stopped. "What has happened?"

Tharbek shook his head. "I do not know," he replied. "But we are no longer able to get through the passes. I have sent warriors back to scout the way but they have not returned." His expression made it clear that they should have been back by now.

"Damn it!" Doomhammer ground his teeth together. "That human betrayed us! I knew one who would sell out his own race could not be trusted!" Still, he had thought the cloaked man too frightened to turn against them. Either the Alliance had shown superior strength, or they had threatened him with something more immediate than Horde domination—or they had discovered his treachery and removed him from whatever position he had held that had enabled him to control those passes. Yes, the last was the most likely. The man had seemed too eager to negotiate to back out now, especially since there would still be Horde warriors nearby. He had been caught and removed, and others now controlled that mountain region.

That did not change the results, however. "How many orcs are trapped up there?" he demanded.

Tharbek shrugged. "Impossible to say," he pointed out. "But at least half the clan, if not more." He glanced around. "We still have many warriors here," he said. "And once Gul'dan and the others arrive we will have more."

Doomhammer laughed bitterly, his mind still reeling. "The others! The others are not coming!" Tharbek looked surprised. "Gul'dan has betrayed us," Doomhammer told his second, barely able to force out the words. "He has taken the ships, and the two clans with them, to the Great Sea."

"But why?" Tharbek asked, genuinely bewildered. "If we lose this war we will all be without a home, him included."

Doomhammer shook his head. "The war was never his first priority." His thoughts flickered back to his encounter with the warlock back in Stormwind, and what Gul'dan had said. "He has found something else, something powerful," he remembered dully. "Something that will make him strong enough to not need the Horde for protection."

"What will we do?" Tharbek asked. He looked over at the city beyond them, studying it anew. "We may not have enough warriors to take it now," he pointed out.

Doomhammer refused to look, but knew his second was right. The city had proven sturdier than expected, and its defenders fiercer. The attack from behind by the

Alliance forces had also taken them by surprise and had reduced their numbers by a large portion. And now they could no longer expect reinforcements from any direction.

But that was not the only matter weighing on him. Gul'dan's treachery was bad enough, but he had taken other orcs with him. They were setting their own goals above those of the Horde, their own selfish desires above the needs of their people. That was what had driven Doomhammer to kill Blackhand and take control in the first place, and he had vowed to end the corruption and restore his people's honor. This betrayal could not be allowed to stand unanswered. No matter what it cost them. Or him.

"Rend! Maim!" Doomhammer bellowed. The Blackhand brothers heard him and approached quickly, perhaps realizing from his tone that they Warchief would brook no delay.

"Take your Black Tooth Grin south," Doomhammer instructed them, remembering the maps his scouts had drawn with the trolls' help. "March back along the lake and from there through the Hillsbrad to the sea. Gul'dan has fled but he would not have needed all the boats, not with only two clans. The rest of our ships should still be there, waiting." He grimaced, showing his tusks. "Pursue the traitors and destroy them to the last orc, leaving their bodies to sink into the water's depths."

"But—this city!" Rend protested. "The war!"

"Our people's honor is at stake!" Doomhammer bellowed, raising his hammer to attack position and growling at the other chieftain, silently daring him to defy the orders. "We must not allow them to go unpunished!" He glared at the Blackhands. "Consider this a chance to regain your honor." Then he took a deep breath and tried to calm himself. "I will lead my clan south more slowly, blocking the Alliance from following you and wreaking havoc across the land as we go. We will keep the route open, all the way back to this city. We will return here afterward," he assured them, "and finish what we started." Though even he had his doubts about that. They had caught the city by surprise this time. That would not happen again.

The Blackhands nodded, though they did not look happy. "It shall be as you say," Maim agreed, and he and his brother turned away to give orders to their warriors.

Doomhammer turned back to Torgus, who had stood nearby, waiting. "Tell Zuluhed to send all dragons to the Great Sea," he instructed the dragon rider. "Fly as fast as you can. You will have your chance to avenge your clanmate's death."

Torgus nodded, grinning at the thought of revenge, and turned back to his dragon, leaving Doomhammer to step back and allow the massive creature room to spread its colossal wings and take flight again. Doomhammer watched them fly away and ground his teeth again, his hands shaking with shock and rage. He had been so close! Another day at most and the city would have been his! Now that chance was gone. His odds of winning this war were slim at best. But honor had to come first.

Teron Gorefiend was standing nearby, and Doom-hammer rounded on the death knight. "What of you, then, you rotting corpse?" Doomhammer demanded of the creature. "You followed Gul'dan once, and he has betrayed us all. Will you run to him now?"

The undead warrior stared at him for a moment with those glowing eyes, then shook his head. "Gul'dan has forsaken our people," Gorefiend replied. "We shall not. The Horde is all, and it retains our loyalty—as do you, as long as you lead it."

Doomhammer nodded brusquely, surprised by the creature's response. "Then go and protect our people as they retreat from the city," he ordered. Gorefiend obeyed, stalking away toward the other death knights and their undead steeds. Tharbek departed as well. For the moment, Doomhammer was alone.

"Gul'dan!" he shouted, raising his hammer high and shaking it at the heavens. "You will die for this! I will see that you suffer for betraying our race and risking our very survival!" The skies did not answer, but Doomhammer felt a little better for the proclamation. He lowered his hammer and turned back toward the war, already forcing himself to think about how best to lead his warriors down south, and how to get the rest of the Horde toward the sea.

Gul'dan leaned out over the prow and sniffed the sea air. He closed his eyes and allowed his mystical senses dominance, questing with his mind for the distinctive tang of magic. It hit him almost at once, so strong he could taste it like the metallic flavor of fresh blood, so powerful it made his skin tingle and his hair crackle.

"Stop!" he shouted over his shoulder, and behind him the clansmen stopped rowing. The boat halted immediately, sitting stock-still on the water, and Gul'dan smiled. "We are here," he announced.

"But—but there's nothing here," one of the orcs, a member of his own Stormreaver clan named Drak'thul, declared. Gul'dan turned, opening his eyes at last, and glared at the young orc warlock.

"No?" He grinned. "Then we will weight you with chains and send you down to the sea bottom to explore it for us. Or would you prefer to sit here and trust that I know what I am doing?" Drak'thul backed away, stammering an apology, but Gul'dan was already ignoring him. Instead he glanced across the water to the boat next to his, and to Cho'gall standing near its prow.

"Inform the others," Gul'dan told his lieutenant. "We will begin at once. Doomhammer may already have learned of our departure, and I do not want to risk him interrupting us before we reach our goal."

The two-headed ogre nodded and turned to shout at the next boat, which then relayed the message to the boat beyond it. Ropes were tossed across and soon the ogre magi and the orc necromancers were climbing into Gul'dan's ship, using the ropes to pull themselves across or guide them while they swam, depending up their skill and comfort in the water.

"The place we seek, an ancient temple, lays below us," Gul'dan explained when all his warlocks had gathered on the deck before him. "And we could attempt to swim down to them, but I do not know how deep the waters are here. Plus it would be dark and cold and not to my liking." He grinned. "Instead we will raise the land itself, bringing the temple to us."

"Can that be done?" one of the new ogre magi asked.

"It can," Gul'dan replied. "Not so long ago on our homeworld we orcs raised another landmass, a volcano in Shadowmoon Valley. I guided the Shadow Council then and I will guide us now." He waited for other questions or objections but there were none and he nodded, pleased. His new subordinates was not only stronger than the old but more obedient, two traits he heartily appreciated.

"When shall we begin?" Cho'gall finally asked.

"Right now," Gul'dan answered. "Why wait?" He turned and led the way to the ship's railing, his assistants ranging themselves to either side of him. Then he closed his eyes and began to reach out toward the power he felt resting deep below. It was easy to grasp and once he had a firm grip upon it Gul'dan began to tug, magically pulling the energy and its source toward him. At the same time he reached out with his mind and cast his magic upon the power's surroundings, lifting them as well. The sky darkened overhead, and the sea around them turned rough.

"I have it," he told his aides through clenched teeth. "Home in on my magic and you will feel it yourself. Pour your own energies into what I have already constructed, and lift with me. Now!"

He felt the shift as first Cho'gall and then the others added their power to his own. A deep red hue suffused the sky and thunder clapped overhead as a hard rain fell and heavy waves rocked the boat. The vast weight he had felt grew lighter, and the tugging became significantly easier. It was still a chore, but now it was bearable instead of excruciating. And with each tug the magic's presence grew stronger and his grasp upon it became firmer, as did his hold on the land around it. All of nature fought against them, but they held firm.

For hours they stood there, unmoving in the eyes of the assembled warriors but engaged in an active struggle against titanic forces. Water drenched them from above and below. Thunder deafened them. Lightning blinded them. The boats were tossed about and warriors clutched at their oars to keep their seats. Several glanced at Gul'dan and the other warlocks for instructions, but none of them moved even when the ship lurched alarmingly.

Then a gout of fire and smoke erupted from the heaving water a short way ahead of the lead ship, filling the air with fire and ash and steam. Through the gritty, burning air they could see something poking up through the water like a chick's beak piercing its egg. The something proved to be rock, and as the warriors watched, too stunned to do more than blink and gasp, it grew larger, rising rapidly from the waves as water and lava dripped down and off it. The small rock became a boulder, the boulder became a small plateau, the plateau became a wide ledge, and the ledge became a small rocky plain. Other shapes emerged as well, rising from the tumultuous sea a short ways from the first, but they all proved to be connected, and as the sea spilled away from it the orcs could see an entire island emerging from the sea's grasp, still spouting flames and dirt and steam. A second, smaller island followed, grinding as it shifted to the surface, and then a third and a fourth.

At last, as the sky overhead shifted from swirling crimson to a mere leaden gray and the waves dropped to heights only as great as a tall ship's mast, Gul'dan opened his eyes. He staggered slightly and leaned against the railing for support, as did a few of his warlocks. But he glanced out over the new island chain, still steaming from the heat of its rapid ascent and still growling and groaning as it settled into a new configuration, and smiled.

"Soon," he said softly, looking upon the land and feeling it with his mind, noting the location of the place he sought. "Soon I will stride across you to the temple I seek, and the great prize that lies within it."

"I see them!" a warrior shouted. "There they are, off those islands!"

Rend Blackhand, one of Black Tooth Grin clan's two

chieftans, looked where the other orc had pointed, near
the place where they had seen the sea and air rolling
madly as they approached. At last he saw the thin spit
of land ahead and to the west, and the dark shapes
alongside it. "Good," he said, nodding and resting his
hands against the handle of his axe. "Increase speed,"
he told his drummer. "I want to reach them before they
have a chance to disappear into some hideout there."
On one of the other boats he saw his brother Maim
speak to his own drummer, no doubt giving similar instructions.

"What will we do if they use magic against us?" one
of his younger warriors asked. Several others nodded
agreement. It was their single greatest fear, even beyond
being captured by the Alliance and being eaten by a
dragon, and Rend could hardly fault them for their concern. He was not thrilled with the idea of battling
Gul'dan and his cronies. Doomhammer had given them
an order, however, and the Blackhand name was at
stake. Rend intended to carry that out—or die trying.

"Their magic is potent," he admitted now, "and
Gul'dan himself could easily kill three or four of us
within minutes. But he needs those minutes. And he
needs physical contact, or to be close by, or to have
something that belongs to the intended victim." He
grinned. "Did any of you loan the chief warlock a waterskin or a pair of gauntlets or a sharpening stone?" That
got chuckles from several, just as he'd hoped. "Then just
steer clear of the warlocks until we are across, do not let

them close to you, and swarm over them before they can cast any spells." He tapped his axe for emphasis. "Despite their powers they are still orcs, and they can still bleed and die. This is no different from hunting an ogre back home—each of them may be stronger than any one or even two of us but we can wear them down and attack in groups and prevent them from fighting back." His warriors nodded. They understood the concept, and now that they were thinking of magic as just another weapon it was no longer as frightening.

"Almost there," the helmsman announced then, and Rend glanced behind him, past the edge of his ship. The island now loomed up along one side, and Rend could tell from the size of the ships that this new land was big, bigger than most of the islands he had already seen on this world. The boats had gone from specks to full-fledged ships, and he could clearly see orcs pouring off them and onto the dark, damp land. Rend repressed the snarl he had felt building in the back of his throat and gave the order: "Prepare to land! Once we do, aim for those warlocks. And kill anyone—anything—that gets in our way."

"We are not alone," Cho'gall pointed out to Gul'dan. Their boat had finally beached on the shore of the new island, which still shuddered and threw off steam and occasional belches of fire and lava.

Gul'dan followed his assistant's gesture and saw a fleet of ships approaching from the far side of the island.

His island. From the way the lead boat moved Gul'dan could tell it was rowed rather than sailed, and that usually meant one thing: orcs. Doomhammer's troops had found them.

"Damn him," Gul'dan muttered. "Why did he always have to be so quick to make decisions? Another day and we would have been here and done before they arrived." He sighed. "Well, there is nothing for it. Tell the warriors to prepare for battle. You will need to fend them off while I enter the temple and find the tomb."

Cho'gall grinned with both his heads. "With pleasure." The massive two-headed ogre was as fanatic as the rest of his clan, and firmly believed in ushering in the end of the world, preferably with violence and bloodshed. All the Twilight's Hammer orcs held the same belief, and would happily fight anyone or anything if doing so would bring the world closer to its ultimate demise. It did not hurt that the demon blood most of them had imbibed back on Draenor had increase their natural bloodlust a hundredfold. "They will not get past us," the ogre promised, drawing the long curve-bladed sword he wore at his side.

Gul'dan nodded. "Good." Then he turned and began picking his way carefully across the island, steam rising from every step he took. Drak'thul and the other necromancers and ogre magi followed quickly behind him.

"Attack!" Rend shouted, his axe clutched in his hands as he ran forward with his warriors. "Kill the traitors!"

"Death to the traitors!" Maim echoed beside him.

"To battle!" Cho'gall bellowed, his scythe-like blade raised so its long sharp blade caught the weak late-afternoon sunlight. "Let this land be awash in their blood," his other head added, "that their deaths may usher in the end times!"

The two forces met with a thunderous impact there on the lava-strewn rocky shore, as orc slammed into orc. Weapons flashed, axes and hammers and swords and spears rising and falling, swinging and stabbing, in a wild display of energy, passion, and violence. Blood sprayed everywhere, filling the thick air with a red mist and turning the nearby waves dark. The ground, still uneven and unsteady, grew slippery, and many warriors lost their balance and met their deaths while struggling to regain their feet.

The battle was fierce. Cho'gall's warriors fought savagely and with no concern for their own safety—their only goal was to inflict as much damage and pain as possible. Doomhammer's soldiers fought for revenge and for justice, avenging Gul'dan's betrayal and the battle it had already cost them. Both sides believed in their goals, and neither was willing to yield.

The one difference between the two sides was numbers. Gul'dan had brought only two clans with him: his own Stormreavers and Cho'gall's Twilight's Hammers. His Stormreavers were the smallest clan and they were all warlocks—every single one of them was with Gul'dan now, leaving only the Twilight's Hammers to block Doomhammer's forces. Rend and Maim Black-hand had brought the bulk of their Black Tooth Grin clan, one of the largest in the Horde. The Twilight's Hammer warriors were outnumbered and they knew it. And as the battle continued, and both sides suffered heavy casualties, that difference began to show.

The fanatic orc warriors refused to surrender, however, and fought to the last orc. They took many of Doomhammer's warriors with them—Cho'gall himself cut one of the strongest Black Tooth Grins's right arm from him as he fell, both of the orc warrior's axes buried in his chest, and another Black Tooth Grin lost an eye to a well-aimed blow from the back spike on a war axe—but in the end the fiery shore was littered with bodies and only the troops the Blackhands had led here still remained.

"Now," Rend said, wiping his axe clean on a fallen orc's chest, blood still dripping from a long gash across his chest, "we go after Gul'dan. The warlock has much to answer for."

Gul'dan was standing at the base of an ancient temple, its outer walls barely visible beneath centuries of moss, fungus, coral, and barnacles. He could still see traces of architecture that matched what he had glimpsed in the Quel'Thalas, both in grandeur and in style. Elves had crafted this structure, and once it had been beautiful and ornate, he was sure. Now, however, its walls were rough and rolling, and the edifice resembled a natural mound of dirt and seaweed and encrustations rather than something that had been built deliberately. But the appearance did not matter to him. What excited him was the pulsing he could feel just behind his eyes, as the power tugged at him so strongly he could almost see its influence quivering the building around it.

"Inside," he told Drak'thul and the others. "We must go inside."

He had debated bringing them beyond the temple's front steps, actually. He knew that the Tomb of Sargeras lay within, and that the Eye of Sargeras housed within it could be tapped for immense, god-like powers. But would he be able to do so alone, or would he be forced to share that potency with the rest of the Shadow Council? What had decided him, finally, was that he did not know what else the ancient temple might contain. Thus Gul'dan had felt it was best to bring his servants and assistants with him into the temple. If necessary he could always kill them when they reached the Tomb itself.

Entering cautiously, Gul'dan created a globe of green light to better see his surroundings. The halls and rooms here were as altered as the building's exterior, the floors coated with sand and grit and seaweed, the walls festooned with more weeds and with shells of various sorts and sizes. Even the doorways had been altered, their outlines smoothed and rounded and distorted by the creatures that had clung to them for all these long years.

"Quickly, you fools," he told his clanmates impatiently, "fan out and search for the primary passageway! We must reach the Chamber of the Eye before the tomb's guardians awaken!"

"Guardians?" one of the warlocks, Urluk Cloud-killer, asked hesitantly. "You said nothing of guardians!"

"Spineless cowards!" Gul'dan railed, slapping the cowering Urluk across the face. "I said move!" His rage mobilized them, at least temporarily overpowering their fear of this strange place and the horrors it might contain, and the warlocks began searching through the building. Finally they found a wide central corridor, and proceeded along it.

As they ventured farther in, however, the depredations lessened. Now Gul'dan could see the fine carvings on the columns and pillars, and the delicate engravings along the walls, as well as the beautiful mosaics that made up the floors and ceilings. Any paint had long since been destroyed by the salt water, of course, but there was still enough decoration to see how beautiful this building had been, a truly elaborate and ornate temple that would have impressed even the most jaded visitors.

Gul'dan had eyes for none of it, however. He was interested in one thing and one thing only, and that was the magic waiting for him in the vault at the very bottom. When he finally reached the vault door he paused, savoring the moment.

"Now, Sargeras," he whispered, "I will claim whatever's left of your power—and bring this wretched world to its knees!"

He could feel the energy already, and it was enough to make his senses dance and his mind quiver in anticipation. The ball of green light, no larger than his hand when he had first conjured it, was now twice the size of his head and made up of roiling green fire so bright he could not bear to look at it directly and so hot he had to keep it to the center of the hall lest it melt its way through a wall. And this was from mere proximity to the source! What would he be capable of once he had actually touched the power, and absorbed it fully into himself?

Wrapped in these thoughts, Gul'dan motioned the others back and they obediently retreated to the far side of the room. Then he reached out and grasped the heavy stone handle of the massive black iron vault door. It was one of the only places in the entire temple that was unadorned, and its stark simplicity gave it a grandeur the statues and carvings had lacked. Clearly, it said, here was a place too important for such fripperies. Eager to see what that place contained, Gul'dan tugged the handle down with all his strength. He felt it stick from centuries of disuse, and also felt a prickle as a spell washed over him. It was not harmful, more a spell trigger than a spell itself, and he could sense the much larger and far more potent spell linked behind it. But the initial spell swept through him and then back out again, and its mate lay untriggered. Just as Sargeras had assured him it would. Aegwynn had warded this vault against intrusion by humans, elves, dwarves, even gnomes—against every race, in short. Every race native to this world. But he was an orc, and Aegwynn had never heard of Draenor. Her spell did not include him, and so he was now able to push the handle the rest of the way, causing a loud click from the door, and then give a mighty yank and swing the door wide open.

Beyond the doorway lay a darkness that even Gul'dan's light could not penetrate. A darkness so cold it froze his fingers numb in an instant and turned his breath to ice. And slowly that darkness took form, coalescing into discreet shapes, scuttling, crawling, writhing shapes with eyes that glowed darker than the rest, so dark it hurt to look upon them. And then these dark shapes smiled as they approached the vault door and exited their eternal prison. Advancing upon the stunned Gul'dan and his warlocks.

Demons. But like none he had seen before. Gul'dan thought he had faced terrible creatures in the past, but these made all others seem mere shadows, harmless and easily dispelled.

No! Gul'dan screamed in his mind, unable to make his mouth work to form the word out loud. *This is not how it is supposed to happen! Sargeras promised!* He tried to summon his magic, to raise his hands, to run—to do anything. But the mere sight of the beings before him had paralyzed him, body and soul, and he who had thought himself master could do nothing but stare and shudder as they crept toward him, their shadowy claws reaching out to caress his face.

That first touch was enough to break his paralysis, and Gul'dan found himself running, falling in his haste to be away from this nightmarish place. Drak'thul and the others had been standing right behind him. Now they were nowhere to be seen; they must have already fled. Screams echoed up from the vault as Gul'dan, too, raced through corridor after corridor. His face burned where the claws had touched him, and it was only after he raised one hand to his cheek that he realized he had been cut there, and deeply.

"Damn you, Sargeras!" he cursed as he stumbled past columns and pillars, through rooms and alcoves. "I won't be beaten like this! I am Gul'dan! I am darkness incarnate! It cannot end . . . like this."

He paused to catch his breath and to listen behind him. Nothing. The screams had stopped. *Blasted, feeble-minded weaklings,* he thought, picturing the Storm-reavers who had followed him down there. "They're all likely dead by now!" His cheek was throbbing now, and he pressed his hand against it, trying to staunch the blood that was leaking from the wound. He was beginning to feel dizzy and his limbs felt weak. "Still, I must press on," he told himself grimly. "My power alone should be enough to—"

Gul'dan stopped speaking to listen carefully. What was that sound? It was faint, and repetitious, and made his skin crawl, but it carried both cruelty and—amusement?

"That laughter . . . Is that you, Sargeras?" he demanded. "You seek to mock me? We'll see who laughs last, demon, when I claim your burning Eye for my own!"

He turned a corner and found himself in a wide room, its walls surprisingly blank. Inspired by something he could not name, Gul'dan crossed to the nearest wall and began writing upon it, scrawling his description of the vault and its guardians with his own blood. Several times he faltered, his hand too heavy to lift.

"Ambushed . . . by the guardians," he wrote heavily. "I am . . . dying." He knew it was true, and struggled to finish writing his tale before death claimed him. But behind him he could already hear the same dry, hungry scrabbling he had heard inside the vault. They were coming for him.

"If my servants had not abandoned me," he wrote, his eyes barely able to focus now, his throat too tight to form words. But he realized now that it was not their fault. It was his own. All this time he had thought he was in control, when in truth he had been little more than a dupe, a pawn, a slave. His very existence had been a sham, a mere joke. And soon it would be over.

I've been a fool, he thought. He stopped writing and turned to run, knowing already that it was too late.

And then the claws bit in deep, and Gul'dan found his voice long enough to scream.

Rend put out an arm and stopped Maim from going any

farther. "No," he said softly. Blood still seeped from beneath the rough binding he had fashioned from a fallen warrior's belt.

"We need to go after Gul'dan," Maim insisted, though he swayed from his own wounds and the rough bandages wrapped around one leg and shoulder were already soaked through with blood.

"There is no need," his brother assured him. "Those . . . creatures have finished the task for us." Something strange had emerged from the building before them, something with too many limbs and too many joints and altogether too many teeth. It had been followed by others and they had attacked the orcs without pause, tearing into them like hunger-crazed animals setting upon fresh prey. Several orcs had been frozen with fear at the sight of the terrible creatures, but others had fought back and they had finally destroyed the last one, though it had taken enough wounds to slay a dozen orcs before it had finally stopped thrashing and biting.

And the creatures had come from within that building. Though only a warrior, Rend had a tenuous feel for magic. And he could sense the magic within the strange old structure before them. It was powerful, immensely so, and evil beyond imagining. And it was filled with hatred, intense and directed toward anything living. Those creatures had only been the barest hint of its strength.

Then something knocked them off their feet, a deafening noise from the building's entrance and a deep rumble like laughter from somewhere far below. Air rushed from the structure, fetid and foul, and something else with it, something that made Rend's hackles rise. He did not see anything, but he was sure he had felt evil itself flowing from that strange place, exploding outward and then unraveling in the warm sunlight. The rumble continued, however, and now the ground was shaking. Cracks began to appear in the rocks beneath their feet. The whole island was coming apart.

"Gul'dan is no longer a threat," Rend said as he clambered back to his feet, and somehow he knew it was true. Whatever Gul'dan had hoped to find here, he had found only his own death. Rend only hoped it had been slow and painful. He was almost certain that had been the case.

"What do we do now, then?" Maim asked as they turned away, leaving the temple behind them.

"We return to Doomhammer," Rend told him. "We still have a war to fight, and now at least we will not need to worry about traitors sapping our strength from within. Let him find fault with that, if he dares." Together the brothers made their way back toward the shore, and the boats waiting there.

CHAPTER EIGHTEEN

"Are we ready?"

"Ready, sir."

Daelin Proudmoore nodded but did not look away from the view past the starboard rail. "Good. Sound for positions. We attack as soon as they fall within range."

"Yes, sir." The quartermaster saluted and moved to the large brass bell that hung near the pilot's wheel and sounded it, ringing it twice in quick succession. Immediately Proudmoore heard the sounds of running feet and sliding ropes and falling bodies as the men on his flagship rushed to their assigned stations. He smiled. He liked order and precision, and his crew knew it. He had hand-picked each and every one of them, and he'd never sailed with a finer group of men. Not that he would ever say that out loud, but they knew it.

Proudmoore returned his attention to the sea beyond his ship, studying the waves and the sky. Raising his brass spyglass again he peered out through it, searching for the small dark shapes he had spotted once already. There. They were noticeably larger now, and he could count more of them distinctly, rather than seeing the spiked shape he had observed before. He was sure the lookout had an even better view of them up in the crow's nest, and guessed that in another ten minutes the shapes would resolve themselves into the unmistakable form of ships.

Orc ships.

The Horde fleet, to be precise.

Proudmoore banged his fist on the hardwood railing, the only outward sign of his agitation. Finally! He had been dreaming of a chance like this since the war had begun. He had almost jumped when he'd received word from Sir Turalyon that the Horde was heading for Southshore, and had been hard pressed to conceal his excitement when lookouts confirmed that the orc ships were on the Great Sea.

The lookouts had also informed him that the orcs were in two separate groups. The first group had sailed on into the sea at once, and the second group had scrambled to catch up. It was unclear whether they were simply in too much of a hurry to coordinate the two halves better—or if the second group was in fact pursuing the first. Could there be such a thing as orc rebels? Proudmoore didn't know, and he didn't care. It did not matter where they had been going or what they had been doing. All he cared about was that the orc ships had turned back and were making their way across the Great Sea once more, back toward Lordaeron.

And that put them within his grasp.

He could see the ships without the spyglass now. They were moving fast despite having no sails—he had seen a few of the orc ships up close and had marveled at the banks of oars they contained, and the speed they must achieve when powerfully built orcs manned all of them in unison. Of course, what they gained in speed they lost in maneuverability. His own ships could literally sail circles around the orc vessels. He had no intention of showing off, however. Naval battles were a deadly serious business, and Proudmoore intended to see the orc fleet sunk as quickly and efficiently as possible.

And now he waited for them behind the island of Crestfall, just northeast of his own beloved Kul Tiras. Waited with his entire fleet behind him, cannons primed and ready, for the orcs to row themselves right into his path.

And they did.

"Fire!" Proudmoore shouted as the tenth orc ship passed their position. If the orcs had seen them waiting quietly between the two islands, sails furled and lanterns covered, they had given no indication, and the first volley of cannon fire took the targeted ship completely by surprise, destroying most of its middle and causing it to tear in half and sink immediately. "Raise sails, all ahead full!" was his next command, and the ship leaped forward across the water as the sails raised and caught the wind. He knew his gunnery crew was already reloading the cannons, but other sailors stood ready with crossbows and with small casks of gunpowder. "Target the next ship in line," Proudmoore instructed them, and the crewmen nodded. The casks were tossed onto the next orc ship and then the crossbow bolts, which had been wrapped in oil-soaked rags, were lit and fired. One of the casks exploded, spreading fires across the deck, and then another, and that ship was soon blazing merrily, its tar-coated planks quickly consumed. Then Proudmoore's ship was past the row of orc vessels and turning back to attack them from the far side.

It was all going as well as Proudmoore had hoped. The orcs were not mariners and knew little about sailing or about naval combat. They were powerful hand-to-hand fighters, and would be dangerous if they could close with one of his ships and board it, but he had instructed his captains to keep themselves well out of boarding range. Several of his ships had followed him through the orc fleet and were now menacing it from the far side, while a second group remained next to Crestfall and struck from there. A third fleet had sailed up and past, and were now turning back to block the orc ships that had already passed the battle, and the fourth fleet had sailed south to complete the circle. Soon the orc ships would be surrounded, attacked on all sides. Already they had lost three ships, and Proudmoore had yet to suffer a single casualty. He allowed himself a rare smile. Soon the seas would be orc-free once more.

Just then the lookout shouted down. "Admiral! There's something heading toward us—and it's coming from the air!"

Proudmoore looked up and saw the sailor, pale and shaking, staring out to the north. He trained his spyglass in that direction, and soon saw what must have sparked the lookout's cry. Small dark specks were heading toward them out of the clouds. They were too far away to make out clearly, but he could tell there were several of them and that they were approaching fast. He didn't know what the Horde had that could fly, but something in his gut warned Proudmoore this battle was far from over.

Derek Proudmoore glanced up from where he stood beside his pilot. "What was that?" he asked the lookout, but the man had fallen back into the crow's nest and appeared to be shaking too badly to respond. Afraid the man had had some sort of fit, Derek grabbed the nearest rigging and swung himself up and over to the central mast. From there he caught the central rigging line and scaled it to the main spar, which he walked to the crow's nest.

"Gerard?" he asked, peering in at the sailor who was curled up there. "Are you all right?"

Gerard looked up at him, tears in his eyes, but only shook his head and huddled more tightly.

"What is it?" Derek climbed over the side and into the crow's nest proper, crouching beside the sailor. He had known Gerard for years and trusted the man implicitly. But now that he was here he could see that Gerard was not sick at all. He was terrified, scared beyond any ability to speak. And the thought of a brave sailor, a veteran of many battles, being that frightened sent a chill down Derek's spine.

"Did you see something?" he asked gently. Gerard nodded, squeezing his eyes shut as if to erase whatever it was from his memory. "Where?" For a second the lookout shook his head, but finally he pointed a shaky hand to the north.

"You rest," Derek told him softly. Then he stood and turned to see what had frightened his friend and crewmate so—and nearly collapsed himself at the sight before him.

There, swooping down out of the clouds, was a dragon, its scales gleaming blood-red in the early morning light. Behind it came a second, and a third, and then several more, until at least a dozen of the massive creatures flew together, their leathery wings beating hard to keep them aloft and drive them closer to their target.

The fleet.

Derek barely noticed the anguish plain in the lead dragon's great golden eyes, or the green-skinned figure perched on its back. His mind was too busy calculating the impact the creatures could have upon this battle. Each one was larger than any ship but a destroyer, considerably faster and more agile, and airborne. Those massive claws could probably tear through hulls with ease, or snap masts like twigs. He had to warn the rest of the fleet—he had to warn his father!

Turning, Derek leaned over the crow's nest to shout down to his pilot. A movement caught his eye as he shifted, however, and he glanced up again. The lead dragon was close now, close enough for Derek to see the grin of the orc on its back, and it opened its long mouth wide. Derek saw a long, serpentine tongue surrounded by sharp triangular teeth almost as tall as he was. Then he saw a glow deep within the dragon's maw. It rushed forward, expanding as it came, and suddenly the world burst around him. He did not even have time to scream before the flames consumed him, and his body crumbled as it fell, burned to mere ash.

In a single swoop the dragons destroyed the Third Fleet, all six ships. Everyone on board perished. And then the dragon riders brought their mounts back around, turning them toward the first fleet and the ships that stood between the orcs and freedom.

"Damn them! Damn them all!" Admiral Proudmoore clung to the railing so hard he thought either his fingers would break or they would gouge out chunks of wood. He watched the last traces of the Third Fleet's destroyer sink beneath the waves, mere cinders upon the sea. He knew there was no chance Derek or any of the other crew had survived.

But grief would come later, if he lived that long. Pushing aside all thoughts of his eldest son, Proudmoore concentrated on the tactical implications. The north was now open once more. The orc ships could simply row on, while the dragons harried his own fleet and forced them to give way. If that happened the orcs would be able to land again at the Hillsbrad or at Southshore, and could rejoin the rest of the Horde. And he would have failed.

That was unacceptable.

"Bring us around!" he ordered, startling his pilot into motion. "I want half our ships sweeping north and blocking their path again! The rest stay where they are and continue the attack!"

The sailor nodded. "But—the dragons," he began, though his hands were already turning the great wheel and bringing the ship around.

"They are foes like any other," Proudmoore replied sharply. "We will simply target them as we would enemy ships."

His men nodded, and jumped to obey his orders. Sails were furled as the ship turned and tacked into the wind. Cannons were reloaded and aimed at an upward angle, with blocks and other objects jammed beneath them to lift them up. Crossbows were reloaded and casks of gunpowder made ready. When the first dragon soared toward them, Proudmoore drew his own sword and raised it high, then brought it down sharply.

"Attack!"

It was a valiant effort—but it failed miserably. The dragon dodged each cannonball, which then sank into the sea. It knocked the casks aside with its wings, and simply ignored the flaming crossbow bolts, which clattered harmlessly from its scales. The ferocity of the attack did make it pull back, however, giving Proudmoore time to ponder other methods.

Fortunately he was spared the need to come up with anything.

As he considered the merits of using ropes and chains to try binding or at least tripping the dragon, several new figures dropped from the clouds. These were considerably smaller than the dragon, perhaps twice the size of a man, with long feathered wings and long tufted tails and proud beaks. And on the back of each of these creatures rode what looked like a short man dressed in strange feathered armor and covered in tattoos and wielding a massive hammer.

"Wildhammers, attack!" Kurdran Wildhammer stood in his saddle and hurled his stormhammer, catching the nearest dragon rider in the chest. The surprised orc did not have time to react but toppled from his own saddle, his chest crushed, both weapon and reins falling from lifeless hands as his body disappeared beneath the waves. His dragon roared in surprise and rage, audible even over the fading thunderclap, but the sound turned to squeals of pain as Sky'ree's sharp claws cut deep into the dragons' flank, slicing neatly through scales and drawing dark blood. Iomhar was beside him, and his own gryphon tore a large chunk from the dragon's left wing with beak and claws, causing the dragon to list dramatically. Then Farand came in on the far side, throwing his own hammer, which struck the dragon a resounding blow to the head. Its eyes lost focus and it fell, sending up a huge wave as it struck the water. It did not resurface.

Kurdran flew over to the largest ship. "We've come to help!" he shouted down at the slender older man standing on the bridge. The man nodded and saluted with the sword in his hand. "We'll handle these beasties," Kurdran assured him. "You take care o' the ships."

Admiral Proudmoore nodded again, and favored him with a tight, nasty grin. "Oh, we will take care of them, sure enough," he told the dwarf. Then he turned back to his pilot. "Keep moving," he ordered. "We'll cut them off as planned, and then tighten the net. I don't want to see a single orc ship escape!"

The Wildhammers attacked the dragons in a fury, killing several and driving the rest back. Proudmoore's remaining ships circled in and began picking off the orc fleet from every side, using cannon and powder and fire to good advantage. He lost another ship when it got too close and the orcs swarmed from their own sinking vessel onto the Alliance ship, slaughtering most of its crew before the dying captain could toss a powder keg into the hold and hole his own ship. And they had lost the Third Fleet and a few scattered others to the dragons. But the orcs lost far more. A handful of their ships made it out of range, but the rest fell before Proudmoore's fury. As for the orcs themselves, a few swam for it or clutched shattered spars and planks, but the rest drowned or died by fire or bolt. Bodies littered the waves.

With the last of the orc fleet disappearing from view, the remaining dragon riders decided there was nothing left to save here. They turned their mounts and fled east toward Khaz Modan, the Wildhammers pursuing them with great whoops and shouts. And Proudmoore surveyed the remains of his fleet, tired but victorious—though at great cost.

"Sir!" one of the sailors shouted. He was leaning over the rail and gesturing at something in the water.

"What is it?" Proudmoore snapped, stepping up beside the man. But his anger changed to hope as he saw what the sailor had seen—someone bobbing in the water, sputtering and clutching to a torn plank.

Someone human.

"Get a rope to him!" Proudmoore ordered, and sailors hastened to obey. "And scan the waters for other survivors!" He wasn't sure how someone from the Third Fleet had wound up this far from where their boats had gone down, but at least one man had. And that meant there could be others.

He could not prevent the tiny flash of hope that Derek might be one of them.

That hope turned to confusion and then to fury, however, when the man was finally hauled aboard. Instead of the green tunic of Kul Tiras, the half-drowned man wore the waterlogged garb of Alterac. And there was only one way one of Perenolde's men could have wound up here in the Great Sea with the orc fleet.

"What were you doing on an orc boat?" Proudmoore demanded, kneeling with his knee on the man's chest. Already weak and out of breath, the man gasped and turned pale. "Speak!"

"Lord Perenolde . . . sent us," the man managed to blurt out. "We . . . guided them to their . . . ships. He told . . . us . . . to render . . . any assistance . . . necessary."

"Traitor!" Proudmoore drew his dagger and laid it across the man's neck. "Conspiring with the Horde! I should gut you like a fish and toss your innards into the sea!" He pressed slightly and watched as a thin red line appeared along the man's skin, the sharp edge parting his flesh easily. But then he drew back and rose to his feet again.

"Such a death is too good for you," Proudmoore announced, resheathing his dagger. "And alive you can provide proof of Perenolde's treachery." He turned to one of the nearby sailors. "Bind him and toss him into the brig," he ordered brusquely. "And search for any other survivors. The more evidence we have, the quicker Perenolde will hang."

"Yes, sir!" The men saluted and hurried about their tasks. It took another hour before they were sure they had scoured the waters completely. They found three more men, all of whom confirmed the first's story.

There were countless orcs in the water as well, but those they let drown.

"Set sail for Southshore," Proudmoore told his pilot after the last Alterac traitor had been hauled aboard. "We will rejoin the Alliance army, and report both our success and Alterac's betrayal. Keep your eyes peeled for those orc ships that escaped our attack." Then he turned away, heading for his cabin, where he could at last give in to his own grief. And, after that, write a letter to his wife, informing her what had befallen their eldest son.

CHAPTER NINETEEN

"They are not coming."

Young Tharbek turned, startled by his leader's sudden pronouncement. "What do you mean?" he asked.

Doomhammer grimaced. "The rest of the Horde. They are not coming."

Tharbek looked around. "You sent them all the way down to the Great Sea," he pointed out carefully, wary of drawing his superior's wrath. "It will take them many days to return."

"They have dragons, you fool!" Doomhammer's fist lashed out, catching Tharbek across the cheek and sending the younger orc staggering back. "The dragon riders would have been here days ago to inform us of the troops' progress! Something has happened! The fleet is gone, and the bulk of our forces with it!"

Tharbek nodded, rubbing his cheek sullenly with one hand, but said nothing. He didn't have to. Doomhammer knew what his Second was thinking—if he had not sent the other clans after Gul'dan in the first place, this would not be an issue now.

Doomhammer ground his teeth together. Why was it no one else among his people understood the reasons behind his decision? He had seen the same look from every other orc these past few days, ever since he had ordered the retreat from Capital City. The gates had already been showing small cracks, and bowed with each strike of the battering ram. The city's guards had long since exhausted their oil supply and were reduced to pouring boiling water on them. The Alliance forces had been pushed back across the lake, and were being held at the bridge. They had almost won! Another day, two at the most, and the city would have cracked. And then he had sent the army away, leaving them too weak to continue here.

Nor had the Alliance been slow to capitalize on the sudden reversal. The humans had poured across the bridge immediately after the Blackhands had led their clan away, crashing through the handful of remaining orc defenders and pushing their way out onto the battlefield. The orcs had found themselves trapped between horsemen and foot soldiers on the one side and entrenched guards on the other. And they had no help in sight. It would take days or even weeks for the rest of the Horde to return, just as Tharbek had said, and that was assuming they were able to defeat Gul'dan and his warlocks and his ogres and whatever else he had conjured to aid him in his treachery. The warriors still trapped in or beyond the mountains he had to assume were dead by now, killed by whatever humans had retaken the passes and closed that route to them. The orcs standing before the city were all he had left for the assault.

So he had ordered the retreat. He had hoped the other clans would encounter them on the way, but the dragons at least should have been here long before. Something had definitely gone wrong. And he blamed Gul'dan for it all. Even if the warlock had not personally killed the Horde warriors, it was his betrayal that had forced Doomhammer to split his forces.

And he had been forced. He had made personal vows to the ancestral spirits that he would not allow his race to continue as it had. He would fight the corruption, the blood lust, the savagery at every turn, using every weapon at his command. Winning the war did not matter. His own survival meant nothing. Without honor they were mere animals, less than animals because they had the potential to be so much more and had a noble history they had thrown away for blood and combat and hatred. If he had allowed Gul'dan to escape unpunished he would have been guilty of allowing such selfishness, even encouraging it, and would have been partially responsible for the further degradation of the entire race.

At least this way he could say he had done his best, Doomhammer decided. He had upheld his honor, and through him the honor of the Horde. They might lose to the humans but they would do so proudly, on their feet and with weapons in their hands, not howling or sniveling.

Besides, the war was not over yet. He was leading his warriors south but to the east instead of the west. Khaz Modan lay there, between Lordaeron and Azeroth. It was the home of the dwarves, and they had marched through that region to reach this land. The dwarves had proven sturdy opponents but their mountain keeps had fallen before the might of the Horde, all except the city of Ironforge, which held fast. Doomhammer had left Kilrogg Deadeye and his Bleeding Hollow clan there to oversee the mining operations that had ultimately produced their ships. If he could lead his own warriors back there and reunite with Kilrogg they would have a substantial force again, enough to turn on the pursuing Alliance and destroy them in turn. The battles would be more difficult, and their conquest would take far longer, but they could still dominate this continent and carve out homes for themselves.

Provided nothing else went horribly wrong.

"Humans!" the orc scout gasped, dropping to his knees from sheer exhaustion. "To the east of us!"

Doomhammer stared at him. "East? Are you sure?" But he didn't need the scout's tired nod to know the orc was not lying. But how did the humans get east of them when they were chasing them the entire way and Lordaeron lay north and west of here?

Then he remembered. The Hinterlands! He had split off some of his forces there, leaving a clan behind to distract the humans while the rest marched on toward Quel'Thalas. The feint had worked and the humans had left half their own forces behind to flush the orcs from the forests there. Apparently those warriors had never made the trek to Capital City, and now they were heading toward them from the east. Which meant, if he was not careful, the two Alliance armies would trap his orcs between them and crush the last chance the Horde had for escape, much less victory.

"How many?" he demanded of the scout, who was gulping water from a skin.

"Hundreds, maybe more," the orc answered finally, frowning in concentration. "And some of those were heavily armored as well."

Doomhammer grimaced and turned away, swinging his hammer about him in great arcs to relieve the anger raging within him. Damn them! That many Alliance warriors could lay waste to his own forces, especially with their horsemen coming up fast from behind. And he was still days away from Khaz Modan. Nor had they seen a single hint of the dragon riders or their other lost brethren.

He had no choice. Doomhammer looked up and caught Tharbek's eye. "Quicken the pace," he told his lieutenant. "Full run, no breaks. We need to reach Khaz Modan as soon as possible."

Tharbek nodded and hurried off to shout orders to

the other orcs, and Doomhammer growled as he watched the younger warrior go. Running felt too much like defeat, and that was something he hated to even consider. But he could not risk an open battle now. He needed to reach the Bleeding Hollow first. Then he could turn and face the restored Alliance army on more equal terms.

"There!" Tharbek pointed, and Doomhammer nodded, having already seen the orc scout crouching atop the cliff.

"Hail, Doomhammer!" the scout shouted, straightening as they approached and raising his axe in salute. "The Bleeding Hollow welcomes you back to Khaz Modan!"

"My thanks," Doomhammer shouted in reply, holding his black stone hammer aloft so the scout would recognize him easily even from this distance. "Where are Kilrogg and the rest?"

"We have made camp in a valley back within the mountains proper," the scout answered, leaping down to a lower ledge so they could converse more easily. "I will run and tell of your approach." He glanced up, and Doomhammer knew he was surveying the mass of warriors behind him. "Where is the rest of the Horde?"

"Dead, most of them," Doomhammer replied bluntly. He bared his tusks as the scout's eyes widened in surprise. "And we have Alliance forces marching fast behind us. Tell Kilrogg to ready his warriors for battle."

The scout seemed about to ask another question,

then thought better of it. Instead he saluted again and
darted back up the cliff, disappearing over the rise at a
run. Doomhammer nodded. At least they would have
the Bleeding Hollow warriors beside them when they
stood to face the humans again. Kilrogg was a clever
old warrior, still powerful despite his years, and his clan
was fierce and warlike. Between the Blackrock and the
Bleeding Hollow they would still be more than a match
for the Alliance.

"We cannot fight them. Not with our full force."

Doomhammer stared at Kilrogg as the older chieftain shook his head, his face glum but resolute.

"What? Why not?" Doomhammer demanded.

"The dwarves," Kilrogg replied curtly.

"The dwarves?" At first he thought the chieftain
meant the gryphon-riders, but Aerie Peak was far from
here. He could only be referring to the dwarves that
lived here in the mountains. "But we crushed their
armies and routed them from their citadels."

"From all but one," Kilrogg corrected, glancing up
so both his good eye and the dead, scarred one stared
at Doomhammer. "We have not been able to crack
Ironforge, and I have lost many good warriors in each
attempt."

"Then leave it," Doomhammer insisted. "We do not
need it now. We must turn on the humans before they
can cross the land bridges and mass on this side of the
channel. Once we have destroyed their army we can

fall upon Ironforge and rip it open, then station our own warriors there while we march north again to finish our conquest there."

But Kilrogg shook his head. "The dwarves are too fierce to leave at our backs," he stated. "I have fought them many times these past few months, and I tell you true, if we let them they will boil from their fortress and fall upon us like angry wasps. Each time we crushed one of their citadels the survivors fled to Ironforge and it took them in—I can only guess how deep its levels run, but the whole of the dwarf nation lurk within it and await a chance for revenge. If we do not guard that place and keep them too busy to emerge we will face not one army but two."

Doomhammer paced, considering this new information. He trusted Kilrogg's judgment, but that meant they would not have enough warriors to stand against the Alliance here and hope to win. He would need to keep moving.

"Stay here," he told Kilrogg finally. "Keep as many warriors as you need to hold the dwarves and harry the humans. I will lead the rest to Blackrock Spire, where we can make our stand from within its sturdy walls." He glanced at the older chieftain. "If you can, bring your warriors there afterward. Perhaps you can fall on the humans from behind. Or perhaps more of our people will appear, either from the sea or from the Dark Portal." He straightened. "But Blackrock Spire is our strongpoint. If we cannot defeat the humans there we cannot hold them anywhere, and this war is lost."

Kilrogg nodded. For a second he eyed the Horde warchief, and when he spoke it was more softly than Doomhammer had ever heard the grizzled old chieftain. "You made the right choice," Kilrogg assured him. "I too know the depths of Gul'dan's treachery. He would have taken us back to the days before the Portal opened, when we were nearly mad with rage and hunger and desperation." He nodded. "Whatever else happens, you have given our people back their honor."

Doomhammer nodded back, feeling a sudden respect and even affection for the one-eyed chieftain he had always feared and disliked. He had always considered Kilrogg a brutish, savage warrior, more interested in glory than in honor. Perhaps he had been wrong all these years.

"Thank you," he said finally. There was nothing more to say and so he turned and walked away, back toward his own clan. There were orders to hand out, and another march to begin. Possibly the last.

CHAPTER TWENTY

"Turalyon!"

Turalyon glanced up at the shout, unable to believe his ears. But there, riding toward him, was a large man in full armor. The lion symbol of Stormwind glittered gold on his battered shield, and the hilt of a massive sword rose above one shoulder.

"Lord Lothar?" Amazed, Turalyon rose from his seat by a campfire and stood staring as the Champion of Stormwind and Commander of the Alliance reined in his horse. Then the older man had dismounted and was clapping him on the back.

"Good to see you, lad!" He could hear the genuine affection in Lothar's voice. "They said I'd find you here!"

"They?" Turalyon glanced around, still confused by his leader's sudden appearance.

"The elves," Lothar explained, pulling off his helm and running a hand over his balding pate. He looked tired but pleased. "I ran across Alleria and Theron and the others as I was turning north. They told me what had happened in Capital City and that you had brought the rest of the army this way, pursuing what's left of the Horde." He clasped him about the shoulders. "Good job, man!"

"I had a lot of help," Turalyon protested, pleased but discomfited by his hero's praise. "And, truth to tell, I'm not entirely sure what happened." He and Lothar sat down again, the older man gratefully accepting some food and a wineskin from Khadgar, and Turalyon explained. He had been as surprised as anyone when the bulk of the Horde forces had turned away from Capital City and marched rapidly south. Then he had received a report from Proudmoore about the naval battle and its outcome. "The rest of the Horde wasn't strong enough to stand against us, especially with King Terenas pounding them every time they approached the city's walls," he concluded, "and their leader must have known it. So he retreated. We've been chasing them ever since."

"He may have been waiting for those orcs to return from the sea," Lothar commented, gnawing on a hunk of cheese. "When they didn't he must have known he was in trouble." He grinned. "Besides, closing the mountains behind him meant no escape route, and no reinforcements from there either."

Turalyon nodded. "You heard about Perenolde, then?"

"Aye." Lothar's expression turned grim. "How a man could turn against his own race I'll never understand. But thanks to Trollbane we don't have to worry about Alterac any more."

"And the Hinterlands?" Khadgar asked.

"Orc-free," Lothar replied. "Took us a while to find all of them—some had burrowed in deep, even carved out homes beneath the ground, where they could disappear when we chased them—but we got them at last. The Wildhammers are still patrolling to make sure, of course."

"And the elves are heading back to Quel'Thalas to clear it as well," Turalyon added. "The orcs seem to have left the forest but the trolls may still be hiding among the trees." He grinned as he thought about Alleria and her kin and their attitude toward the forest trolls. "I would not want to be them when they and the rangers meet again." He glanced around. "But where are Uther and the other Paladins?"

"I sent them up to Lordaeron," Lothar answered, draining the wineskin and tossing it aside. "They'll make sure that region's safe again, and then they'll follow after us." He smiled a little. "Uther may be upset if we don't leave him anyone to fight."

Turalyon nodded, imagining how his zealous fellow Paladin would react to discovering he had missed the end of the war. And though the orcs were still numerous it felt as if the war was winding down. He had thought they were all finished there by Capital City, but when the bulk of the Horde had left it had changed everything. And the Horde had been growing smaller and more desperate ever since.

"They may try to hole up here in Khaz Modan," Khadgar was saying, but Turalyon shook his head. He was pleased to see Lothar doing the same. "They'll have the dwarves to reckon with if they do," the Champion explained. "Ironforge still stands unconquered, and the dwarves will be twitching for a chance to take the fight back to the orcs and reclaim their mountains for good."

"We should give it to them," Turalyon commented, pausing as both Lothar and Khadgar turned to give him their full attention. "We can detour to Ironforge if the orcs aren't going there themselves, and use the gryphon riders to keep tabs on the Horde's path. If we free the dwarves, they can hold the mountains, preventing any chance of the orcs returning this way. They'll also hunt down any orcs still hiding among the peaks."

Lothar nodded. "It's a good plan," he said with a smile. "Let the troops know, and we'll begin our march in the morning." He stood and straightened slowly. "For me, I need sleep," he explained, sounding a little annoyed at himself. "It was a long ride, and I'm not as young as I was." But he favored Turalyon with a serious glance before turning away. "You've handled yourself and the troops well was I was gone," he said. "As I knew you would." Lothar paused, and a look of mixed sorrow and respect crossed his face. "Llane," he said softly. "You remind me of him. You have his courage." Turalyon stared, unable to respond.

Khadgar stepped up beside Turalyon as the older warrior walked away. "Looks like you've won his respect after all," the mage teased him. He knew how much Turalyon valued the Champion's good opinion, and how he'd worried that he would fail the Alliance commander.

"Shut up," Turalyon said absently, shoving Khadgar lightly. But he was smiling as he arranged his own bedroll, collapsed upon it, and closed his eyes, trying to get a little rest before they moved out again.

"Attack!" Lothar shouted. He had his greatsword out, its golden runes catching the sunlight as they charged up the wide path curving around the snow-topped mountain peak. Near the top of the peak the rock had been planed and polished and carved into a massive wall, complete with windows that pierced the stone far above. Set into that wall atop a short flight of stairs were a pair of truly gargantuan doors, easily fifty feet high, the image of a mighty dwarven warrior chiseled into their face. Above the doors soared a majestic arch, and within it was engraved the image of a heavy anvil. It was an awe-inspiring sight, the entrance to Ironforge.

The heavy doors were closed fast, of course, and no other entrances or openings were visible. Which did not stop the orcs from pounding against both that portal and the rocks around it, trying in vain to batter down the dwarves' ancient defenses.

It was these orcs Lothar and his soldiers targeted now as they reached the top of the path and emerged onto the wide snowy ledge facing those colossal doors. The orcs spun around, surprised—they had been so busy with their own attack that between that and the winds that whipped past the peak they had not heard the Alliance's approach. Now they tried desperately to bring weapons to bear against this new enemy, but the first row of orcs were mowed down before they could even turn around to face their attackers.

"Do not let up!" Lothar shouted, his sword lopping off one orc's arm and then splitting another up the middle. "Drive them back against the rocks!" His men raised their shields accordingly and advanced steadily, using swords and spears to strike at any orcs that tried to breach their line and otherwise content to move them bodily back against the very edifice they had been trying to breach.

But, as Lothar had hoped, the dwarves were well prepared. The mammoth black doors swung open with only a faint sigh and short, sturdy fighters in heavy mail poured through the opening, hammers and axes and pistols at the ready. They fell upon the orcs from the rear, and between them and the humans the orcs were quickly cut down.

"Our thanks," one of the dwarves proclaimed, singling Lothar out. "I am Muradin Bronzebeard, brother to King Magni, and the dwarves of Ironforge are in your debt." His thick beard's hue matched his name, and his axe was notched from many battles.

"Anduin Lothar, Commander of the Alliance," Lothar

introduced himself, offering his hand. Muradin's grasp was as strong as he'd expected. "We are happy to help. Our goal is to rid all our lands of the Horde and their influence."

"Aye, as it should be," Muradin agreed, nodding. He frowned. "Alliance? It was you who sent missives to us months ago, from Lordaeron?"

"Indeed." Lothar realized King Terenas must have sent messengers here as well as Quel'Thalas. The king of Lordaeron had apparently left no potential ally untouched. "We have banded together for this common cause."

"And whither are ye bound now?" a second dwarf asked, stepping close enough to join the conversation. His face was less lined than Muradin's but he had similar features and a matching beard.

"My brother Brann," Muradin explained.

"We are following the remainder of the Horde," Lothar answered. "Many of them have already fallen to us, both on land and by sea, and we now seek to vanquish the rest and end this war."

The brothers looked at each and nodded. "We'll be accompanying ye," Muradin announced. "Many of our kin will be after combing these mountains, reclaiming our ancestral strongholds and making sure no orcs remain within Khaz Modan." He grinned. "But we'll bring some lads and join your Alliance to make sure these orcs dinna trouble any of us again."

"We welcome your help," Lothar said honestly. He

had met dwarves once or twice before, back in Stormwind, and had always been impressed by their strength and endurance. And if these Bronzebeard dwarves were as good in combat as their Wildhammer cousins, a contingent of them would be valuable indeed.

"Good. We'll be sending someone to inform our brother, and to catch up to us with supplies." Muradin shouldered his axe and glanced around. "Which way did the Horde go?"

Lothar glanced at Khadgar, who grinned. Then he shrugged, smiled, and pointed south.

"They be heading to Blackrock Spire," Kurdran announced, hopping down from his gryphon near where Lothar and his lieutenants sat in a ring around a small campfire. He and the other Wildhammers with them had been scouting and had just returned to report.

"Blackrock Spire? You're sure?" Muradin asked. Turalyon had noticed that the Wildhammers and the Bronzebeards did not get along well. No, that wasn't quite fair. They were like quarrelsome siblings, he thought—they liked each other but could not resist arguing and trying to show each other up.

"Of course I'm sure!" Kurdran snapped, and Sky'ree cawed a soft warning beside him. "I followed them, didn't I?" Then a sly look came over his face. "Or would you rather be seeing for yourself?" Muradin, and Brann beside him, blanched and stepped back a pace, drawing an evil chuckle from Kurdran. The Bronzebeards were as fond of flying as the Wildhammers were of going underground, which was not at all.

"Blackrock Spire," Lothar mused. "That's the fortress on the mountain summit?" The others nodded. "A strong position," he admitted. "Good vantage all around, solid fortifications, easy to defend from the surrounding mountains, probably easy to control the routes in and out." He shook his head. "Whoever their leader is, he knows what he's doing. This won't be easy."

"Aye, and it be cursed as well," Muradin added. "Well, it is," the dwarf continued when the others looked at him, though Turalyon noticed both Brann and Kurdran were nodding. "Our Dark Iron cousins"— he paused to spit as if their very name was distasteful— "built that fortress, but something far darker lives there now, beneath the surface." He and the other dwarves shuddered.

"If there were something else there, it didn't disturb the orcs," Lothar pointed out. "They'll fall back there, and getting past their defenses will be a problem."

"But we can do it," Turalyon surprised himself by saying. "We have the numbers and the skill to take them down."

Lothar smiled at him. "Yes, we can do it," he agreed. "It will be challenging, but anything worth doing usually is." He was about to say something else when they heard the unmistakable sound of plate mail creaking, and turned to see a man striding toward them. His armor was battered but still gleamed and on its breastplate was the same symbol Turalyon wore, the image of the Silver Hand. As the man drew closer to them, the light of the campfire shone off his flame-red hair and beard.

"Uther!" Lothar stood and offered his hand to the Paladin, who clasped it firmly.

"My lord," Uther answered. He clasped Turalyon's hand as well, and nodded to the others. "We came as soon as we could."

"Lordaeron is clean?" Khadgar asked as Uther lowered himself onto a rock beside them. He looked tired.

"It is," he replied, quiet pride shining in his storm-blue eyes. "My fellows and I have made sure of it. No orcs remain within that land, nor are there any in the mountains alongside." For a second Turalyon felt a strange pang, as if he should have been with the rest of his order. But he had been assigned a different task by Faol himself, and was doing his duty the same as Uther and the others.

"Excellent." Lothar smiled. "And you have arrived at a good time, Sir Uther. We have just learned the orcs' final position, and we will reach it within—?" He turned to the dwarven brothers next to him. They were the most accustomed to this region and would best know the distances involved.

"Five days," Brann replied after pondering a moment. "Provided they have left us no surprises along the way." He glanced at his brother and nodded. "And if ye're going to Blackrock, we'll be going with you. We'll not leave ye to face that lot alone."

"I dinna see any ambushes," Kurdran said, frowning as if the question were a slight to his scouting ability. "The entire Horde, such as it is, is moving in a solid mass back to the Spire." He glanced at Lothar, as if sensing the Champion's next question. "Aye, the Wildhammers will stay with ye as well. And altogether we outnumber them, though not by a large margin," he confirmed.

"I don't need a large margin," Lothar replied. "Just a fair fight." His face was stern. "Five days, then," he told the rest of them. "In five days we finish this."

To Turalyon the words had a ring of finality, even of doom. He just hoped the doom was not their own.

CHAPTER TWENTY-ONE

"The humans are here!"

Doomhammer glanced up from his reverie, annoyed at the fear he heard in Tharbek's voice. When had his fierce subchieftain become so weak?

"I know they are here," he growled in reply, standing and glancing behind the other orc. They were standing upon a rough ledge that had been carved from the mountaintop, in front of the fortress itself and high above the rocky plain, and from here he could see the remaining Horde spread below. The last time he had had this vantage his warriors had carpeted the plain below, leaving not a hint of the rock beneath. Now there were large patches of black rock between the green and brown, and he could pick out each family where it grouped together, slightly apart from the rest. When had his Horde grown so thin? What had he led them to? Why had he not listened to Durotan sooner and heeded his old friend's words? Everything he had been warned about was coming true!

"What will we do?" Tharbek demanded, stepping up behind him. "We do not have the numbers to repel them, not anymore."

Doomhammer glared at his second so fiercely the other orc backed away. It was true that they were fewer now, and that their forces were no longer so numerous as to blanket the world. But they were still orcs, by the ancestors! "What do we do?" he hissed at his lieutenant, pulling his hammer from its place on his back. "We fight, of course!"

Turning away from the quivering Tharbek, Doom-hammer stepped farther onto the ledge. "Hear me, my people!" he bellowed, raising his hammer high. Some turned to look up but others did not, and that incensed him. He struck the cliff face a mighty blow with his weapon, and the resounding crack brought him the Horde's immediate and undivided attention.

"Hear me!" he shouted again. "I know that we have suffered defeats and setbacks, and our numbers are sorely diminished! I know that Gul'dan's treachery has cost us dearly! But still we are orcs! Still we are the Horde! And our footsteps shall shake this world!" A cheer rose from the warriors below, but it was ragged and weak.

"The humans have followed us to this place," he continued, spitting each word as if it disgusted him—which it did. "They think us beaten! They think we came here because we were fleeing their might, as a dog would flee its master! But they are wrong!" He raised his hammer again. "We came here because this is our stronghold, our place of strength. We came here because from here we can spill forth once more, covering this land with our steps. We came here so that we might pour out upon them again, and make them once more tremble at our name!" This time the cheer was louder, and Doomhammer let it wash over him. The warriors were standing and waving their weapons aloft, and he could tell they were getting worked up again. Good.

"We will not wait for them to come upon us," he told his people. "We will not sit here idly and let them dictate this battle. No. We are orcs! We are the Horde! We will bring the fight to them, and they will learn to regret ever pursuing us here! And when we have crushed them beneath us, we will march back over their corpses and once more claim their lands as our own!" He held his hammer over him with both hands, swinging it about above his head, and the cheer now shook the rocks and the very stone upon which he stood. Doomhammer felt a smile crease his face, and exulted in it. These were his people! They would not go down sniveling and pleading! If they fell, it would be in battle, and with blood on their hands.

"Ready the warriors of our clan," he told the stunned Tharbek. "My elite guard and I will lead the charge ourselves. The rest of the Horde will follow." Turning, Doomhammer glanced at the bulky figures that stood in the shadows, waiting. Each of them straightened and nodded as he caught their gaze, and Doomhammer nodded in return. These were his elite guard, and they were all ogres.

Doomhammer was a proper orc and had been raised to hate the ogres, but these were different. They were more intelligent than most of their kind, for one, but they were warriors and not warlocks. Equally as important, they were intensely loyal to him and him alone. He knew they admired his strength and courage—they seemed to see him as a small ogre himself, and had pledged themselves to his personal command. He, in turn, had come to respect their strength and rely upon their support. He knew they would die for him if necessary, and was surprised to realize he would give his life for them as well.

And now they would all risk their lives, as the Horde's victory hung in the balance.

At least the portal was safe. Rend and Maim Blackhand had survived the battle with Gul'dan and an attack by the Alliance fleet, along with some of their clanmates. They had sent a scout to Doomhammer, finding him on his way here from Khaz Modan, and he had ordered them to join the rest of their clan at the portal. He still did not trust the brothers but they proven themselves loyal to the Horde, at least, and he needed strong warriors to protect their access to Draenor. Not that he would ever consider fleeing, even if the battle turned against them.

He nodded at his ogres again. Then he made his way

off the ledge, leading down toward the plain below, and the battle that awaited them.

The Alliance was not prepared for the orcs to attack. Just as Doomhammer had hoped, the humans had positioned themselves for a siege, expecting to wait the orcs out and take out any lone warriors foolish enough to show themselves beyond the protective cliffs that ringed Blackrock Mountain itself. Doomhammer's charge took them completely by surprise.

"Orcs!" a soldier shouted, running back to where Lothar and his lieutenants stood. "They've overrun our position!"

"What?" Lothar kicked his steed into motion and galloped across the black valley where he had stationed the bulk of the Alliance troops. Turalyon and the others followed close behind.

Sure enough, as he approached the front lines he heard the unmistakable sounds of battle. Then he saw them. They were orcs, but orcs like he had never seen. These were massive creatures, with thick arms and stout legs, and their hair was worn in spikes that rose above them like bird crests or horse manes. The orcs had no armor, wearing only loincloths, shoulderpads, and furry boots, and wielded their weapons with mad abandon, hacking and stabbing everything within their reach. Their green skin was heavily tattooed, and most of them had jagged bits of metal or small bits of what looked like bone shoved through ears, noses, brows, lips, and even nipples. They were savages, and the men were falling back before their frothing attack.

"Uther!" Lothar shouted, and the Paladin strode forward. He lowered his sword, indicating the orcs, and that was enough. The Paladin nodded, beckoning the other members of the Silver Hand to follow him as he lowered his helm and raised his warhammer.

"By the Holy Light!" Uther shouted, a glow springing up around him and his weapon. "We shall not suffer such beasts to live!" And he dove into the fray, his hammer slamming down upon the nearest orc's head and shattering its skull.

The sky here was always thick with clouds and soot, casting heavy shadows and blood-tinged light upon everything. But not now. The clouds parted and a beam of pure sunlight lanced down, limning Uther as he waded into the assembled Horde. The Paladin became a figure of pure light, awesome and terrifying, his every blow crushing orc warriors left and right.

The other Paladins joined him, his light suffusing them as well. The Silver Hand had expanded in the months since the war had begun, and now numbered twelve under Uther's command and not counting Turalyon. Those twelve waded into the combat, their hammers and axes and swords glowing with their faith, and the rest of the Alliance soldiers pulled back to give them space.

The orcs turned and faced their new foes. It was a brutal battle, savages versus zealots, shining mail against tattoos and piercings. The orcs were strong, tough, and crazed enough to not notice pain. But the Paladins were filled with righteous anger and the power of their faith, and their holy auras caused more than one orc to turn away when attacking. With this advantage the Paladins ringed the savage orcs, cutting down one after another until the last lay dead at their feet.

"Good work," Lothar was saying when another sentry ran up to him. *What now?* he wondered wearily. *Another attack?*

"Another attack!" the soldier gasped, echoing his thought. "This time to the west!"

"Damn them," Lothar muttered, spurring his horse again and racing toward the new location. They were smart, he had to give them that. He had not expected an attack and his men were not ready for it. Most of them had relaxed, counting on a long slow siege, and some had even removed their armor, though he had ordered them to stay alert just in case. Now they were paying the price for their laxity. And if the orcs were able to weaken enough spots along their line with these sudden attacks, they could break through and escape into the rest of the mountain range. It could take months, even years to track all of them down, and that would give the Horde time enough to rebuild and try again.

He could not allow that to happen.

He burst upon the new battle, trampling an orc that did not move aside quickly enough, and then wheeled his horse around and reined in, studying the situation.

This was a much larger attack than the last one, a full three score of them or more. Even more daunting were the six ogres in their midst. They fought savagely but not as mindlessly as the last attackers, and showed some sense of tactics. Particularly the giant orc in their midst, whose long hair hung in ornamented braids that danced as he swung a massive black hammer left and right, crushing Alliance soldiers with each blow. Something about the way the giant moved, quickly but carefully, even gracefully despite the massive black plate armor encasing him, struck Lothar. This, he somehow knew, was their leader. He was urging his horse into the fray when the giant glanced up and looked right at him. Those eyes were not the glowing red Lothar had grown accustomed to seeing in his foes—they were gray, and full of intelligence. And they widened slightly, as if in recognition.

There! Doomhammer grinned as he studied the large human perched on the horse nearby. That one, with the shield and the enormous sword and the clever sea-blue eyes. He was their leader. He was the one Doomhammer had been hoping to find. If he could take out this man, the army's resolve would crumble.

"Move aside!" Doomhammer bellowed, smashing a human soldier in his path and kicking one of his own orcs out of the way as well. The man, he saw, was charging into the fray as well, laying about him with that sword, barely looking at the carnage he was creating. The human leader's eyes were locked on him.

Combat raged all around him, but Doomhammer kept his own gaze fixed on his foe. He stalked forward, his hammer clearing space through the crush of bodies, not caring if he struck orc or human. All that mattered was reaching that man. The human was only slightly more careful, not actively striking any of his own people but expecting them to dodge his horse and his blows all the same. Finally there were no more warriors between them, and Doomhammer faced the man at close range.

Mounted, the human had the advantage. Doomhammer solved that problem at once. His hammer arced out, its massive stone head smashing full force into the horse's head. The steed collapsed, blood pouring from its shattered skull, its legs twitching. The human did not fall. Instead he kicked free of his stirrups and leaped to one side as his horse fell, then hurdled the body to confront Doomhammer directly. The rest of the battle faded away as the two leaders raised their weapons and collided without words, each intent upon only one thing—the other's death.

It was a titanic battle. Lothar was a large, powerful man, easily as big and as strong as most orc warriors. But Doomhammer was larger still, and stronger, and younger. What Lothar lacked in youth and speed, however, he made up for in skill and experience.

Both wore heavy plate armor, the battered mail of Stormwind versus the black plate of the Horde. And both carried weapons lesser warriors could never have wielded, the glittering rune-etched blade of Stormwind and the black-stone hammer of the Doomhammer line. And both were determined to win, no matter the cost.

Lothar struck first. His sword swept in from the side, angling suddenly to weave below Doomhammer's block, and carved a furrow in the orc's heavy armor. The Horde warchief grunted from the impact and retaliated by bringing his hammer down fast, missing Lothar only because the Champion danced back a step. But Doomhammer reversed his grip suddenly and swept the weapon back up, catching Lothar a glancing blow under the chin and sending him stumbling backward. A quick hammer blow followed, but Lothar brought his sword up in time to block it, catching the heavy weapon on its handle. For a second the two warriors struggled, Doomhammer to bring his hammer down and Lothar to knock it aside, and the weapons quivered but did not move.

Then Lothar twisted his blade and succeeded in sending the hammer wide. He stepped in close while Doomhammer was bringing the massive weapon back around and struck the orc in the face with the flat of his blade, stunning the warchief for an instant. But Doomhammer lashed out with his free hand, catching Lothar a ringing blow in the neck, and regained his weapon and his composure while the Alliance commander staggered from that impact.

Turalyon was battling orcs of his own, but a powerful hammer blow dropped one opponent and over the falling warrior he saw Lothar and the massive orc locked in battle. "No!" Turalyon shouted, seeing his leader and hero facing the monstrous black-armored orc. He began striking with renewed force, his hammer crushing orcs with each sweeping blow, as he desperately fought his way toward the two commanders.

They both stepped in again, hammer and sword swinging. Lothar took Doomhammer's hit full upon his lion-head shield, which crumpled from the impact and nearly drove him to his knees, but his sword caught the orc hard across the chest and dented the heavy breastplate deeply. Doomhammer stepped back, his lips pulling back in a snarl of pain and frustration, and ripped the ruined armor from his torso just as Lothar rose to his feet again and tossed his useless shield to the side. Then both bellowed and charged again.

Doomhammer was faster now without the armor, but Lothar had his sword in both hands and could dance it around the orc's defenses. Both took solid blows, Doomhammer a nasty gash across his stomach and Lothar a heavy blow to his right side, and both staggered slightly as they parted for the third time. Around them other orcs and humans fought their own savage battles, as the two powerful leaders struck out again and again, each seeking a weak point in his opponent's defense, each delivering punishing attacks and receiving them in return.

The two closed again, and Doomhammer slammed Lothar in the chest with one heavy fist, the impact rocking the Champion on his heels and denting his breastplate. Before he could recover fully Doomhammer stepped back himself and brought his massive hammer down with both hands, all his strength behind the blow. Lothar swung his sword up to block the vicious attack, and took the full force of the swing upon his blade—

—which shattered from the impact.

A gasp escaped Turalyon as pieces of the legendary sword fell to the ground. And Doomhammer's blow, now unimpeded, continued its glittering downward arc, striking the top of Lothar's helm with a sickening crunch. The Lion of Azeroth swayed, bringing his ruined sword down reflexively, and laid open Doomhammer's chest with the jagged half-blade before collapsing himself. There was utter silence as both sides stopped fighting and stared at the Alliance commander splayed upon the ground, his body twitching as the life fled him. And then nothing moved save the pool of blood spreading rapidly from beneath his ruined head.

Doomhammer took an unsteady step, one hand rising to press against the gaping wound across his torso. Blood leaked out around his fingers, but still he stood straight and, with an effort, raised his hammer high above his head.

"I have conquered!" he proclaimed in a hoarse whisper, swaying and spitting blood but still victorious. "And so shall all our foes die, until your world belongs to us!"

CHAPTER TWENTY-TWO

"**N**O!" The word burst from Turalyon's lips as he shoved through the crowd and dropped to his knees beside the dead body of his hero, his mentor, his commander. Then his gaze switched to the orc towering above him, and something within him clicked into place.

For months Turalyon had been struggling with his faith, and with one particular question: How could the Holy Light unite all creatures, all souls, when something as monstrous, as cruel, and as purely evil as the orc Horde walked this world? Unable to reconcile the two he had been unsure of himself and of the Church's teachings, and had looked on with envy as Uther and the other Paladins gave blessings and shone bright with zeal, knowing he could not match their abilities.

But something this orc, this Doomhammer, had just said had registered on some level below conscious thought, and Turalyon tried to trace it. "Until your world belongs to us," the Horde warchief had gloated. "Your world," not "our world" or even "this world."

And that was the answer.

He had remembered the Dark Portal, of course—Khadgar had told him about it when they had first met, while describing the orc menace, and it had been mentioned several times since then. But for some reason the truth of it had never really sunk in. Until now.

The orcs were not of this world.

They were foreign to this planet, to this very plane of existence. They came from elsewhere, and were powered by demons from even farther beyond.

The Holy Light did unite all life, everyone in this world. But not the orcs, who did not belong here.

And that meant his task was clear. He was charged with upholding the Holy Light and using its blazing glory to scour this world clean of all threats from without, and to maintain the purity within.

The orcs did not belong here. And that meant he could strike them down with impunity.

"By the Light, your time here has ended!" he shouted, rising to his feet. And a brilliant glow sprang up around him, so bright orcs and humans alike turned away, shielding their eyes. "You are not of this world, not of the Holy Light. You do not belong here! Begone!"

The Horde warchief grimaced and backed away a step, a hand shielding his eyes. Turalyon took advantage of the moment to crouch again beside Lothar's body.

"Go with the Light, my friend," he whispered,

touching a forefinger to the fallen Champion's shattered forehead, his own tears dripping down to mix with the dead warrior's blood. "You have earned a place among the holy, and the Light welcomes you into its loving embrace." An aura sprang up around the body, glowing a pure white, and he thought the features of his dead friend relaxed slightly, growing calm, even quietly content.

Then Turalyon rose again, and now he held in one hand the shattered greatsword. "And you, foul creature," he declared, turning toward the dazzled Doomhammer. "You will pay for your crimes upon this world and its peoples!"

Doomhammer must have recognized the threat in his tone, for the orc leader gripped his hammer with both hands and swung it up, blocking the blow he sensed was coming. But Turalyon had both hands wrapped around the broken sword's hilt and brought the blade down in a blinding flash of light—

—and the ruined weapon slammed hard into the massive warhammer's black stone head, the impact traveling down the heavy wooden handle and shaking it free of its master's grip. The hammer fell harmlessly to the side. Doomhammer's eyes widened as he realized what had happened, and then he closed them and gave a faint nod, waiting for the rest of the blow to fall.

But Turalyon had turned the blade at the last second, and struck the orc with the flat instead of the edge. The impact drove Doomhammer to his knees, and then he collapsed alongside Lothar, but Turalyon could see the rise and fall of the warchief's back.

"You will stand trial for your crimes," he told the unconscious orc, the light building around him. "You will stand in Capital City, in chains"—it was brighter than the brightest day now, and every orc turned away, cowering from the blinding light—"as the leaders of the Alliance decide your fate, and there you will acknowledge your full defeat."

Then he turned and glanced up, this time at the other orc warriors, who had stood frozen as they had watched their leader's apparent victory converted to stunning defeat. "But you will not be so lucky," Turalyon intoned, leveling the shattered sword at them. Light lanced from it and from his hand, his head, his eyes. The black rock around him was blanched white by the power that poured from his body. "You will die here, with the rest of your kind, and this world will be rid of your taint forever!" And with that he leaped forward, the sun-bright blade already in motion. It caught the first orc in the throat before he could even react, and the brute fell, blood spurting from the wound, as Turalyon charged past him toward the other half-blinded Horde warriors.

That broke the paralysis, and the other orcs and humans finally were able to move again. Uther and the other Silver Hand Paladins had joined the throng during Lothar and Doomhammer's battle and now they ran forward to follow their fellow, auras springing up around them as well as they dove into the gathered Horde. The rest of the Alliance forces followed.

The battle that followed was surprisingly quick. Many of the orcs had seen Doomhammer's defeat, and their leader's collapse sent them into a panic. Many fled. Others dropped their weapons and surrendered—these were rounded up for imprisonment and, despite his earlier statement, Turalyon found he did not have it in himself to kill helpless prisoners, no matter what they done beforehand. Many did stand and fight, of course, but they were disorganized and dazed and proved little match for the resolute Alliance soldiers.

"A band of them, perhaps four hundred strong, is fleeing south through the Redridge Mountains," Khadgar reported an hour later, after the combat had ended and the valley and grown quiet save for the rustling of the men, the moans of the wounded, and the growling of the prisoners.

"Good," Turalyon replied. He was tearing a long strip from his cloak and wound that around his waist as a sash, then stuck Lothar's shattered sword through it. "Form up ranks and pursue them, but not too quickly. Let the unit leaders know. We don't want to catch them."

"We don't?"

Turalyon turned and looked at his friend, reminding himself again that for all his talents the mage was no tactician. "Where is this Dark Portal that leads back to the orcs' world?" he asked.

Khadgar shrugged. "We don't know exactly," he admitted. "Somewhere in the swamplands."

"And now that the Horde has suffered an undeniable defeat, where will those few survivors go?"

The old-seeming mage grinned. "Back home."

"Exactly." Turalyon straightened. "And we will follow them back to this portal, and destroy it once and for all."

Khadgar nodded and turned to seek the unit leaders, but stopped as Uther approached them.

"There are no orcs left save those who have given themselves into our custody," the Paladin announced.

Turalyon nodded. "Good work. A handful escaped, but we will pursue them and destroy or capture them as well."

Uther studied him. "You have assumed command," he said softly.

"I suppose I have." Turalyon considered it. He hadn't really thought about it before. He had simply gotten used to giving orders for the army, both at Lothar's request and when the Commander was in the Hinterlands with the rest of the troops. Now he shrugged. "If you'd prefer we can send a gryphon rider to Lordaeron to ask King Terenas and the other kings who should assume command."

"There's no need," Khadgar said, stepping back to stand beside him. "You were Lothar's lieutenant and sub-commander. You were given charge of half the army when we divided the forces. You are the only choice to command now that he is gone." The mage turned toward Uther with a glare, clearly daring him to contradict the statement.

But to Turalyon's surprise, Uther nodded. "It is so," he agreed. "You are our commander, and we will follow your lead as we did Lord Lothar's." Then he moved closer and rested a friendly hand on Turalyon's shoulder. "And happy I was to see your faith finally emerge, my brother." The compliment seemed genuine, and Turalyon smiled, pleased to have the older Paladin's approval.

"And I thank you, Uther the Lightbringer," Turalyon replied, and he saw the older Paladin's eyes widen at the new title. "For so shall you be known henceforth, in honor of the Holy Light you brought us this day." Uther bowed, clearly pleased, then turned without another word and walked back toward the other knights of the Silver Hand, no doubt to tell them their marching orders.

"I thought he'd argue for taking control," Khadgar said quietly.

"He doesn't want it," Turalyon replied, still watching Uther. "He wants to lead, yes, but only by example. He's comfortable leading the Order only because they're Paladins as well."

"And you?" his friend asked bluntly. "Are you comfortable leading us all?"

Turalyon pondered that, then shrugged. "I don't feel I've earned it, but I know Lothar trusted me with it.

And I believe in him and his judgment." He nodded and met Khadgar's gaze. "Now let's be after those orcs."

It took them a week to reach what Khadgar said were called the Swamp of Sorrows. They could have moved more quickly but Turalyon had cautioned his soldiers not to overtake the orcs yet. They needed to know the location of that portal first. Then they could strike.

Lothar's death had shocked everyone, but it had also galvanized them. Men who had been weary were now focused, hard, and resolute. They had all taken the loss of their commander personally, and seemed determined to avenge his death. And they all accepted Turalyon as his chosen successor, especially those who had followed him to Quel'Thalas and back.

Slogging through the marshes was difficult and unpleasant, but other than muttering a little no one complained. Their scouts kept the orcs in sight and then reported back, allowing the Alliance troops to move at a slow pace and still not worry about losing their quarry. The Horde remnant was in general disarray, all the orcs heading the same direction but not marching together, simply jogging or walking at their own paces and with a handful of companions amid the larger group. Turalyon just hoped that remained the case. He assumed the Horde leader, that Doomhammer, had left troops and a lieutenant in charge of the portal itself. If that leader was strong enough he could fuse the defeated orcs back into a solid fighting force, along with whatever warriors he had with him already. Turalyon warned his lieutenants to keep the men alert and not let them get complacent. Assuming this would be an easy fight could get them all killed.

They spent another week in the swamps before finally reaching an area called the Black Morass. But here even Khadgar was in for a surprise.

"I don't understand," the mage commented, crouching to study the ground. "This should all be marsh! It should be just like what we've already been through, soggy and filthy and smelly." He tapped the hard red stone before him and frowned. "This is definitely not right."

"It looks almost igneous," said Brann Bronzebeard, who stood beside him. The dwarves had insisted on accompanying them the rest of the way, and Turalyon had been glad for both their battle prowess and their company. He found he liked the two brothers, with their bluff good cheer and their equal appreciation for a good fight, a good ale, and a fine woman. Brann was certainly the more scholarly of the two, and he and Khadgar had spent several evenings talking about obscure texts while the rest of them discussed less academic subjects. And all the dwarves from Ironforge were experts on rocks and gems, so for Brann to not recognize the rock beneath them was unsettling, to say the least. "But no fire I know could do this," he added, scraping at it with one blunt fingernail. "And certainly not to such a large expanse." For the red stone stretched ahead of them as far as they could see. "I've never seen the like."

"Unfortunately, I have," Khadgar replied, standing again. "But not on this world." He did not explain further and something in his expression warned the others not to press him.

Muradin started to ask anyway, but his brother stopped him. "Do ye know what your name means in Dwarven, lad?" Brann asked Khadgar. "It means 'trust.'" The mage nodded. "We trust ye, lad. You'll tell us when you're ready."

"Well, it's almost certainly tied to the orcs," Turalyon pointed out, "and we'll have an easier time pursuing them across stone than we would through more marshland, so I'm not opposed to the change in scenery." The others nodded, though Khadgar still looked thoughtful, and they mounted up again and continued on.

A few nights later, Khadgar glanced up from the campfire and suddenly announced, "I think we have a problem." The others all turned to listen to the young-old mage. "I have consulted with the other magi and we think we know what's caused the ground to change," he explained. "It's the Dark Portal itself. Its very presence is affecting our world, starting with the lands immediately around it. And I think it's spreading."

"Why would this portal cause such an alteration?" Uther asked. The Silver Hand leader had never been very comfortable with magi, sharing the common perception that their magic was unholy and possibly even demonic, but he had learned to at least accept and possibly even respect Khadgar during the long war.

But the mage shook his head. "I'd have to see it to be certain," he replied. "But I'd guess the portal is linking our two worlds, this one and the orcs' homeworld of Draenor, and it's doing more than just forming a bridge. Somehow it's melding the two together, at least right at its entry point."

"And their world is made of red stone?" Brann guessed.

"Not entirely," Khadgar answered. "Some time ago I had a vision of Draenor, however, and what I saw of it was a bleak place, with ground much like this. There is little life left there, as if nature itself has been stripped away. I think it may be their magics, which taint the land itself. That taint is spreading through the portal, and every time the orcs use their magics here it grows worse."

"All the more reason to destroy it, then," Turalyon announced. "And the sooner the better."

His friend nodded. "Yes, I agree. The sooner the better."

It was three more days before the scouts came back and announced that the orcs had stopped moving. "They're all holed up in a large valley just ahead," one of them announced. "And there's some kind of gateway in the center."

Khadgar exchanged a glance with Turalyon, Uther, and the Bronzebeard brothers. That had to be the Dark Portal.

"Tell the men," Turalyon said softly, drawing Lothar's broken sword with one hand and hefting his own hammer with his other. "We attack at once." Khadgar marveled once again at the changes the last few months had caused in his friend. Turalyon had become more stern, more commanding, more sure of himself—he had gone from being an untried youth to a seasoned warrior and an experienced commander. But since Lothar's death he had also had an aura about him, a sense of calm and wisdom and even majesty. Uther and the other Paladins had similar feels but more removed, as if they were above the problems of this world. Turalyon seemed to be more at one with the world around him, more attuned to his surroundings. It was a magic Khadgar did not understand, but one he respected a great deal. In many ways it was the opposite of his own magic, which sought to control the elements and other forces. Turalyon was not controlling anything, but by opening himself to those same forces he gained the ability to tap them, with less control but more subtlety than any mage.

The soldiers were readied, and they all crept forward, leading their horses to keep them at least quieter on the hard red stone. The ground rose up slightly and then dropped abruptly into a deep valley whose far walls reared even higher. At the center of the valley, as the scout had said, stood a massive gate, not set in any wall or structure but freestanding, and Khadgar gasped as he saw it fully. The Dark Portal—it could hardly be anything else—was easily a hundred feet high and almost as wide, and was crafted from some greenish gray stone. It had harsh, swirling patterns carved on either side, each based around a scowling skull, with two wickedly curved barbs along the outer edges. The centerpiece had a crude ornamental border below but was plain and unmarked above. Four wide steps led up to the portal itself, which glowed green and black and crackled with energy. And to Khadgar's senses it was a maelstrom, radiating power and a strange sense of vast distance. He could also feel it reaching out, digging into the land and pulling tendrils of energy into its gaping maw.

The orcs were milling about before the portal, as if unsure what to do now. There were more here than they had been following, so clearly Turalyon had been right—Doomhammer had left orcs here to guard the place. But the Alliance still outnumbered them. And the orcs were separated into distinct clusters, as if they no longer had reason to trust one another and so had reverted to their own families and hunting parties. This was not an army but a collection of small bands.

"Now!" Turalyon shouted, and he leaped over the edge of the cliff and slid down the long slope, landing almost on top of several orcs sitting there. Lothar's sword stabbed forward, impaling one orc on its jagged half-length, and then Turalyon' hammer struck another orc, crushing his skull and sending him careening into the first, who fell free of the sword and toppled to the ground. Then Uther and the rest of the Paladins were there as well, flanking Turalyon as he stood and stalked toward the other orcs, and the rest of the Alliance was right behind them.

Khadgar knew he was less useful in battle than wielding his magic, so he stayed upon the cliff with the other magi, watching the fight. It was quick and decisive. Lothar and Turalyon had forged the Alliance troops into a powerful unified force, and it fought as one now, with the men working together against a common foe. Pikemen were defending by swordsman and axe-wielders, and the archers watched over all of them and provided ranged support as needed. The orcs were too disorganized to work together, and each cluster stood and fought alone. That made it easy for Turalyon to send in his men, surround one orc band at a time, and either slaughter them or take them prisoner. He worked his way methodically across the valley, defeating orc after orc, and as many huddled in chains as lay dead upon the ground. By this time a large number of orcs, death knights, and others had fled through the portal rather than face death or capture. Only a small ragged group remained behind, standing its ground to cover the others' retreat.

Finally Turalyon had reached the bottom of the portal's bottom step. Two stocky, muscular orcs stood on the top step, each wielding massive, jagged axes. They had medals and bones hanging from their hair, their noses, their ears, their brows, and all over their armor, and their hair rose in a single mass of short dark spikes atop their heads, as if those too were weapons.

One of the orcs had bloodstained bandages around his left shoulder and leg. Nevertheless, both orcs seemed arrogant and confident of victory, evidently unmoved by their leader's recent defeat.

"You face Rend and Maim Blackhand, of the Black Tooth Grin," one of them shouted as they stomped down the steps toward Turalyon. "Our father, Blackhand, led the Horde until that upstart Doomhammer slew him unjustly. Now he is gone we will rebuild the Horde until it is even larger than before, and we will smash you out of existence!"

"I think not," Turalyon replied, his words ringing across the valley. Against the backdrop of the portal's swirling energy he glowed a brilliant white, small and piercing. "Your leader is captured, your army destroyed, your clans in disarray, and what remains of your Horde gathered here in this one valley, which we have surrounded." He raised both hammer and sword. "Face me, if you dare. Or turn and flee back to your own world and never return."

The taunt worked, and the two brothers charged down the last step, leaping upon Turalyon with fierce battle cries. But the young Paladin and recent commander did not flinch. He took a quick step back and brought both hammer and sword down hard, knocking the orcs' axes down to the ground. Then he closed again and swept his own weapons back up, catching both orcs under the chin. The one to the left staggered back a pace, stunned, but his brother reeled, blood flying from the deep cut beneath his chin.

As Khadgar watched the two orcs growled and lashed out again, but their attacks were clumsier this time, more wild, and Turalyon avoided them both by the simple expedient of darting forward, between and past the two orcs. He struck them each in the stomach as he passed, doubling them over from the impact, and then kicked them both from behind, sending them tumbling from the ramp to the hard stone ground. He was right behind them, his weapons whistling as they arced through the air.

Unfortunately, the brothers were not alone.

"Clanmates, to us!" one of the brothers bellowed. "Kill the human!"

Two more orcs leaped into the fray, giving the Blackhands space to pull back. The brothers swung at some of the men approaching them, but to Khadgar their blows seemed half-hearted. They had clearly reconsidered their chances. A gap appeared in the Alliance forces approaching the portal and the orc brothers took advantage of it and ran. A handful of their brethren followed their example. But Turalyon was too busy to chase after them, however. Many of the other orcs remained to fight, some even spitting at and cursing the fleeing Blackhands. And the two who had moved to the Blackhands' aid were still menacing Turalyon himself.

"Rargh!" one of the newcomers growled, sweeping out with his axe. Turalyon blocked the blow with his hammer and battered the heavy orc weapon aside, then stabbed in with the broken sword, the blade piercing armor and flesh alike and driving deep into the orc's middle. The orc dropped his weapon and stiffened, gasping as his hands clutched at the blood-slick blade, and then he crumpled to the ground, his eyes already glazing over.

"Die!" the other orc howled and threw himself at Turalyon. But Turalyon had pulled the sword free of the first orc and now swung it at the second, catching him in the throat with the jagged tip. It was not enough to stop the charging warrior but Turalyon knocked his axe blow aside with the hammer and then swung again, the heavy hammer connecting solidly with the orc's head. The impact must have been tremendous because the orc warrior collapsed, blood pouring from his shattered temple, and did not move again.

Turalyon glanced down at the two dead bodies for a second, then toward the Blackhands disappearing at the far end of the valley. Then he looked up toward the ledge until he spotted Khadgar. "Do it now!" the Paladin shouted, pointing Lothar's blade at the portal. "Destroy it!"

"Get back!" Khadgar shouted in reply. "I don't know what will happen!" He barely noticed his friend nodding and trotting clear of the massive stone structure. Instead he and the eleven magi with him were already concentrating on the object.

He could feel its power, and its link to both this world and Draenor, and the rift it had fashioned to allow access between the two. The rift would simply swallow their magic, he suspected. And the worlds themselves were too large and too powerful for them to affect, even all of them together. Which left the physical gate itself. Because no matter how powerful it was, stone was still stone. And stone could be shattered.

Concentrating, Khadgar summoned the power to him, filling himself up with magical might. There was little power left in these lands but the Dark Portal itself had ample energy and nothing to safeguard that reservoir, to prevent people like the magi from tapping that power for their own ends. Khadgar and the other magi did so now, draining the portal's reserves utterly and directing all the energy into Khadgar himself. His hair stood on end and energy crackled across his face and along his fingers. The wind howled around him, and he thought he saw lightning nearby, though it could have simply been the energy arcing across and even through his eyes. He just hoped it was enough.

Facing the Dark Portal, Khadgar closed his eyes and opened his arms wide, his hands turned palm-up. He gathered all the magic he had just absorbed, every last bit of it, and bound it into something like a mystical ball that hung, pulsing and beaming, before his eyes. He could feel the ball, feel how it throbbed, and feel how loosely it was assembled. Perfect. He shifted his senses toward the portal, toward the energies there, and then he aligned himself with its position.

Then at last he opened his eyes.

And slammed his hands together, turning them at the last second so they met palm-to-palm. And the ball of energy was propelled forward, flattening and elongating and transforming from a simple sphere to a long slim shape, very like a different kind of spear.

A spear that lanced the portal right in the center, its energy pouring out and into the Dark Portal and across the stone slabs that formed its sides and top. The explosion rocked most of the Alliance soldiers and many of the remaining orcs from their feet, and Khadgar himself staggered on his perch. But the portal's heavy lintel and squared columns were blown apart. Fortunately for the Alliance forces nearby, the explosion drove most of the larger stone fragments into the portal's depths.

Then the portal itself vanished, the roiling colors replaced by simple empty space. And Khadgar felt the world draw breath again as whatever had bound it to Draenor snapped, ending the tug of that dying world and letting nature reassert itself.

Glancing down, Khadgar saw Turalyon picking himself up off the ground. The Paladin was covered with rock dust and small rock chips but looked otherwise unharmed, and he grinned up at Khadgar as he wiped the dust from his face, arms, and chest.

"I don't think they will be using that again," he called up, and they both laughed, their humor born of profound relief.

The war was over. And the Alliance had won. Their world was safe.

Epilogue

"It will be an impressive monument," Turalyon co-mented. He and Khadgar sat their horses near the cliff's edge, looking out over the same plain where Lothar had fought his final battle months before. The landscape was bleak, brutal, and harsh, all black stone and hardened lava except where fresh lava glowed red amid the shadows. The air was thick with ash and soot, and the sky seemed perpetually overcast. The mountains loomed like disapproving guardians. Blackrock Spire rose at the far end.

"It will," Khadgar agreed. "His sacrifice will always shine as a symbol of loyalty and bravery, even after other traces of this war have vanished."

Turalyon nodded, his gaze still focused upon the statue that was being raised before Blackrock Spire. Regent Lord Anduin Lothar, Champion of Stormwind and Commander of the Alliance, stood with sword raised and shield at the ready, looking to the skies as if daring them to battle. He was dressed in full armor but without his helm, and his strong features stared out across the valley, his gaze stern but kind.

"At least it's over," Khadgar said.

It was true. That battle at the Dark Portal had been the last. Those few orcs who had survived had surrendered and been taken prisoner. No one was quite sure what to do with them, and for now they had been put to work hauling materials for Lothar's monument, an irony Turalyon appreciated. Once this was done, perhaps the orcs would be sent to do more hard labor elsewhere. He doubted they would be slaughtered but neither could they be set loose, in case they dreamed of creating a Horde once more. Some, including the Blackhands, had escaped, but they lacked the numbers to pose a serious threat now.

Still, that was not his concern. Terenas and the other kings would make that decision, when the time came. After Lordaeron had been cleansed Terenas had marched his forces into Alterac and declared martial law, deposing the traitorous Perenolde and imprisoning him. Alterac's fate was still uncertain, but the Alliance would continue, and the remaining monarchs had asked Turalyon to remain as its Commander. He had accepted, feeling Lothar would have wanted him to continue in that role. His friend and mentor had only wanted to protect the land and its people, and he vowed to do the same.

"You're thinking heavy thoughts," Khadgar commented, nudging him in the arm.

"Only about the future and what it may bring," Turalyon replied.

"No one knows the future," his friend said, though a strange look crossed his face. "Though I suspect we have not seen the last of the Horde or its world."

"I hope you are wrong," Turalyon told him. "But if you are right, we will be here waiting for them when they return. And we will drive them back again, just as we did this time. This world is ours, and by the Holy Light we will keep it safe, now and forever."

The mage laughed. "A noble statement, good Turalyon," he teased. "Perhaps that is what they will carve on your statue, when the time comes."

"A statue?" Turalyon laughed. "What could either of us possibly do to earn statues?"

ACKNOWLEDGMENTS

As always, massive thanks go to Chris for starting the tide and to Marco for controlling it. I'd also like to thank Evelyn for her sharp eyes and kind words. Most importantly I'd like to thank the *World of Warcraft* fans, without whom Lothar and Orgrim and the others would have no one to tell their tale.

ABOUT THE AUTHOR

AARON ROSENBERG is originally from New Jersey and New York. He returned to New York City in 1996 after stints in New Orleans and Kansas. He has taught college-level English and worked in corporate graphics and book publishing.

Aaron has written novels for *Star Trek*, *StarCraft*, *Warcraft*, *Warhammer*, and *Exalted*. He also writes role-playing games and has worked on the *Star Trek*, *War-Craft*, and *Warhammer* games. He writes educational books as well.

Aaron lives in New York City with his family. For more information about his writing you can visit him online at www.rosenbergbooks.com.